WINSTON S. CHURCHILL

P.C., O.M., C.H., M.P.

SELECTIONS FROM
HIS WRITINGS AND SPEECHES

CHOSEN AND EDITED BY

GUY BOAS, M.A.

MACMILLAN AND CO. LIMITED
ST. MARTIN'S STREET, LONDON
1952

ACKNOWLEDGMENTS

THE compiler and his publishers are indebted to Messrs. Cassell & Company, Ltd. for permission to reprint in this volume the passages from *Into Battle, The Unrelenting Struggle, The End of the Beginning, Secret Session Speeches, Onwards to Victory, The Dawn of Liberation,* and the first two volumes of *The Second World War—The Gathering Storm* and *Their Finest Hour*; and to Odhams Press, Ltd., as proprietors of the copyright, for the passages from *My Early Life,* the volumes of *The World Crisis* (including *The Eastern Front* and *The Aftermath*), *Great Contemporaries,* and *Thoughts and Adventures.* The extracts from the Victory speeches are quoted from the reports published in *The Times* of May 9th, 1945.

WINSTON S. CHURCHILL

SELECTIONS FROM
HIS WRITINGS AND SPEECHES

CONTENTS

From *My Early Life*

From *Thoughts and Adventures*

From *The World Crisis*, 1911–1914

From *The World Crisis: The Eastern Front*

INTRODUCTION

It is hard to guess the ultimate stature of a contemporary. There is no reason to suppose that the Elizabethans conceived that Shakespeare would conquer the world, and who can prophesy what in a hundred years' time will be Bernard Shaw's rank in the Temple of Fame? Yet it is difficult, even while he is still among us, not to think of Winston Churchill as already secure among the immortals. Literary and artistic reputation is subject to changing taste, but historic actions are immutable : nothing can alter the fact that when Europe and civilisation were threatened in 1940 by Hitler's intention that they should be subjected for a thousand years, one nation prevented the occurrence, and the soul of that nation was epitomized in the leadership of one man.

During the long subsequent struggle Winston Churchill, as he has himself written, may not always on every occasion have taken the right decision, and in the years which followed the war he may not always as a politician have equalled his greatness as a statesman. But to read his speeches during the first two months of his premiership, when the enemy was at the gates, and all but courage seemed lost, is to be conscious of a single supreme will at work which saved the course of history.

Human genius is individual, and one great figure only resembles another in respect of magnitude. Nevertheless, it is hard to resist setting the qualities of Churchill beside those of giants of the past. As a man of action and letters he compares with Julius Caesar ; as statesman and strategist with Napoleon ; and as a leader of the English people with Cromwell and the younger Pitt.

The military achievements of Caesar, fighting as he was against enemies and weapons so much more primitive, can hardly be reckoned beside warfare against Hitler, but Caesar's books lie as open to us still as Churchill's volumes ; and though the style of the former may be more concise, what reader does not find the writings of Churchill more alluring? Napoleon, architect of the *Code Napoléon*, was a great administrator who, if his conception of a United States of Europe had fructified, might have saved the twentieth century from two world convulsions : yet always in Napoleon burned personal ambition, which in the end sent him to the shadows of St. Helena. Pitt laid and maintained the civil foundations of victory, but it was Nelson who brought the enemy to bay. Probably with Cromwell, not only the victor of Edgehill and Marston Moor but author of the finest letters in the English language, Churchill most nearly disputes the bays.

Between 1906 and 1940, when he first became Prime Minister, Churchill held eight of the chief offices of state, including the Home Secretaryship, First Lordship of the Admiralty, the Secretaryship of State for War and the Chancellorship of the Exchequer. Since the occasion of his brilliant maiden speech on the South African War in the House of Commons on January 26th, 1901, he has been a pre-eminent Member of Parliament. Before becoming a politician at the age of 25 he was professional soldier, war correspondent and author. His subsequent literary output has been continuous and prodigious, and in itself would give him a lasting reputation as historian and literary artist. His epic accounts of the two World Wars are assured classics. His massive Life and vindication of his ancestor the First Duke of Marlborough is also of classic quality, and his many essays on subjects ranging from Moses to Lord Birkenhead possess the same vitality, sanity, lucidity, and wit. In two of his more personal essays he has described how in later life painting became his hobby, and one who has been made an Honorary Academician Extraordinary is an amateur of more than normal talent.

As an orator in the classical style he has had no equal during his lifetime : his innumerable speeches have a quality of literature, as all that he has written bears the mark of rhetoric in the high sense of that art. Finally, it is not, perhaps, always recognised that he is the finest humorist of our time, whose wit contributed as much as his courage and comprehension to carrying the nation safely through the valley of the shadow.

"Power tends to corrupt," said Lord Acton, " and absolute power corrupts absolutely." Between 1940 and 1945 Churchill came as near to having powers of dictatorship as the English constitution allows, yet no trace of corruption ever became evident, while as his power expanded his character seemed to mellow, his benevolence and sympathy to increase.

In the turmoil of party politics Churchill would not have thriven without the stimulus of hard knocks received as well as given. After the disaster of Gallipoli his reputation fell to its lowest. In the years preceding Hitler's war his Cassandra-like warnings were regarded as warmongering rather than patriotism, and in 1945 in the hour of victory—his victory—a majority of his countrymen expelled him with no more apparent reason than the Greeks exiled Aristides because they could no longer bear hearing him called The Just.

There is no greater proof of Churchill's grandeur than that he has harboured no bitterness nor resentment—

I think the sun where he was born
Drew all such humours from him.

Such are the qualities of the man from whose writings and speeches the following extracts are taken. Words throughout his life have been the mainspring of his self-expression and also of his actions. The trouble with most writers, said Bagehot, is that they have never done anything. Churchill is a splendid exception, and it is characteristic that his style has never reached greater heights than at the moment of his country's greatest peril, and when action was most imperative:

" I would say this to the House as I said to those who have joined this Government : ' I have nothing to offer but blood, toil, tears and sweat! ' . . .

" Long dark months of trials and tribulations lie before us. Not only great dangers, but many more misfortunes, many shortcomings, many mistakes, many disappointments will surely be our lot. Death and sorrow will be the companions of our journey ; hardship our garment ; constancy and valour our only shield. . . .

" Let us therefore brace ourselves to our duties, and so bear ourselves that, if the British Empire and its Commonwealth last for a thousand years, men will still say, ' This was their finest hour.' "

G. B.

CHILDHOOD

When does one first begin to remember? When do the waving lights and shadows of a dawning consciousness cast their print upon the mind of a child? My earliest memories are Ireland. I can recall scenes and events in Ireland quite well, and, sometimes dimly, even people. Yet I was born on November 30, 1874, and I left Ireland early in the year 1879.

In one of these years we paid a visit to Emo Park, the seat of Lord Portarlington, who was explained to me as a sort of uncle. Of this place I can give very clear descriptions, though I have never been there since I was four or four and a half. The central point in my memory is a tall white stone tower which we reached after a considerable drive. I was told it had been blown up by Oliver Cromwell. I understood definitely that he had blown up all sorts of things and was therefore a very great man.

My nurse, Mrs Everest, was nervous about the Fenians. I gathered these were wicked people and there was no end to what they would do if they had their way. On one occasion when I was out riding on my donkey, we thought we saw a long dark procession of Fenians approaching. I am sure now it must have been the Rifle Brigade out for a route march. But we were all very much alarmed, particularly the donkey, who expressed his anxiety by kicking. I was thrown off and had concussion of the brain. This was my first introduction to Irish politics!

In the Phoenix Park there was a great round clump of trees with a house inside it. In this house there lived a personage styled the Chief Secretary or the Under Secretary, I am not clear which. But at any rate from this house there came a man called Mr. Burke. He gave me a drum. I cannot remember what he looked like, but I remember the drum. Two years afterwards when we were back in England, they told me he had been murdered by the Fenians in this same Phoenix Park we used to walk about in every day. Everyone round me seemed much upset about it, and I thought how lucky it was the Fenians had not got me when I fell off the donkey.

It was at " The Little Lodge " I was first menaced with Education. The approach of a sinister figure described as " the Governess " was announced. Her arrival was fixed for a certain day. In order to prepare for this day Mrs. Everest produced a book called *Reading without Tears*. It certainly did not justify its title in my case. I was made aware that before the Governess arrived I must be able to read without tears. We toiled each day. My nurse pointed with a pen at the different letters. I thought it all very tiresome. Our preparations were by no means completed when the fateful hour struck and the Governess was due to arrive. I did what so many peoples have done in similar circumstances : I took to the woods. I hid in the extensive shrubberies—forests they seemed—which surrounded " The Little Lodge ". Hours passed before I was retrieved and handed over to the Governess. We continued to toil every day, not only at letters but at words, and also at what was much worse, figures. Letters after all had only got to be known, and when they stood together in a certain way one recognised their formation and that it meant a certain sound or word which one uttered when pressed sufficiently. But the figures were tied into all sorts of tangles and did things to one another which it was extremely difficult to forecast with complete accuracy.

You had to say what they did each time they were tied up together, and the Governess apparently attached enormous importance to the answer being exact. If it was not right, it was wrong. It was not any use being " nearly right ". In some cases these figures got into debt with one another : you had to borrow one or carry one, and afterwards you had to pay back the one you had borrowed. These complications cast a steadily gathering shadow over my daily life. They took one away from all the interesting things one wanted to do in the nursery or in the garden. They made increasing inroads upon one's leisure. One could hardly get time to do any of the things one wanted to do. They became a general worry and preoccupation. More especially was this true when we descended into a dismal bog called " sums ". There appeared to be no limit to these. When one sum was done there was always another. Just as soon as I managed to tackle a particular class of these afflictions, some other much more variegated type was thrust upon me.

TO SCHOOL

The school my parents had selected for my education was one of the most fashionable and expensive in the country.

When the last sound of my mother's departing wheels had died away, the Headmaster invited me to hand over any money I had in my possession. I produced my three half-crowns, which were duly entered in a book, and I was told that from time to time there would be a " shop " at the school with all sorts of things which one would like to have, and that I could choose what I liked up to the limit of the seven and sixpence. Then we quitted the Headmaster's parlour and the comfortable private side of the house, and entered the more bleak apartments reserved for the instruction and accommodation of the pupils. I was taken into a Form Room and told to sit at a desk. All the other boys were out of doors, and I was alone with the Form Master. He produced a thin greeny-brown-covered book filled with words in different types of print.

" You have never done any Latin before, have you? " he said.

" No, sir."

" This is a Latin grammar." He opened it at a well-thumbed page. " You must learn this," he said, pointing to a number of words in a frame of lines. " I will come back in half an hour and see what you know."

Behold me then on a gloomy evening, with an aching heart, seated in front of the First Declension.

Mensa	a table
Mensa	O table
Mensam	a table
Mensae	of a table
Mensae	to or for a table
Mensa	by, with or from a table

What on earth did it mean? Where was the sense in it? It seemed absolute rigmarole to me. However, there was one thing I could always do : I could learn by heart. And I thereupon proceeded, as far as my private sorrows would allow, to memorise the acrostic-looking task which had been set me.

In due course the Master returned.

" Have you learnt it?" he asked.

" I think I can *say* it, sir," I replied ; and I gabbled it off.

He seemed so satisfied with this that I was emboldened to ask a question.

" What does it mean, sir?"

" It means what it says. Mensa, a table. Mensa is a noun of the First Declension. There are five declensions. You have learnt the singular of the First Declension."

" But," I repeated, " what does it mean?"

" Mensa means a table," he answered.

" Then why does mensa also mean O table," I enquired, " and what does O table mean?"

" Mensa, O table, is the vocative case," he replied.

" But why O table?" I persisted in genuine curiosity.

" O table,—you would use that in addressing a table, in invoking a table." And then seeing he was not carrying me with him, " You would use it in speaking to a table."

" But I never do," I blurted out in honest amazement.

" If you are impertinent, you will be punished, and punished, let me tell you, very severely," was his conclusive rejoinder.

Such was my first introduction to the classics from which, I have been told, many of our cleverest men have derived so much solace and profit.

HARROW

However, by being so long in the lowest form I gained an immense advantage over the cleverer boys. They all went on to learn Latin and Greek and splendid things like that. But I was taught English. We were considered such dunces that we could learn only English. Mr. Somervell—a most delightful man, to whom my debt is great—was charged with the duty of teaching the stupidest boys the most disregarded thing—namely, to write mere English. He knew how to do it. He taught it as no one else has ever taught it. Not only did we learn English parsing thoroughly, but we also practised continually English analysis. Mr. Somervell had a system of his own. He took a fairly long sentence and broke it up into its components by means of black, red, blue and green inks. Subject, verb, object: Relative Clauses, Conditional Clauses, Conjunctive and Disjunctive Clauses! Each had its colour and its bracket. It was a kind of drill. We did it almost daily. As I remained in the Third Fourth (β) three times as long as anyone else, I had three times as much of it. I learned it thoroughly. Thus I got into my bones the essential structure of the ordinary British sentence—which is a noble thing. And when in after years my schoolfellows who had won prizes and distinction for writing such beautiful Latin poetry and pithy Greek epigrams had to come down again to common English to earn their living or make their way, I did not feel myself at any disadvantage. Naturally I am biassed in favour of boys learning English. I would make them all learn English: and then I would let the clever ones learn Latin as an honour, and Greek as a treat. But the only thing I would whip them for is not knowing English. I would whip them hard for that.

I first went to Harrow in the summer term. The school possessed the biggest swimming-bath I had ever seen. It was more like the bend of a river than a bath, and it had two bridges across it. Thither we used to repair for hours at a time, and bask between our dips, eating enormous buns, on the hot asphalt margin. Naturally it was a good joke to come up behind some naked friend, or even enemy, and push him in. I made quite a habit of this with boys of my own size or less. One day when I had been no more than a month in the school, I saw a boy standing in a meditative posture wrapped in a towel on the very brink. He was no bigger than I was, so I thought him fair game. Coming stealthily behind, I pushed him in, holding on to his towel out of humanity, so that it should not get wet. I was startled to see a furious face emerge from the foam, and a being evidently of enormous strength making its way by fierce strokes to the shore. I fled : but in vain. Swift as the wind my pursuer overtook me, seized me in a ferocious grip and hurled me into the deepest part of the pool. I soon scrambled out on the other side, and found myself surrounded by an agitated crowd of younger boys. " You're in for it," they said. " Do you know what you have done? It's Amery ; he's in the Sixth form. He is Head of his House ; he is champion at Gym ; he has got his football colours ". They continued to recount his many titles to fame and reverence, and to dilate upon the awful retribution that would fall upon me. I was convulsed not only with terror, but with the guilt of sacrilege. How could I tell his rank when he was in a bath-towel and so small? I determined to apologise immediately. I approached the potentate in lively trepidation. " I am very sorry," I said. " I mistook you for a Fourth Form boy. You are so small." He did not seem at all placated by this ; so I added in a most brilliant recovery, " My father, who is a great man, is also small ". At this he laughed, and after some general remarks about my " cheek " and how I had better be careful in the future, signified that the incident was closed.

SANDHURST

I learned several things at Sandhurst which showed me how to behave and how officers of different ranks were expected to treat one another in the life and discipline of a regiment. My company commander, Major Ball, of the Welsh regiment, was a very strict and peppery martinet. Formal, reserved, frigidly courteous, punctilious, impeccable, severe, he was held in the greatest awe. It had never been his fortune to go on active service, but we were none the less sure that he would have had to be killed to be beaten.

The rule was, that if you went outside the college bounds, you first of all wrote your name in the company leave-book, and might then assume that your request was sanctioned. One day I drove a tandem (hired) over to Aldershot to see a friend in a militia battalion then training there. As I drove down the Marlborough lines, whom should I meet but Major Ball himself driving a spanking dog-cart home to Sandhurst. As I took off my hat to him, I remembered with a flash of anxiety that I had been too lazy or careless to write my name in the leave-book. However, I thought, " there is still a chance. He may not look at it until Mess ; and I will write my name down as soon as I get back'. I curtailed my visit to the militia battalion and hastened back to the college as fast as the ponies could trot. It was six o'clock when I got in. I ran along the passage to the desk where the leave-book lay, and the first thing that caught my eyes were the Major's initials " O.B. " at the foot of the leaves granted for the day. I was too late. He had seen me in Aldershot and had seen that my name was not in the book. Then I looked again, and there to my astonishment was my own name written in the Major's hand-writing and duly approved by his initials.

This opened my eyes to the kind of life which existed in the old British Army and how the very strictest discipline could be maintained among officers without the slightest departure from the standards of a courteous and easy society. Naturally after such a rebuke I never was so neglectful again.

THE FOURTH HUSSARS

In those days the principle was that the newly-joined officer was given a recruit's training for the first six months. He rode and drilled afoot with the troopers and received exactly the same instruction and training as they did. At the head of the file in the riding-school, or on the right of the squad on the Square, he had to try to set an example to the men. This was a task not always possible to discharge with conspicuous success. Mounting and dismounting from a bare-backed horse at the trot or canter; jumping a high bar without stirrups or even saddle, sometimes with hands clasped behind one's back; jogging at a fast trot with nothing but the horse's hide between your knees, brought their inevitable share of mishaps. Many a time did I pick myself up shaken and sore from the riding-school tan and don again my little gold-braided pork-pie cap, fastened on the chin by a boot-lace strap, with what appearance of dignity I could command, while twenty recruits grinned furtively but delightedly to see their officer suffering the same misfortunes which it was their lot so frequently to undergo. I had the

ill-luck, at an early stage in these proceedings, to strain my
tailor's muscle on which one's grip upon a horse depends.
In consequence I suffered tortures. Galvanic treatment
was then unknown ; one simply had to go on tearing at a
lacerated muscle with the awful penalty of being thought
a booby, if one begged off even for a day.

INDIA

The time was now come for us to embark for the East.
We sailed from Southampton in a trooper carrying
about 1,200 men, and after a voyage of twenty-three days
cast anchor in Bombay Harbour and pulled up the curtain
on what might well have been a different planet.

It may be imagined how our whole shipful of officers
and men were delighted after being cooped up for nearly
a month to see the palms and palaces of Bombay lying
about us in a wide crescent. We gazed at them over the
bulwarks across the shining and surf-ribbed waters. Every
one wanted to go on shore at once and see what India was
like. The delays and formalities of disembarkation which
oppress the ordinary traveller are multiplied for those who
travel at the royal expense. However, at about three
o'clock in the afternoon orders were issued that we were to
land at eight o'clock when it would be cool ; and in the
meantime a proportion of officers might go ashore independently. A shoal of tiny boats had been lying around us
all day long, rising and falling with the swell. We eagerly
summoned some of these. It took about a quarter of an
hour to reach the quays of the Sassoon Dock. Glad I was
to be there ; for the lively motion of the skiff to which I

and my two friends had committed ourselves was fast becoming our main preoccupation. We came alongside of a great stone wall with dripping steps and iron rings for hand-holds. The boat rose and fell four or five feet with the surges. I put out my hand and grasped at a ring ; but before I could get my feet on the steps the boat swung away, giving my right shoulder a sharp and peculiar wrench. I scrambled up all right, made a few remarks of a general character, mostly beginning with the earlier letters of the alphabet, hugged my shoulder and soon thought no more about it.

Let me counsel my younger readers to beware of dis-located shoulders. In this, as in so many other things, it is the first step that counts. Quite an exceptional strain is required to tear the capsule which holds the shoulder joint together ; but once the deed is done, a terrible liability remains. Although my shoulder did not actually go out, I had sustained an injury which was to last me my life, which was to cripple me at polo, to prevent me from ever playing tennis, and to be a grave embarrassment in moments of peril, violence and effort. Since then, at irregular intervals my shoulder has dislocated on the most unexpected pretexts : sleeping with my arm under the pillow, taking a book from the library shelves, slipping on a staircase, swimming, etc. Once it very nearly went out through a too expansive gesture in the House of Commons, and I thought how astonished the members would have been to see the speaker to whom they were listening suddenly for no reason throw himself upon the floor in an instinctive effort to take the strain and leverage off the dis-placed arm-bone.

This accident was a serious piece of bad luck. However, you can never tell whether bad luck may not after all turn out to be good luck. Perhaps if in the charge of Omdurman I had been able to use a sword, instead of having to adopt a modern weapon like a Mauser pistol, my story might not have got so far as the telling. One must never forget when misfortunes come that it is quite possible they are saving one from something much worse ; or that when you make some great mistake, it may very easily serve you better than the best-advised decision. Life is a whole, and luck is a whole, and no part of them can be separated from the rest.

OMDURMAN

September 2nd 1896

The collision was now very near. I saw immediately before me, not ten yards away, the two blue men who lay in my path. They were perhaps a couple of yards apart. I rode at the interval between them. They both fired. I passed through the smoke conscious that I was unhurt. The trooper immediately behind me was killed at this place and at this moment, whether by these shots or not I do not know. I checked my pony as the ground began to fall away beneath his feet. The clever animal dropped like a cat four or five feet down on to the sandy bed of the watercourse, and in this sandy bed I found myself surrounded by what seemed to be dozens of men. They were not thickly-packed enough at this point for me to experience any actual collision with them. Whereas Grenfell's troop next but one on my left was brought to a complete standstill and suffered very heavy losses, we seemed to push our way through as one has sometimes seen mounted policemen break up a crowd. In less time than it takes to relate, my pony had scrambled up the other side of the ditch. I looked round.

Once again I was on the hard, crisp desert, my horse at a trot. I had the impression of scattered Dervishes running to and fro in all directions. Straight before me a man threw himself on the ground. The reader must remember that I had been trained as a cavalry soldier to believe that if ever cavalry broke into a mass of infantry, the latter would be at their mercy. My first idea therefore was that the man was terrified. But simultaneously I saw the gleam of his curved sword as he drew it back for a ham-stringing cut. I had room and time enough to turn my pony out of his reach, and leaning over on the off side I fired two shots into him at about three yards. As I straightened myself in the saddle, I saw before me another figure with uplifted sword. I raised my pistol and fired. So close were we that the pistol itself actually struck him. Man and sword disappeared below and behind me. On my left, ten yards away, was an Arab horseman in a bright-coloured tunic and steel helmet, with chain-mail hangings. I fired at him. He turned aside. I pulled my horse into a walk and looked around again.

In one respect a cavalry charge is very like ordinary life. So long as you are all right, firmly in your saddle, your horse in hand, and well armed, lots of enemies will give you a wide berth. But as soon as you have lost a stirrup, have a rein cut, have dropped your weapon, are wounded, or your horse is wounded, then is the moment when from all quarters enemies rush upon you. Such was the fate of not a few of my comrades in the troops immediately on my left. Brought to an actual standstill in the enemy's mass, clutched at from every side, stabbed at and hacked at by spear and sword, they were dragged from their horses and cut to pieces by the infuriated foe. But this I did not at the time see or understand. My impressions continued to be sanguine. I thought we were masters of the situation, riding the enemy down, scattering them and killing them. I pulled my horse up and looked about me. There was a mass of Dervishes about forty or fifty yards away on my left. They were huddling and clumping themselves together, rallying for mutual protection. They seemed wild with excitement, dancing about on their feet, shaking their spears up and down. The whole scene seemed to flicker. I have an impression, but it is too fleeting to define, of brown-clad Lancers mixed up here and there with this surging mob. The scattered individuals in my immediate neighbourhood made no attempt to molest me. Where was my troop? Where were the other troops of the squadron? Within a hundred yards of me I could not see a single officer or man. I looked back at the Dervish mass. I saw two or three riflemen crouching and aiming their rifles at me from the fringe of it. Then for the first time that morning I experienced a sudden sensation of fear. I felt myself absolutely alone. I thought these riflemen would hit me and the rest devour me like wolves. What a fool I was to loiter like this in the midst of the enemy! I crouched over the saddle, spurred my horse into a gallop and drew clear of the *mêlée*. Two or three hundred yards away I found my troop all ready faced about and partly formed up.

The other three troops of the squadron were re-forming close by. Suddenly in the midst of the troop up sprang a Dervish. How he got there I do not know. He must have leaped out of some scrub or hole. All the troopers turned upon him thrusting with their lances : but he darted to and fro causing for a moment a frantic commotion. Wounded several times, he staggered towards me raising his spear. I shot him at less than a yard. He fell on the sand, and lay there dead. How easy to kill a man! But I did not worry about it. I found I had fired the whole magazine of my Mauser pistol, so I put in a new clip of ten cartridges before thinking of anything else.

I was still prepossessed with the idea that we had inflicted great slaughter on the enemy and had scarcely suffered at all ourselves. Three or four men were missing from my troop. Six men and nine or ten horses were bleeding from spear thrusts or sword cuts. We all expected to be ordered immediately to charge back again. The men were ready, though they all looked serious. Several asked to be allowed to throw away their lances and draw their swords. I asked my second sergeant if he had enjoyed himself. His answer was " Well, I don't exactly say I enjoyed it, Sir ; but I think I'll get more used to it next time." At this the whole troop laughed.

But now from the direction of the enemy there came a succession of grisly apparitions ; horses spouting blood, struggling on three legs, men staggering on foot, men bleeding from terrible wounds, fish-hook spears stuck right through them, arms and faces cut to pieces, bowels protruding, men gasping, crying, collapsing, expiring. Our first task was to succour these ; and meanwhile the blood of our leaders cooled. They remembered for the first time that we had carbines. Everything was still in great confusion. But trumpets were sounded and orders shouted, and we all moved off at a trot towards the flank of the enemy. Arrived at a position from which we could enfilade and rake the watercourse, two squadrons were dismounted and in a few minutes with their fire at three hundred yards compelled the Dervishes to retreat. We therefore remained in possession of the field. Within twenty minutes of the time when we had first wheeled into line and begun our charge, we were halted and breakfasting in the very watercourse that had so nearly proved our undoing. There one could see the futility of the much vaunted *Arme Blanche*. The Dervishes had carried off their wounded, and the corpses of thirty or forty enemy were all that could be counted on the ground. Among these lay the bodies of over twenty Lancers, so hacked and mutilated as to be mostly unrecognisable. In all out of 310 officers and men the regiment had lost in the space of about two or three minutes five officers and sixty-five men killed and wounded, and 120 horses—nearly a quarter of its strength.

WAR CORRESPONDENT : PRISONER OF THE BOERS

We agreed that the engine should go slowly back along the line with all the wounded, who were now numerous, and that the Dublins and the Durban men should retreat on foot, sheltering themselves behind the engine which would go at a foot's pace. Upwards of forty persons, of whom the greater part were streaming with blood, were crowded on the engine and its tender, and we began to move slowly forward. I was in the cab of the engine directing the engine-driver. It was crammed so full of wounded men that one could scarcely move. The shells burst all around, some striking the engine, others dashing the gravel of the track upon it and its unhappy human freight. The pace increased, the infantry outside began to lag and then to be left behind. At last I forced the engine-diver to stop altogether, but before I could get the engine stopped we were already 300 yards away from our infantry. Close at hand was the bridge across the Blue Krantz River, a considerable span. I told the engine-driver to cross the bridge and wait on the other side, and forcing my way out of the cab I got down on to the line and went back along it to find Captain Haldane, and to bring him and his Dublin Fusiliers along.

But while these events had been taking place everything else had been in movement. I had not retraced my steps 200 yards when, instead of Haldane and his company, two figures in plain clothes appeared upon the line. " Plate-layers! " I said to myself, and then with a surge of realiz-ation, " Boers! " My mind retains its impression of these tall figures, full of energy, clad in dark, flapping clothes, with slouch, storm-driven hats, poising on their levelled rifles hardly a hundred yards away. I turned again and ran back towards the engine, the two Boers firing as I ran between the metals. Their bullets, sucking to right and left, seemed to miss only by inches. We were in a small cutting with banks about six feet high on either side. I flung myself against the bank of the cutting. It gave no cover. Another glance at the two figures ; one was now kneeling to aim. Movement seemed the only chance. Again I darted forward : again two soft kisses sucked in the air ; but nothing struck me. This could not endure. I must get out of that cutting—that damnable corridor! I jigged to the left and scrambled up the bank. The earth sprang up beside me. I got through the wire fence unhurt. Outside the cutting was a tiny depression. I crouched in this, struggling to get my breath again.

Fifty yards away was a small platelayers' cabin of masonry; there was cover there. About 200 yards away was the rocky gorge of the Blue Krantz River; there was plenty of cover there. I determined to make a dash for the river. I rose to my feet. Suddenly on the other side of the railway, separated from me by the rails and two uncut wire fences, I saw a horseman galloping furiously, a tall, dark figure, holding his rifle in his right hand. He pulled up his horse almost in its own length and shaking the rifle at me shouted a loud command. We were forty yards apart. That morning I had taken with me, Correspondent-status notwithstanding, my Mauser pistol. I thought I could kill this man, and after the treatment I had received I earnestly desired to do so. I put my hand to my belt, the pistol was not there. When engaged in clearing the line, getting in and out of the engine, etc., I had taken it off. It came safely home on the engine. I have it now! But at this moment I was quite unarmed. Meanwhile, I suppose in about the time this takes to tell, the Boer horseman, still seated on his horse, had covered me with his rifle. The animal stood stock still, so did he, and so did I. I looked towards the river, I looked towards the platelayers' hut. The Boer continued to look along his sights. I thought there was absolutely no chance of escape, if he fired he would surely hit me, so I held up my hands and surrendered myself a prisoner of war.

"When one is alone and unarmed," said the great Napoleon, in words which flowed into my mind in the poignant minutes that followed, "a surrender may be pardoned". Still he might have missed; and the Blue Krantz ravine was very near and the two wire fences were still uncut. However, the deed was done. Thereupon my captor lowered his rifle and beckoned to me to come across

to him. I obeyed. I walked through the wire fences and
across the line and stood by his side. He sprang off his
horse and began firing in the direction of the bridge upon
the retreating engine and a few straggling British figures.
Then when the last had disappeared he re-mounted and at
his side I tramped back towards the spot where I had left
Captain Haldane and his company. I saw none of them.
They were already prisoners. I noticed that it was raining
hard. As I plodded through the high grass by the side of
my captor a disquieting and timely reflection came into
my mind. I had two clips of Mauser ammunition, each
holding ten rounds, in two little breast pockets one on
each side of my khaki coat. These cartridges were the
same as I had used at Omdurman, and were the only kind
supplied for the Mauser pistol. They were what are called
" soft-nosed bullets". I had never given them a thought
until now ; and it was borne in upon me that they might
be a very dangerous possession. I dropped the right-hand
clip on the ground without being seen. I got the left-hand
clip in my hand and was about to drop it, when my
captor looked down sharply and said in English, " What
have you got there? "

" What is it? " I said, opening the palm of my hand, "I
picked it up. "

He took it, looked at it and threw it away. We continued
to plod on until we reached the general gang of prisoners
and found ourselves speedily in the midst of many hundreds of mounted Boers who streamed into view, in long
columns of twos and threes, many holding umbrellas over
their heads in the pouring rain.

B

ESCAPE

The State Model Schools stood in the midst of a quadrangle, and were surrounded on two sides by an iron
grille and on two by a corrugated-iron fence about ten feet
high. These boundaries offered little obstacle to anyone
who possessed the activity of youth, but the fact that they
were guarded on the inside by sentries, fifty yards apart,
armed with rifle and revolver, made them a well-nigh in-
superable barrier. No walls are so hard to pierce as living
walls.

After anxious reflection and continual watching, it was
discovered by several of the prisoners that when the
sentries along the eastern side walked about on their beats
they were at certain moments unable to see the top of a
few yards of the wall near a small circular lavatory office.
The electric lights in the middle of the quadrangle
brilliantly lighted the whole place, but the eastern wall
was in shadow. The first thing was therefore to pass the
two sentries near the office. It was necessary to hit off the
exact moment when both their backs should be turned
together. After the wall was scaled we should be in the
garden of the villa next door. There the plan came to an
end. Everything after this was vague and uncertain. How
to get out of the garden, how to pass unnoticed through
the streets, how to evade the patrols that surrounded the
town, and above all how to cover the two hundred and
eighty miles to the Portuguese frontier, were questions
which would arise at a later stage.

Together with Captain Haldane and Lieutenant Brockie
I made an abortive attempt, not pushed with any decision,
on December 11. There was no difficulty in getting into
the circular office. But to climb out of it over the wall

was a hazard of the sharpest character. Anyone doing so must at the moment he was on the top of the wall be plainly visible to the sentries fifteen yards away, if they were in the right place and happened to look! Whether the sentries would challenge or fire depended entirely on their individual dispositions, and no one could tell what they would do. Nevertheless I was determined that nothing should stop my taking the plunge the next day. As the 12th wore away my fears crystallized more and more into desperation. In the evening, after my two friends had made an attempt, but had not found the moment propitious, I strolled across the quadrangle and secreted myself in the circular office. Through an aperture in the metal casing of which it was built I watched the sentries. For some time they remained stolid and obstructive. Then all of a sudden one turned and walked up to his comrade, and they began to talk. Their backs were turned.

Now or never! I stood on a ledge, seized the top of the wall with my hands, and drew myself up. Twice I let myself down again in sickly hesitation, and than with a third resolve scrambled up and over. My waistcoat got entangled with the ornamental metal-work on the top. I had to pause for an appreciable moment to extricate myself. In this posture I had one parting glimpse of the sentries still talking with their backs turned fifteen yards away. One of them was lighting his cigarette, and I remember the glow on the inside of his hands as a distinct impression which my mind recorded. Then I lowered myself lightly down into the adjoining garden and crouched among the shrubs. I was free! The first step had been taken, and it was irrevocable. It now remained to await the arrival of my comrades. The bushes in the garden gave a good deal of cover, and in the moonlight their shadows fell dark on the ground. I lay here for an hour in great impatience and anxiety. People were continually moving about the garden, and once a man came and apparently looked straight at me only a few yards away. Where were the others? Why did they not make the attempt?

Suddenly I heard a voice from within the quadrangle say, quite loud, " All up." I crawled back to the wall. Two officers were walking up and down inside, jabbering Latin words, laughing and talking all manner of nonsense —amid which I caught my name. I risked a cough. One of the officers immediately began to chatter alone. The other said, slowly and clearly, " They cannot get out. The sentry suspects. It's all up. Can you get back again? " But now all my fears fell from me at once. To go back was impossible. I could not hope to climb the wall unnoticed. There was no helpful ledge on the outside. Fate pointed onwards. Besides, I said to myself, " Of course, I shall be recaptured, but at least I will have a run for my money ". I said to the officers, " I shall go on alone ".

Now I was in the right mood for these undertakings— failure being almost certain, no odds against success affected me. All risks were less than the certainty. The gate which led into the road was only a few yards from another sentry. I said to myself, " *Toujours de l'audace*," put my hat on my head, strode into the middle of the garden, walked past the windows of the house without any attempt at concealment, and so went through the gate and turned to the left. I passed the sentry at less than five yards. Most of them knew me by sight. Whether he looked at me or not I do not know, for I never turned my head. I restrained with the utmost difficulty an impulse to run. But after walking a hundred yards and hearing no challenge, I knew that the second obstacle had been sur-mounted. I was at large in Pretoria.

RELIEF OF LADYSMITH
February 28th 1900

In spite of the vexatious course of the war, the two months' fighting for the relief of Ladysmith makes one of the most happy memories of my life. Although our irregular cavalry brigade was engaged with the enemy on at least three days out of five, our losses except in Thorney-croft's regiment at Spion Kop were never severe. We had one skirmish after another with casualties running from half a dozen to a score. I saw all there was to see. Day after day we rode out in the early morning on one flank or another and played about with the Boers, galloped around or clambered up the rocky hills, caught glimpses of dart-ing, fleeting horsemen in the distance, heard a few bullets whistle, had a few careful shots and came safe home to a good dinner and cheery, keenly-intelligent companions. Meanwhile I dispatched a continual stream of letters and cables to the *Morning Post*, and learned from them that all I wrote commanded a wide and influential public. I knew all the generals and other swells, had access to everyone, and was everywhere well received. We lived in great com-fort in the open air, with cool nights and bright sunshine, with plenty of meat, chickens and beer. The excellent Natal newspapers often got into the firing line about noon and always awaited us on our return in the evening. One lived entirely in the present with something happening all the time. Care-free, no regrets for the past, no fears for the future ; no expenses, no duns, no complications, and all the time my salary was safely piling up at home! When a prisoner I had thought it my duty to write from Pretoria to the *Morning Post* releasing them from their contract, as it seemed they could get no more value out of me. They did not accept my offer ; but before I knew this, I was already free. My relations with them continued to be of the best ; and one could not serve better employers.

It was a great joy to me to have my brother Jack with me, and I looked forward to showing him round and doing for him the honours of war. This pleasure was, however, soon cut short. On February 12 we made a reconnaissance 6 or 7 miles to the east of the railway line and occupied for some hours a large wooded eminence known to the army as Hussar Hill. Buller and the Headquarters staff, it seemed, wished to examine this ground. Using our whole brigade we drove away the Boer pickets and patrols, set up an outpost line of our own, and enabled the general to see what he wanted. As the morning passed, the rifle fire became more lively, and when the time came to go home the Boers followed on our tail and we had some loss in disengaging ourselves.

After quitting Hussar Hill and putting at a gallop a mile between us and the enemy, our squadrons reined into a walk and rode slowly homewards up a long smooth grass slope. I was by now a fairly experienced young officer and I could often feel danger impending from this quarter or from that, as you might feel a light breeze on your cheek or neck. When one rode for instance within rifle shot of some hill or watercourse about which we did not know enough, I used to feel a draughty sensation. On this occasion as I looked back over my shoulder from time to time at Hussar Hill or surveyed the large brown masses of our rearmost squadrons riding so placidly home across the rolling veldt, I remarked to my companion, " We are still much too near those fellows ". The words were hardly out of my mouth when a shot rang out, followed by the rattle of magazine fire from two or three hundred Mauser rifles. A hail of bullets whistled among our squadrons, emptying a few saddles and bringing down a few horses. Instinctively our whole cavalcade spread out into open order and scampered over the crest now nearly two hundred yards away. Here we leapt off our horses, which were hurried into cover, threw ourselves on the grass, and returned the fire with an answering roar and rattle.

If the Boers had been a little quicker and had caught us a quarter of a mile farther back we should have paid dearly for the liberty we had taken : but the range was now over 2,000 yards ; we were prone, almost as invisible as the enemy, and very little harm was done. Jack was lying by my side. All of a sudden he jumped and wriggled back a yard or two from the line. He had been shot in the calf, in this his very first skirmish, by a bullet which must have passed uncommonly near his head. I helped him from the firing line and saw him into an ambulance. The fusillade soon ceased and I rode on to the field hospital to make sure he was properly treated. The British army doctors were in those days very jealous of their military rank ; so I saluted the surgeon, addressed him as " Major ", and had a few words with him about the skirmish, and then mentioned my brother's wound. The gallant doctor was in the best of tempers, promised chloroform, no pain, and every attention, and was certainly as good as his word.

But now here was a curious coincidence. While I had

been busy in South Africa my mother had not been idle at home. She had raised a fund, captivated an American millionaire, obtained a ship, equipped it as a hospital with a full staff of nurses and every comfort. After a stormy voyage she had arrived at Durban and eagerly awaited a consignment of wounded. She received her younger son as the very first casualty treated on board the hospital ship *Maine*. I took a few days' leave to go and see her, and lived on board as on a yacht. So here we were all happily reunited after six months of varied experiences. . . .

February 27 was the anniversary of Majuba, and on this day the Natal army delivered its final attack. All the big guns were now back again on the big hills, and the Brigades, having passed the river by the Boer bridge which was undamaged, attacked the Boer position from the right. First Barton's Hill was stormed. This drew with it the capture of Railway Hill ; and lastly the dreaded position of the Inniskilling Hill, already half turned and to some extent commanded, was carried by the bayonet. The last row of hills between us and Ladysmith had fallen. Mounting in haste we galloped to the river, hoping to pursue. The Commander-in-Chief met us at the bridge and sternly ordered us back. " Damn pursuit! " were said to be the historic words he uttered on this occasion. As one might say " Damn reward for sacrifices! Damn the recovery of debts overdue! Damn the prize which eases future struggles! "

The next morning, advancing in leisurely fashion, we crossed the river, wended up and across the battle-scarred heights, and debouched upon the open plain which led to Ladysmith six miles away. The Boers were in full retreat ; the shears were up over their big gun on Bulwana Hill, and the dust of the wagon-trains trekking northward rose from many quarters of the horizon. The order " Damn pursuit! " still held. It was freely said that the Commander-in-Chief had remarked " Better leave them alone now they are going off". All day we chafed and fumed, and it was not until evening that two squadrons of the S.A.L.H. were allowed to brush through the crumbling rearguards and ride into Ladysmith. I rode with these two squadrons, and galloped across the scrub-dotted plain, fired at only by a couple of Boer guns. Suddenly from the brushwood up rose gaunt figures waving hands of welcome. On we pressed, and at the head of a battered street of tin-roofed houses met Sir George White on horseback, faultlessly attired. Then we all rode together into the long-beleaguered, almost starved-out, Ladysmith. It was a thrilling moment.

I dined with the Headquarters staff that night. Ian Hamilton, Rawlinson, Hedworth Lambton, were warm in their welcome. Jealously preserved bottles of champagne were uncorked. I looked for horseflesh, but the last trek ox had been slain in honour of the occasion. Our pallid and emaciated hosts showed subdued contentment. But having travelled so far and by such rough and devious routes, I rejoiced to be in Ladysmith at last.

THE HOUSE OF COMMONS

January 26th 1901

It was an honour to take part in the deliberations of this famous assembly which for centuries had guided England through numberless perils forward on the path of empire. Though I had done nothing else for many months but address large audiences, it was with awe as well as eagerness that I braced myself for what I regarded as the supreme ordeal. As I had not been present at the short winter session, I had only taken my seat for four days before I rose to address the House. I need not recount the pains I had taken to prepare, nor the efforts I had made to hide the work of preparation. The question in debate, which raised the main issue of the war, was one upon which I felt myself competent to argue or advise. I listened to counsel from many friendly quarters. Some said " It is too soon ; wait for a few months till you know the House ". Others said " It is your subject : do not miss the chance ". I was warned against offending the House by being too controversial on an occasion when everyone wished to show goodwill. I was warned against mere colourless platitude. But the best advice I got was from Mr. Henry Chaplin, who said to me in his rotund manner, " Don't be hurried ; unfold your case. If you have anything to say, the House will listen."

I learned that a rising young Welshman, a pro-Boer, and one of our most important bugbears, named Lloyd George, who from below the gangway was making things very difficult for the leaders of the Liberal party, would probably be called about nine o'clock. He had a moderately phrased amendment on the paper, but whether he would move it was not certain. I gathered that I could, if I wished, have the opportunity of following him. In those days, and indeed for many years, I was unable to say anything (except a sentence in rejoinder) that I had not written out and committed to memory beforehand. I had never had the practice which comes to young men at the University of speaking in small debating societies impromptu upon all sorts of subjects. I had to try to foresee the situation and to have a number of variants ready to meet its possibilities. I therefore came with a quiverful of arrows of different patterns and sizes, some of which I hoped would hit the target. My concern was increased by the uncertainty about what Mr. Lloyd George would do. I hoped that the lines I had prepared would follow fairly well from what he would probably say.

The hour arrived. I sat in the corner seat above the gangway, immediately behind the Ministers, the same seat from which my father had made his speech of resignation and his terrible Piggott attack. On my left, a friendly counsellor, sat the long-experienced Parliamentarian, Mr. Thomas Gibson Bowles. Towards nine o'clock the House began to fill. Mr. Lloyd George spoke from the third bench below the gangway on the Opposition side, surrounded by a handful of Welshmen and Radicals, and backed by the Irish Nationalist party. He announced forthwith that he did not intend to move his amendment, but would instead speak on the main question. Encouraged by the cheers of the " Celtic fringes " he soon became animated and even violent. I constructed in succession sentence after sentence to hook on with after he should sit down. Each of these poor couplings became in turn obsolete. A sense of alarm and even despair crept across me. I repressed it with an inward gasp. Then Mr. Bowles whispered " You might say ' instead of making his violent speech without moving his moderate amendment, he had better have moved his moderate amendment without making his violent speech ' ". Manna in the wilderness was not more welcome! It fell only just in time. To my surprise I heard my opponent saying that he " would curtail his remarks as he was sure the House wished to hear a new member ", and with this graceful gesture he suddenly resumed his seat.

I was up before I knew it, and reciting Tommy Bowles's rescuing sentence. It won a general cheer. Courage returned. I got through all right. The Irish—whom I had been taught to detest—were a wonderful audience. They gave just the opposition which would help, and said nothing they thought would disturb. They did not seem the least offended when I made a joke at their expense. But presently when I said " The Boers who are fighting in the field—*and if I were a Boer, I hope I should be fighting in the field*—. . . ." I saw a ruffle upon the Treasury bench below me. Mr. Chamberlain said something to his neighbour which I could not hear. Afterwards George Wyndham told me it was "That's the way to throw away seats!" But I could already see the shore at no great distance, and swam on vigorously till I could scramble up the beach, breathless physically, dripping metaphorically, but safe. Everyone was very kind. The usual restoratives were applied and I sat in a comfortable coma till I was strong enough to go home. The general verdict was not unfavourable. Although many guessed I had learnt it all by heart, this was pardoned because of the pains I had taken. The House of Commons, though gravely changed, is still an august collective personality. It is always indulgent to those who are proud to be its servants.

After this debate I first made the acquaintance of Mr. Lloyd George. We were introduced at the Bar of the House of Commons. After compliments, he said " Judging from your sentiments, you are standing against the Light ". I replied " You take a singularly detached view of the British Empire ". Thus began an association which has persisted through many vicissitudes.

THE BATTLE OF SIDNEY STREET
January 3rd 1911

At about ten o'clock on the morning of January 3 I was in my bath, when I was surprised by an urgent knocking at the door.

" There is a message from the Home Office on the telephone absolutely immediate. "

Dripping wet and shrouded in a towel I hurried to the instrument, and received the following news :

" The Anarchists who murdered the police have been surrounded in a house in the East End—No. 100 Sidney Street—and are firing on the police with automatic pistols. They have shot one man and appear to have plenty of ammunition. Authority is requested to send for troops to arrest or kill them."

I replied at once, giving the necessary permission and directing the police to use whatever force was necessary. In about twenty minutes I was at the Home Office. There I found my principal adviser, Mr. Ernley Blackwell, who told me that no further information had been received, except that the Anarchists had been effectually surrounded, but were still firing in all directions. No one knew how many Anarchists there were or what measures were going to be taken. In these circumstances I thought it my duty to see what was going on myself, and my advisers concurred in the propriety of such a step. I must, however, admit that convictions of duty were supported by a strong sense of curiosity which perhaps it would have been well to keep in check.

We started at once in a motor-car. Down the Strand, through the City towards Houndsditch, until at length at about noon we reached the point where all traffic was stopped. We got out of the car. There was a considerable crowd of angry and alarmed people, and I noticed the unusual spectacle of Metropolitan constables armed with shotguns hastily procured from a local gunsmith. The attitude of the crowd was not particularly friendly, and there were several cries of " Oo let 'em in? " in allusion to the refusal of the Liberal Government to introduce drastic laws restricting the immigration of aliens. Just at this moment, however, a shot rang out perhaps a couple of hundred yards away, followed by another and another, until there was a regular fusillade. Accompanied by an inspector, we proceeded down the empty street, turned a corner, turned another corner, and reached a group of policemen, several of whom were armed, and a number of onlookers and journalists who had found themselves within the police cordon when it was originally closed and had been permitted to remain. Another street ran at right angles across our path. Up this street fifty or sixty yards to the left was the house (No. 100) in which the murderers had barricaded themselves. On the opposite side in front of us, police, Scots Guardsmen, and spectators were crouching behind the projecting corners of the buildings ; and from both sides of the street, from the street itself, and from numerous windows, policemen and other persons were firing rifles, pistols, and shotguns with increasing frequency at the house which harboured the desperadoes. These replied every minute or two, shooting sometimes up and down the street and sometimes at their assailants in front. The bullets struck the brickwork and ricochetted hither and thither. We have since become only too familiar with scenes of this kind, and the spectacle of street fighting has long lost its novelty in Europe. But nothing of the sort had ever been seen within living memory in quiet, law-abiding, comfortable England ; and from this point of view at least my journey was well repaid.

But the situation almost immediately became embarrassing. Some of the police officers were anxious to storm the building at once with their pistols. Others rightly thought it better to take more time and to avoid the almost certain loss of three or four valuable lives. It was no part of my duty to take personal control or to give executive decisions. From my chair in the Home Office I could have sent any order and it would have been immediately acted on, but it was not for me to interfere with those who were in charge on the spot. Yet, on the other hand, my position of authority, far above them all, attracted inevitably to itself direct responsibility. I saw now that I should have done much better to have remained quietly in my office. On the other hand, it was impossible to get into one's car and drive away while matters stood in such great uncertainty, and moreover were extremely interesting.

Being anxious to have a direct view of the besieged house, I now crossed the street and took shelter in the doorway of a warehouse on the opposite side. Here I found Lord Knutsford, the Chairman of the London Hospital, and together we watched the closing scenes of the drama.

Plans were now made to storm the building from several sides at once. One party, emerging from the next-door house, was to rush the front door and charge up the stairs ; another party of police and soldiers would break into the second floor at the back through a window ; a third, smashing in the roof, would leap down on the assassins from above. There could be no doubt about the result of such an attack, but it certainly seemed that loss of life would be caused, not only by the fire of the Anarchists, but also from shots fired by the attackers in the confusion. My own instincts turned at once to a direct advance up the staircase behind a steel plate or shield, and search was made in the foundries of the neighbourhood for one of a suitable size. Meanwhile, however, the problem settled itself. At about half-past one a wisp of smoke curled out of the shattered upper windows of the besieged house, and in a few minutes it was plainly on fire. The conflagration gained apace, burning downwards. To the crackling of wood succeeded the roar of flames. Still the Anarchists, descending storey by storey, kept up their fire, and bullets continued to strike the brickwork of the surrounding houses and pavement.

Now occurred a curious incident, which, for the first time, made my presence on the spot useful. The ordinary functions of British life had been proceeding inflexibly to within a few feet of the danger-zone, and the postman on his rounds actually delivered his letters at the house next door. Suddenly, with a stir and a clatter, up came the fire brigade, scattering the crowds gathered on the approaches to the scene and thrusting through them until they reached the police cordon at the beginning of the danger-zone. The inspector of police forbade further progress, and the fire brigade officer declared it his duty to advance. A fire was raging, and he was bound to extinguish it. Anarchists, automatic pistols, danger-zones, nothing of this sort was mentioned in the Regulations of the London Fire Brigade. When the police officer pointed out that his men would be shot down, he replied simply that orders were orders and that he had no alternative. I now intervened to settle this dispute, at one moment quite heated. I told the fire-brigade officer, on my authority as Home Secretary, that the house was to be allowed to burn down and that he was to stand by in readiness to prevent the conflagration from spreading. I then returned to my coign of vantage on the opposite side of the road.

The flames were now beginning to invade the ground floor of the doomed house. Some minutes had passed without a shot being fired by the Anarchists. No human being could live longer in the building. Everyone expected to see the Anarchists—how many there were was not known for certain—sally out, pistol in hand, into the open street. A hundred rifles, revolvers, and shotguns were levelled at the smouldering doorway. The minutes passed in intense excitement, and the flames invaded the whole ground floor. At last it became certain that these human fiends had perished. Suddenly, upon a spontaneous impulse which led everyone into the open, a detective inspector walked quickly to the door and kicked it open. I followed a few yards behind, accompanied by a police sergeant with a double-barrelled shotgun. There was nothing but smoke and flame inside the building. The firemen rushed forward into the empty street with their hoses, and behind them surged a crowd of soldiers, journalists, photographers, and spectators. It was already three o'clock, and leaving the now-dying fire to be dealt with by the fire brigade and the ruins to be searched by the police, I went home.

Besides the police inspector shot in the morning, a colour-sergeant of the Guards and three civilians had been wounded by bullets, and a police sergeant struck, but not seriously injured, by a ricochet. Up to this moment no lives had been lost except those of the murderers. Alas, the day was not yet done! A falling wall injured five of the firemen, two in the most grave manner. There were found in the ruins of Sidney Street two charred bodies, one shot by a British bullet and one apparently suffocated by smoke. These were established to be the corpses of Fritz Svaars and Jacob Vogel, both members of " Peter the Painter's " Anarchist gang, and both certainly concerned in the police murders. One Browning and two Mauser pistols and six gun-metal bomb-cases were found amid the ruins, together with many cartridges.

Thus ended the battle of Sidney Street. Of " Peter the Painter " not a trace was ever found. He vanished completely. Rumour has repeatedly claimed him as one of the Bolshevik liberators and saviours of Russia. Certainly his qualities and record would well have fitted him to take an honoured place in that noble band. But of this Rumour is alone the foundation.

Party controversy was then at its height in England, and I was much criticized in the newspapers and in Parliament for my share in this curious episode. Mr. Balfour in the House of Commons was especially sarcastic.

" We are concerned to observe," he said in solemn tones, " photographs in the illustrated newspapers of the Home Secretary in the danger-zone. I understand what the photographer was doing, but why the Home Secretary? "

And with this not altogether unjust reflection I may bring the story to an end.

WORLD CRISIS

It was the custom in the palmy days of Queen Victoria for statesmen to expatiate upon the glories of the British Empire, and to rejoice in that protecting Providence which had preserved us through so many dangers and brought us at length into a secure and prosperous age. Little did they know that the worst perils had still to be encountered and that the greatest triumphs were yet to be won.

Children were taught of the Great War against Napoleon as the culminating effort in the history of the British peoples, and they looked on Waterloo and Trafalgar as the supreme achievements of British arms by land and sea. These prodigious victories, eclipsing all that had gone before, seemed the fit and predestined ending to the long drama of our island race, which had advanced over a thousand years from small and weak beginnings to a foremost position in the world. Three separate times in three different centuries had the British people rescued Europe from a military domination. Thrice had the Low Countries been assailed : by Spain, by the French Monarchy, by the French Empire. Thrice had British war and policy, often maintained single-handed, overthrown the aggressor. Always at the outset the strength of the enemy had seemed overwhelming, always the struggle had been prolonged through many years and across awful hazards, always the victory had at last been won : and the last of all the victories had been the greatest of all, gained after the most ruinous struggle and over the most formidable foe.

Surely that was the end of the tale as it was so often the end of the book. History showed the rise, culmination, splendour, transition and decline of States and Empires. It seemed inconceivable that the same series of tremendous events through which since the days of Queen Elizabeth we had three times made our way successfully, should be repeated a fourth time and on an immeasurably larger scale. Yet that is what has happened, and what we have lived to see.

The [First] Great War through which we have passed differed from all ancient wars in the immense power of the combatants and their fearful agencies of destruction, and from all modern wars in the utter ruthlessness with which it was fought. All the horrors of all the ages were brought together, and not only armies but whole populations were thrust into the midst of them. The mighty educated States involved conceived with reason that their very existence was at stake. Germany having let Hell loose kept well in the van of terror ; but she was followed step by step by the desperate and ultimately avenging nations she had assailed. Every outrage against humanity or international law was repaid by reprisals often on a greater scale and of longer duration. No truce or parley mitigated the strife of the armies. The wounded died between the lines : the dead mouldered into the soil. Merchant ships and neutral ships and hospital ships were sunk on the seas and all on board left to their fate, or killed as they swam. Every effort was made to starve whole nations into submission without regard to age or sex. Cities and monuments were smashed by artillery. Bombs from the air were cast down indiscriminately. Poison gas in many forms stifled or seared the soldiers. Liquid fire was projected upon their bodies. Men fell from the air in flames, or were smothered, often slowly, in the dark recesses of the sea. The fighting strength of armies was limited only by the manhood of their countries. Europe and large parts of Asia and Africa became one vast battlefield on which after years of struggle not armies but nations broke and ran. When all was over, Torture and Cannibalism were the only two expedients that the civilised, scientific, Christian States had been able to deny themselves : and these were of doubtful utility.

But nothing daunted the valiant heart of man. Son of the Stone Age, vanquisher of nature with all her trials and monsters, he met the awful and self-inflicted agony with new reserves of fortitude. Freed in the main by his intelligence from mediaeval fears, he marched to death with sombre dignity. His nervous system was found in the twentieth century capable of enduring physical and moral stresses before which the simpler natures of primeval times would have collapsed. Again and again to the hideous bombardment, again and again from the hospital to the front, again and again to the hungry submarines, he strode unflinching. And withal, as an individual, preserved through these torments the glories of a reasonable and compassionate mind. . . .

One rises from the study of the causes of the [First] Great War with a prevailing sense of the defective control of individuals upon world fortunes. It has been well said, " there is always more error than design in human affairs." The limited minds even of the ablest men, their disputed authority, the climate of opinion in which they dwell, their transient and partial contributions to the mighty problem, that problem itself so far beyond their compass, so vast in scale and detail, so changing in its aspect—all this must surely be considered before the complete condemnation of the vanquished or the complete acquittal of the victors can be pronounced. Events also got on to certain lines, and no one could get them off again. Germany clanked obstinately, recklessly, awkwardly towards the crater and dragged us all in with her. But fierce resentments dwelt in France, and in Russia there were wheels within wheels. Could we in England perhaps by some effort, by some sacrifice of our material interests, by some compulsive gesture, at once of friendship and command, have reconciled France and Germany in time and formed that grand association on which alone the peace and glory of Europe would be safe? I cannot tell. I only know that we tried our best to steer our country through the gathering dangers of the armed peace without bringing her to war or others to war, and when these efforts failed, we drove through the tempest without bringing her to destruction.

A TALK WITH THE GERMAN AMBASSADOR

August 1911

One night the German Ambassador, still Count Metternich, whom I had known for ten years, asked me to dine with him. We were alone, and a famous hock from the Emperor's cellars was produced. We had a long talk about Germany and how she had grown great; about Napoleon and the part he had played in uniting her; about the Franco-German War and how it began and how it ended. I said what a pity it was that Bismarck had allowed himself to be forced by the soldiers into taking Lorraine, and how Alsace-Lorraine lay at the root of all the European armaments and rival combinations. He said these had been German provinces from remote antiquity until one day in profound peace Louis XIV had pranced over the frontier and seized them. I said their sympathies were French: he said they were mixed. I said anyhow it kept the whole thing alive. France could never forget her lost provinces, and they never ceased to call to her. The conversation passed to a kindred but more critical subject.

Was he anxious about the present situation? He said people were trying to ring Germany round and put her in a net, and that she was a strong animal to put in a net. I said, how could she be netted when she had an alliance with two other first-class Powers, Austria-Hungary and Italy? *We* had often stood quite alone for years at a time without getting flustered. He said it was a very different business for an island. But when you had been marched through and pillaged and oppressed so often and had only the breasts of your soldiers to stand between you and invasion, it ate into your soul. I said that Germany was frightened of nobody, and that everybody was frightened of her.

Then we came to the Navy. Surely, I said, it was a great mistake for Germany to try to rival Britain on the seas. She would never catch us up. We should build two to one or more if necessary, and at every stage antagonism would grow between the countries. Radicals and Tories, whatever they might say about each other, were all agreed on that. No British Government which jeopardized our naval supremacy could live. He said Mr. Lloyd George had told him very much the same thing, but the Germans had no thought of naval supremacy. All they wanted was a Fleet to protect their commerce and their colonies. I asked what was the use of having a weaker Fleet? It was only another hostage to fortune. He said that the Emperor was profoundly attached to his Fleet, and that it was his own creation. I could not resist saying that Moltke had pronounced a very different opinion of Germany's true interest.

I have recorded these notes of a pleasant though careful conversation, not because they are of any importance, but because they help to show the different points of view. I learned afterwards that the Chancellor of the Exchequer in similar circumstances had spoken more explicitly, saying that he would raise a hundred millions in a single year for the British Navy if its supremacy were really challenged.

Count Metternich was a very honourable man, serving his master faithfully but labouring to preserve peace, especially peace between England and Germany. I have heard that on one occasion at Berlin in a throng of generals and princes, some one had said that the British Fleet would one day make a surprise and unprovoked attack upon Germany. Whereupon the Ambassador had replied that he had lived in England for nearly ten years, and he knew that such a thing was absolutely impossible. On this remark being received with obvious incredulity, he had drawn himself up and observed that he had made it on the honour of a German officer and that he would answer for its truth with his honour. This for a moment had quelled the company.

It is customary for thoughtless people to jeer at the old diplomacy and to pretend that wars arise out of its secret machinations. When one looks at the petty subjects which have led to wars between great countries and to so many disputes, it is easy to be misled in this way. Of course such small matters are only the symptoms of the dangerous disease, and are only important for that reason. Behind them lie the interests, the passions and the destiny of mighty races of men ; and long antagonisms express themselves in trifles. "Great commotions," it was said of old, "arise out of small things, but not concerning small things." The old diplomacy did its best to render harmless the small things : it could not do more. Nevertheless, a war postponed may be a war averted. Circumstances change, combinations change, new groupings arise, old interests are superseded by new. Many quarrels that might have led to war have been adjusted by the old diplomacy of Europe and have, in Lord Melbourne's phrase, " blown over." If the nations of the world, while the sense of their awful experience is still fresh upon them, are able to devise broader and deeper guarantees of peace and build their houses on a surer foundation of brotherhood and interdependence, they will still require the courtly manners, the polite and measured phrases, the imperturbable demeanour, the secrecy and discretion of the old diplomatists of Europe.

TO THE ADMIRALTY

October 1911

The Agadir crisis came, however, peacefully to an end. It terminated in the diplomatic rebuff of Germany. Once more she had disturbed all Europe by a sudden and menacing gesture. Once more she had used the harshest threats towards France. For the first time she had made British statesmen feel that sense of direct contact with the war peril which was never absent from Continental minds. The French, however, offered concessions and compensations. An intricate negotiation about the frontiers of French and German territory in West Africa, in which the *Bec de Canard* played an important part, had resulted in an agreement between the two principals. To us it seemed that France had won a considerable advantage. She was not, however, particularly pleased. Her Prime Minister, Monsieur Caillaux, who had presided during those anxious days, was dismissed from office on grounds which at the time it was very difficult to appreciate here, but which viewed in the light of subsequent events can more easily be understood. The tension in German governing circles must have been very great. The German Colonial Secretary, von Lindequist, resigned rather than sign the agreement. There is no doubt that deep and violent passions of humiliation and resentment were coursing beneath the glittering uniforms which thronged the palaces through which the Kaiser moved. And of these passions the Crown Prince made himself the exponent. The world has heaped unbounded execrations upon this unlucky being. He was probably in fact no better and no worse than the average young cavalry subaltern who had not been through the ordinary mill at a public school nor had to think about earning his living. He had considerable personal charm, which he lavished principally upon the fair sex, but which in darker days has captivated the juvenile population of Wieringen. His flattered head was turned by the burning eyes and guttural words of great captains and statesmen and party leaders. He therefore threw himself forward into this strong favouring current, and became a power, or rather the focus of a power, with which the Kaiser was forced to reckon. Germany once more proceeded to increase her armaments by land and sea.

" It was a question," writes von Tirpitz, " of our keeping our nerve, *continuing to arm on a grand scale*, avoiding all provocation, and waiting without anxiety *until our sea power was established* and forced the English to let us breathe in peace." Only to breathe in peace! What fearful apparatus was required to secure this simple act of respiration!

Early in October Mr. Asquith invited me to stay with

him in Scotland. The day after I had arrived there, on our way home from the links, he asked me quite abruptly whether I would like to go to the Admiralty. He had put the same question to me when he first became Prime Minister. This time I had no doubt what to answer. All my mind was full of the dangers of war. I accepted with alacrity. I said, " Indeed I would." He said that Mr. Haldane was coming to see him the next day and we would talk it over together. But I saw that his mind was made up. The fading light of evening disclosed in the far distance the silhouettes of two battleships steaming slowly out of the Firth of Forth. They seemed invested with a new significance to me.

That night when I went to bed, I saw a large Bible lying on a table in my bedroom. My mind was dominated by the news I had received of the complete change in my station and of the task entrusted to me. I thought of the peril of Britain, peace-loving, unthinking, little prepared, of her power and virtue, and of her mission of good sense and fair play. I thought of mighty Germany, towering up in the splendour of her Imperial State and delving down in her profound, cold, patient, ruthless calculations. I thought of the army corps I had watched tramp past, wave after wave of valiant manhood, at the Breslau manoeuvres in 1907 ; of the thousands of strong horses dragging cannon and great howitzers up the ridges and along the roads around Wurzburg in 1910. I thought of German education and thoroughness and all that their triumphs in science and philosophy implied. I thought of the sudden and successful wars by which her power had been set up. I opened the Book at random and in the 9th Chapter of Deuteronomy I read :

" Hear, O Israel : Thou art to pass over Jordan this day,

to go in to possess nations greater and mightier than thyself, cities great and fenced up to heaven,

" 2. A people great and tall, the children of the Anakims, whom thou knowest, and of whom thou hast heard say, Who can stand before the children of Anak!

" 3. Understand therefore this day, that the Lord thy God is he which goeth over before thee ; as a consuming fire he shall destroy them, and he shall bring them down before thy face : so shalt thou drive them out, and destroy them quickly, as the Lord hath said unto thee.

" 4. Speak not thou in thine heart, after that the Lord thy God hath cast them out from before thee, saying, For my righteousness the Lord hath brought me in to possess this land : but for the wickedness of these nations the Lord doth drive them out from before thee.

" 5. Not for thy righteousness, or for the uprightness of thine heart, dost thou go to possess their land : but for the wickedness of these nations the Lord thy God doth drive them out from before thee, and that he may perform the word which the Lord sware unto thy fathers, Abraham, Isaac, and Jacob."

It seemed a message full of reassurance.

THE SAFEGUARD OF FREEDOM

I recall vividly my first voyage from Portsmouth to Portland, where the Fleet lay. A grey afternoon was drawing to a close. As I saw the Fleet for the first time drawing out of the haze a friend reminded me of " that far-off line of storm-beaten ships on which the eyes of the Grand Army had never looked ", but which had in their day " stood between Napoleon and the dominion of the world ". In

Portland Harbour the yacht lay surrounded by the great ships ; the whole harbour was alive with the goings and comings of launches and small craft of every kind, and as night fell ten thousand lights from sea and shore sprang into being and every masthead twinkled as the ships and squadrons conversed with one another. Who could fail to work for such a service? Who could fail when the very darkness seemed loaded with the menace of approaching war.

For consider these ships, so vast in themselves, yet so small, so easily lost to sight on the surface of the waters. Sufficient at the moment, we trusted, for their task, but yet only a score or so. They were all we had. On them, as we conceived, floated the might, majesty, dominion and power of the British Empire. All our long history built up century after century, all our great affairs in every part of the globe, all the means of livelihood and safety of our faithful, industrious, active population depended upon them. Open the sea-cocks and let them sink beneath the surface, as another Fleet was one day to do in another harbour far to the North, and in a few minutes—half an hour at the most—the whole outlook of the world would be changed. The British Empire would dissolve like a dream ; each isolated community struggling forward by itself ; the central power of union broken ; mighty provinces, whole Empires in themselves, drifting hopelessly out of control, and falling a prey to strangers ; and Europe after one sudden convulsion passing into the iron grip and rule of the Teuton and of all that the Teutonic system meant. There would only be left far off across the Atlantic unarmed, unready, and as yet uninstructed America, to maintain, single-handed, law and freedom among men.

Guard them well, admirals and captains, hardy tars and tall marines ; guard them well and guide them true.

THE EMPEROR FRANCIS JOSEPH

The creaking and straining system of the Dual Monarchy revolved ponderously around the person of the aged Emperor. Francis Joseph had ascended his throne in 1848 amid executions, martial law and the rigorous suppression of revolt. He had sustained every kind of public tribulation and domestic tragedy. His brother the Emperor Maximilian had been executed in Mexico by a rebel firing party. His only son Rudolf, heir to the throne, had perished tragically in 1889. His wife had been stabbed through the heart on a jetty at Geneva by an Italian anarchist. He had never declared a foreign war he did not lose, nor bent himself to a domestic policy which was not evidently failing. In 1859 the fields of Solferino and Magenta had stripped him of north Italy. In 1866 the battle of Sadowa had transferred the hegemony of Germany from Austria to Prussia. Hungary against whom he had warred with severity asserted a challenging separatism in the heart of the Empire. Bohemia, whom he would never recognize as a partner, chafed bitterly under his hands.

However, he lived and thrived. He had sat on the throne for more than sixty years when King Edward VII died. At seventy-five he was not only well preserved, but vigorous. He walked far ; he could still ride : his chief amusement was shooting boar and bears and deer. He had borne his bereavements stoically. He was jealous of his brother Maximilian ; he did not love his wife ; he had been on bad terms with all his family, some of whom had incurred a public notoriety which by his rigid standards was beyond any pardon ; he politely acquiesced in the existence of his nephew, the new heir, the Archduke Franz

Ferdinand ; but he could never forgive him for his love-marriage. General Marchenko, Russian Military Attaché at Vienna from 1905 to 1911, in memoirs which are a definite contribution to history, says that a colleague, Major von Bülow, the German Attaché (brother of the German Ex-Chancellor, and afterwards killed in Belgium), remarked upon the Emperor's troubles : " He is used to all that. Without a misfortune in the day's work he would be bored." Marchenko himself says that Francis Joseph " regarded his defeats and reverses as sacrifices to fortune." A courtly, sagacious, crabbed, disillusioned old gentleman, reared in the purple, harassed from youth up by awful public responsibilities, with an ever-present self-questioning about their adequate discharge.

In the closing phase of his reign he had become almost an automaton. He discharged routine duties without pleasure, indeed with distaste, punctually and assiduously, literally from dawn to dusk. He rose usually at four in the morning, and, dressed in his sky-blue uniform, drank his coffee at his desk amid official portfolios and files. His wish was to go to sleep not later than eight o'clock at night. He resented keenly all functions which interrupted this rule. When compelled to entertain company he dined as late as five or even six o'clock in the afternoon. Otherwise, although in Vienna the usual hour was between eight and nine o'clock, the Emperor took his evening meal between three and four. Alone upon his rocky pinnacle from which the tides of time had sunk, this venerable, conscientious functionary continued in harness pulling faithfully at the collar, mostly in the right direction, to the last gasp.

THE TRAGEDY OF SARAJEVO
June 24th 1914

The Serbian officers who had cut to pieces King Alexander and Queen Draga at Belgrade in 1903 had
banded themselves together for mutual protection in a
secret society called " The Black Hand ". This deadly
association nourished a fierce patriotism with the discipline
of the early Jesuits and the methods of the Russian Nihilists. They were concerned at many points with Serbian
governing circles. It was even said that the Crown Prince
Alexander, Pashitch the Prime Minister, and Putnik, the
Commander-in-Chief, had at one time or another been
with them ; and their leader, Colonel Dimitriyevitch, was
actually at this time the head of the Serbian Intelligence
branch. Amid many obscurities there is little doubt that
Dimitriyevitch organized the plot to murder the Archduke
during his visit to Bosnia. A number of fanatical youths,
most of them not yet twenty, were incited to go to Sarajevo. They were provided under his authority with bombs
and Browning pistols which they were taught to use. They
were given money for their journey and maintenance. They
were given cyanide of potassium for suicide in the last
resort. There seems no doubt from post-war revelations
that Pashitch and several of his colleagues learned what
was afoot. The Serbian Government at that time was at
variance with the " Black Hand " organization upon the
administration of the newly-acquired Macedonian territory. It is said on their behalf that they sent orders to their
frontier authorities to prevent the conspirators passing
into Bosnia ; but that these frontier authorities being
themselves members of the Black Hand sped them on
their way. It is also suggested that the Government

endeavoured to warn Vienna that the Archduke would be in danger during his visit to Bosnia and Sarajevo. Indeed the Serbian Minister in Vienna, Yovanovitch, almost certainly made a vaguely-worded statement to one of Berchtold's subordinates to this effect. So far as this was regarded at all, it was regarded as an impertinence. The Archduke was alive to the dangers of his visit, and he attempted without success to dissuade his wife from coming with him. As a Prince and a soldier, he himself felt bound to fulfil his engagements.

In these circumstances it might have been expected that the most stringent police and military precautions would have been taken. Instead the neglect and carelessness were such as to foster the insulting suspicion that the Archduke's life was not much valued in the highest spheres of the Austro-Hungarian Government. At this point General Potiorek presents himself for closer examination. After Conrad he was the leading military personage in the Austro-Hungarian Empire. Conrad himself when invited to become Chief of the Staff in 1908 had proposed Potiorek instead. A dapper, keen-looking soldier of almost monastic self-discipline, with a strong element of mysticism in his nature, and an intimate and carefully developed connection with the Emperor's aged court, Potiorek stood on firm ground. He was at this moment as the military Governor of Bosnia responsible above all others for the safety of the Heir-Apparent during his visit to its capital. Whether maliciously or through sheer incompetence, he grossly neglected his duty. His subsequent military record favours the more charitable view. But of course he knew how strongly the Court disapproved of royal honours being accorded to the Duchess Sophie. It was understood she was not to be unduly exalted. Few police were im-

c

ported, no troops lined the streets, no reserve of gendar-
merie was at hand. The arrangements invited disaster,
and, such as they were, they were muddled in execution.

On the afternoon of June 28 the Archduke and his wife
entered Sarajevo. The murder had been carefully planned.
At least seven assassins had taken their stations at various
points upon the probable royal route. Every one of the
three bridges had its two or three murderers in waiting.
The first attempt was made on the way to the Town Hall ;
but the bomb slid off the back of the motor-car and its
explosion only wounded two officers of the suite. After
the miscreant had been caught, the Archduke proceeded
to the Town Hall and received in a mood of natural
indignation the addresses of welcome. The police precautions had seemed to be lax, and the owner of the motor-
car, Count Harrach, who sat beside the driver, accosted
the Governor, Potiorek : " Has not your Excellency
arranged for a military guard to protect his Imperial High-
ness? " to which the Governor replied impatiently, " Do
you think Sarajevo is full of assassins, Count Harrach? "
The Archduke proposed to alter the return route and to
visit the hospital to which the wounded officers had been
taken. When told that the bomb-thrower had been captured, he is said to have remarked, " Hang him as quickly
as possible or Vienna will give him a decoration ". A
strangely bitter saying! Almost his last! Count Harrach
wished to stand on the left footplate to protect the Archduke. " Don't make a fool of yourself," said Franz
Ferdinand. The four cars moved out into the dense
crowds in the original order, but at a faster pace. At the
entrance to Franz Josef Street the crowd, uncontrolled
by the police, made a lane and by a fatal error the cars
turned back to the original route. Governor Potiorek, who

sat facing the Royal visitors, told the chauffeur he had taken the wrong turning. The car slowed down and came close to the right-hand pavement. A young man fired two shots at three yards' range. The Archduke continued to sit upright : his wife sank upon his breast. A few murmured words passed between them. For a few moments no one realized they had been shot. But the Archduke had been pierced through the artery of his neck and the Duchess through the abdomen. Both sank into unconsciousness and expired within a quarter of an hour. The assassin, a Serbian student named Princip, was seized by the crowd. He died in prison, and a monument erected in recent years by his fellow-countrymen records his infamy and their own. Such was the tragedy of Sarajevo. . . .

The crime of Sarajevo roused widespread fury throughout the Austro-Hungarian Empire, and its various races were united with their government in rage and hatred of Serbia. To judge their feelings we must imagine our own in a similar case. Suppose that Ireland had been a republic growing in power and hostility ; that it was not an island, but lay with frontiers actually joining Wales and Scotland ; that there was a vehement, active pan-Celtic scheme to unite Ireland, Scotland and Wales into a separate foreign combination against England ; that the Prince of Wales had gone to Carnarvon on official duty, and that he had been murdered by a band of assassins organized and sent by an Irish secret society and armed with weapons supplied from the Dublin Arsenal! That would have been a not-unfair parallel to the situation now created in the Hapsburg dominions. For some days the anger of the peoples of Austria expressed itself in violent demonstrations against Serbia and attacks upon Serbian representatives and establishments. The British Consul-General at Buda-Pest reported that Hungarian feeling was even more incensed. " A wave of blind hatred for Serbia and everything Serbian is sweeping over the country." The Hungarian nation he thought " willing to go to any lengths to revenge itself on the despised and hated enemy."

The Emperor, though shocked at assassination in principle, and loathing Serbia, was decidedly resigned and even cool upon the personal aspects of the tragedy. His first remark to Count Paar on hearing the news reveals his distinctive point of view. " Horrible! The Almighty does not allow Himself to be challenged with impunity. . . . A higher Power has restored the old order, which I unfortunately was unable to uphold." This, then, was the punishment administered by Providence as guardian of the Hapsburg dynasty to an Heir-Apparent who had fallen into a morganatic marriage.

The opportunity for which Conrad had waited so long and pleaded so often had now come. He demanded, as usual, immediate war upon Serbia. Mobilize at once and march in! Those who had restrained him in the past were gone. Aerenthal was dead ; the Archduke was dead ; and Conrad found in Count Berchtold not opposition, but agreement. Berchtold had already made up his mind. As Foreign Minister he was not, however, free to act alone under the Emperor. The constitution required that he should procure the agreement of the two Minister-Presidents of Austria and of Hungary. The Hungarian, Count Tisza, was an outstanding figure, a man of force and personality, clear-sighted, resolute, severe in speech, and with political influence far beyond the authority of his high office. On July 1 Berchtold told Count Tisza that he meant to make " the horrible deed at Sarajevo the occasion for a reckoning with Serbia." Tisza objected ; he warned his colleague of the measureless consequences which might follow what he stigmatized as " a fatal mistake ". He wrote to the Emperor the same day that Serbia's guilt was not proved and that if the Serbian government were able to furnish satisfactory explanations the Empire would have exposed herself before the whole world as a disturber of the peace, besides having to begin a great war in the most unfavourable circumstances. He insisted upon an inquiry. He dwelt upon the unsatisfactory attitude of Roumania. He advocated a treaty of Alliance with Bulgaria as a vital precaution before a breach with Serbia. On the other side, Conrad and the generals clamoured incessantly for war.

THE GERMAN PROMISE

When on the morning of Sunday, July 5, Count Hoyos reached Berlin [from Vienna] he consulted with the Austro-Hungarian Ambassador, Count Szögyény, who asked forthwith for an audience of the Kaiser in order to deliver the letter of the Emperor Francis Joseph. The Kaiser invited the Ambassador to luncheon at Potsdam. Count Hoyos proceeded to the Foreign Office and had a lengthy conversation with Zimmermann. Meanwhile Szögyény reached Potsdam and delivered his letter and memorandum. The Kaiser read them both, and said at first that he had expected some serious step against Serbia, but that possible European complications made it necessary for him to consult the Imperial Chancellor before giving a definite answer. After luncheon, however, William II, without waiting for Bethmann-Hollweg's arrival, made the following momentous statement, which he authorized the

Ambassador to convey to Francis Joseph as a personal message from Sovereign to Sovereign.

The Kaiser, according to the Ambassador, said that Austria might rely on Germany's full support. He must first hear the opinion of the Chancellor ; but he did not in the least doubt that Herr von Bethmann-Hollweg would agree with him, especially in the matter of the action against Serbia. It was the Kaiser's opinion that this action must not be delayed. Russia's attitude would doubtless be hostile, but he had been prepared for this for years ; and should it come to war between Austria-Hungary and Russia, Austria could be assured that Germany would stand by her side with her accustomed loyalty. As things stood to-day, however, Russia was in no way prepared for war, and would certainly think twice before appealing to arms, although she would incite the Powers of the Triple Entente against Austria, and add fuel to the fire in the Balkans. " He understood very well that it would be hard for his Imperial and Royal Majesty, with his well-known love of peace, to march into Serbia ; but if we had really recognized the necessity of war against Serbia, he would regret it if we did not make use of the present moment, which is all in our favour."

It did not take Count Szögyény very long to return to Berlin and telegraph these declarations to Vienna.

The Kaiser was under no illusions upon the gravity of the step he had taken. He had, in fact, decided to court the general European war. He had urged Austria to invade Serbia and had promised to defend her against Russian interference. As the German defence of Austria against Russia meant the immediate German invasion of France and violation of Belgian neutrality, the whole fearful panorama was unrolled. Of course he hoped it would not come to war. Austria would punish Serbia, and be once more indebted to Germany. France and England, in fear of war or love of peace, or from moral or material unpreparedness, would persuade Russia to stand aside ; and Russia, convinced at last of the worthlessness of their friendship or alliance, would abandon the Triple Entente. The Central Empires would tower up, united and triumphant, over a bloodless field. For the future they would have only isolated opponents to confront. The " mailed fist " and the " shining armour " would once again have done their work, and he, the Kaiser, would have proved his mettle to the satisfaction even of his most exacting subjects. But if not, so much the worse for them all!

He was to leave at 9.15 the next morning upon his yachting cruise in the Norwegian fjords. Before that, there was much to do. He had already summoned the Chancellor and the heads of the fighting services. General von Falkenhayn, the Prussian Minister of War, arrived at 5 p.m., Bethmann-Hollweg at six, and Captain Zenker, representing the Naval Staff, a little after seven. Admiral von Capelle, representing the Admiralty in the absence of Tirpitz, and General von Bertrab, the senior General Staff Officer then present in Berlin, arrived between eight and nine the next morning. Baron Krupp, head of the armament works, was commanded to dine with the Emperor at Kiel the following night. To each of these functionaries the Emperor spoke separately, and all of them have recorded their impressions of what he said. On July 5 Falkenhayn wrote to Moltke, the Chief of the Staff, who was taking a cure, that His Majesty had informed him that " Austria-Hungary appears determined not to tolerate any longer the plots hatched against Austria in the Balkan peninsula, and if necessary to accomplish this end, to begin by marching into Serbia ; even if Russia will not tolerate this, Austria is not disposed to give way. . . . Considerable time will elapse before the treaty with Bulgaria is concluded. So Your Excellency hardly need curtail your stay at Carlsbad. Nevertheless I thought it desirable, although I have had no instructions to do so, to let you know that the situation is acute, in order that you may not be quite unprepared for surprises which in the end may come about." To the Kaiser's direct question whether the army was ready for all contingencies, Falkenhayn had replied briefly and unconditionally that it was ready.

THE BLANK CHEQUE

Berchtold and Conrad now proceeded to fill in the blank cheque. They made it out for all the assets of the German people and appointed a speedy date for payment. In the pigeon-holes of the Ballplatz there lay a document prepared three years before for use against Serbia should occasion arise. This was the celebrated ultimatum. It expressed all that Austria felt against its foe and all that she had never until now dared to say aloud. Only a few minor changes in the wording were necessary to bring it up to date and make it fit the circumstances of the hour.

In the course of July 8 Conrad, too, visited Berchtold. He found with him Barons Burian and Macchio, and Counts Forgach and Hoyos. He writes :

" I received information as to the demands which were to be handed to Serbia in an ultimatum with the short time-limit of either twenty-four or forty-eight hours. It was to be expected that Serbia would refuse the demands, so that on the expiry of the time-limit, mobilization for war would ensue."

" BERCHTOLD. What happens if Serbia lets things go as far as mobilization and then gives way all along the line?

CONRAD. Then we march in.

BERCHTOLD. Yes—but if Serbia does nothing at all?

CONRAD. Then Serbia remains occupied until the costs of the war have been paid.

BERCHTOLD. We will not hand in the ultimatum until after the harvest and after the close of the Sarajevo Inquiry.

CONRAD. Rather today than tomorrow, so long as the situation is what it is. So soon as our opponents get wind of it they will get ready.

BERCHTOLD. Care will be taken that the secret is kept most carefully and that no one knows anything of it.

CONRAD. When is the ultimatum to go out?

BERCHTOLD. In fourteen days—on the 22nd July. It would be a good thing if you and the War Minister would go on leave for a time, in order to preserve the appearance that nothing is happening.

We then spoke about the attitude of Roumania and the possible intervention of Russia.

CONRAD. As to whether we are to go to war with Russia we must be perfectly clear at once. If Russia orders a general mobilization, then the moment has come for us to declare ourselves against Russia.

BERCHTOLD. If we enter Serbia and have occupied sufficient territory—what then?

CONRAD. With the occupation of territory nothing has been attained ; we must proceed until we have struck down the Serbian army.

BERCHTOLD. And if it retires?

CONRAD. Then we demand demobilization and disarmament. Once things have got that far, the rest follows.

BERCHTOLD. Only take no measures now which could give us away ; nothing must be done which would attract attention."

Sentence of death had thus been signed, sealed and delivered upon the Empire of the Hapsburgs, upon the Russia of Peter and of Catherine the Great, and upon the Germany of Bismarck. The end of the world of Queen Victoria was at hand.

But now it is summer-time and all over Europe families of every class are looking forward to their holidays. The Kaiser is cruising among the fjords of Norway ; his generals and ministers are at watering-places, salt or medicinal. Francis Joseph rests in his shooting-lodge at Ischl. Conrad, as arranged, departs for Tirol. Russian royalties and generals preen themselves at Homburg or Marienbad. The French President and his Premier are banqueting and parading with the Czar at St. Petersburg. London and Lancashire folk are thinking of Margate or the Isle of Man. Only the English Cabinet is tethered to Westminster by the Irish troubles, and the Admiralty is busy with its test mobilization, about which it had been fussing, and with the Royal Review of the entire British Fleet appointed for the third week in July. All is calm and the skies are blue and the weather genial. Nevertheless a certain piece of foolscap covered with typewriting is lying in Berchtold's portfolio. It will be despatched to its address on July 23.

FRONTS AND COMBATANTS

This fortnight of sunshine and peace was the last which many millions of men and women were ever to enjoy. It was the respite of the nations. Let us look beneath the fair-seeming surface of Europe, into those chambers and recesses in which the agencies of destruction have been prepared and stored. Let us survey the regions about to be rent by the explosion. Let us measure the forces gathered during the generations of wealth and science for the torment of mankind, and describe the conditions, combinations and directions under which when liberated they will work their will.

Let us first examine with a military eye the theatre of impending action. The prime characteristic is its size. In the West the armies were too big for the country; in the East the country was too big for the armies. The enormous masses of men which were repeatedly flung at each other were dwarfed and isolated by the scale of the landscape. Sixteen or seventeen armies, each approaching two hundred thousand men, were in constant movement against the enemy, sometimes grouped in twos and threes, sometimes acting in convergent combination, yet always separated by wide gaps of undefended and almost unwatched country from one another. Everywhere and always the flanks and often the rear of these huge organizations were exposed to hostile strategy or manoeuvres. No large force on either side could advance far without intense and growing anxiety, lest some other powerful body were advancing swiftly from an unexpected angle and would suddenly manifest itself in unknown strength, marching upon the vital communications. Each of these armies comprised the population of a large city, consuming men, food and highly-refined, costly manufactures at an incredible rate. None could live for more than a week without a copious flow of supplies. The capture by surprise of some key fortress, the cutting of an important railway line, a blown-up bridge or a blown-in tunnel, the seizure of some mountain pass or gap in a chain of lakes, might spell not only the failure of gigantic operations but the ruin and disintegration of larger and far more highly organized forces than Napoleon had led from Europe into Russia.

Here was War in all its old unlimited hazard, but on an unexampled scale. No endless succession of trench lines, range behind range, fortified with every device or carefully studied for eventual defence, all backed by a prodigious artillery and batteries everywhere supporting each other, all laced together by a close network of railways—none of this reduced the liabilities of the commanders or set bounds to the consequences of a victory. There were all the dramatic, dumbfounding situations, all the movement, all the disproportionate forfeits of accident and chance of the campaigns in the Shenandoah Valley. It was the same fierce, primordial game multiplied fifty-fold and with whole ponderous armies instead of mobile brigades as counters. No long-prepared, elaborately mounted offensives, no months of preparation for resistance as in the West : here it was " catch as catch can," as in the wars of Marlborough, Frederick and Napoleon. But the pitch was also raised by the strong multiplying power of railways capable of producing now here, now there, an irresistible development of hostile forces. In this wide scene and amid these dire conditions Austria flagged, Russia toiled, suffered and finally collapsed ; while the German Titan, equipped with science and armed with terror, darted from point to point with cruel, flashing sword.

THE CALL OF WAR

Such were the plans and compacts which underlay the civilization of Europe. All had been worked out to the minutest detail. They involved the marshalling for immediate battle of nearly twelve million men. For each of these there was a place reserved. For each there was a summons by name. The depots from which he would draw his uniform and weapons, the time-tables of the railways by which he would travel, the roads by which he would march, the proclamations which would inflame or inspire him, the food and munitions he would require, the hospitals which would receive his torn or shattered body—all were ready. Only his grave was lacking ; but graves do not take long to dig. We know no spectacle in human history more instinct with pathos than that of these twelve million men, busy with the cares, hopes and joys of daily life, working in their fields or mills, or seated these summer evenings by their cottage doors with their wives and children about them, making their simple plans for thrift or festival, unconscious of the fate which now drew near, and which would exact from them their all. Only a signal is needed to transform these multitudes of peaceful peasants and workmen into the mighty hosts which will tear each other to pieces year after year with all the machinery of science, with all the passions of races, and all the loyalties of man.

Yet it should not be supposed by future generations that much direct compulsion was required. Of all the millions who marched to war in August 1914, only a small proportion went unwillingly away. The thrill of excitement ran through the world, and the hearts of even the simplest masses lifted to the trumpet-call. A prodigious event had happened. The monotony of toil and of the daily round was suddenly broken. Everything was strange and new. War aroused the primordial instincts of races born of strife. Adventure beckoned to her children. A larger, nobler life seemed to be about to open upon the world. But it was, in fact, only Death.

THE BURDEN OF RESPONSIBILITY

To read many modern writers one would suppose that the war came by itself, and that no person in authority ever thought of such a wicked thing. Berchtold did this and Conrad did that, and Jagow was on his honeymoon, and Tschirschky was snubbed by the Kaiser, and Bethmann-Hollweg did not understand the situation, and the Russians got excited and Moltke alarmed, and then all of a sudden all the greatest nations in the world fell upon each other with fire and sword. It was a case of spontaneous combustion. The theory that it all happened by itself, that Germany carelessly gave Austria a blank cheque to correct Serbia, that Russia was indignant at the spectacle, that Germany was alarmed because Russia mobilized, that France and England did not tell Russia she must give in, that England did not tell Germany in time that she would fight, that all Berchtold wanted was his little private war with Serbia, that all Germany wanted was not to be forced to desert her ally, that all the Kaiser wanted was a diplomatic triumph—all these cases find ample documentary support. Still certain stark facts which no elaboration can veil stand forth for all time.

Berchtold and his circle meant to use armed violence

upon Serbia. The Kaiser encouraged and urged them to do so. Both parties knew that such an event must arouse not only the Czar and his government, but the Russian nation. Both decided to accept this risk and whatever else it might entail. The Kaiser, having given Berchtold and Vienna a free hand, deliberately absented himself until the ultimatum to Serbia had been dispatched. The German Chancellor and Foreign Secretary instructed their Ambassador to declare that Germany considered the ultimatum right and proper, before they had even seen its terms. When the Serbians returned a soft answer, Jagow and others delayed the presentation of this document to the Kaiser until it was too late for him to prevent Austria declaring war upon Serbia. Berchtold issued his declaration of war with precipitate haste and obtained its signature from the Emperor Francis Joseph partly under false pretences. Every request for delay was refused by Vienna. Every proposal, whether for conference of the Powers or direct negotiations between Austria and Russia, was refused or resisted until too late. At St. Petersburg the Russian Government, Court and military men extracted first a partial and then a complete mobilization decree from the reluctant Czar. Germany fastened upon Russia a deadly quarrel about her mobilization. Germany sent an ultimatum to Russia requiring her to cancel it within twelve hours. At this moment the German mobilization, although not officially proclaimed, was already in progress. Germany declared war upon Russia. Germany summoned France to repudiate the terms of the Franco-Russian Alliance and hand over to German keeping her key fortresses as gages of faithful neutrality. Germany declared war upon France. Germany violated the treaty protecting the Duchy of Luxembourg. Germany violated

received no news. He was darkly hopeful. The map was produced. The dense massing of German divisions west of the Belgian Meuse and curling round the left flank of the Anglo-French line was visible as a broad effect. So was the pivot of Namur, in front of which this whole vast turning movement seemed precariously to be hinged. He had in his mind a great French counterstroke—a thrust at the shoulder, as it were, of the long, straining, encircling arm which should lop it off or cripple it fatally. He said of the Germans : " They are running a grave risk. No one can set limits to what a well-disciplined army can do ; but if the French were able to cut in here, " he made a vigorous arrow N.W. from Namur, " the Germans might easily have a Sedan of their own on a larger scale." I had a pleasing vision of the first phase of Austerlitz, with the Austrians stretching and spreading their left far out to the villages of Tellnitz and Sokolnitz, while Napoleon remained crouched for his spring at the Pratzen plateau. But had France a Napoleon? One had marched through Charleroi ninety-nine years before. Was there another? And were the Germans like the Austrians and Russians of Austerlitz? However, we went anxiously but hopefully to our slumbers.

At 7 o'clock the next morning I was sitting up in bed in Admiralty House working at my boxes, when the door of my bedroom opened and Lord Kitchener appeared. These were the days before he took to uniform, and my recollection is that he had a bowler hat on his head, which he took off with a hand which also held a slip of paper. He paused in the doorway and I knew in a flash and before ever he spoke that the event had gone wrong. Though his manner was quite calm, his face was different. I had the subconscious feeling that it was distorted and discoloured as if it had been punched with a fist. His eyes rolled more than ever. His voice, too, was hoarse. He looked gigantic. " Bad news," he said heavily and laid the slip of paper on my bed. I read the telegram. It was from Sir John French.

" My troops have been engaged all day with the enemy on a line roughly east and west through Mons. The attack was renewed after dark, but we held our ground tenaciously. I have just received a message from G.O.C. 5th French Army that his troops have been driven back, that Namur has fallen, and that he is taking up a line from Maubeuge to Rocroi. I have therefore ordered a retirement to the line Valenciennes-Longueville-Maubeuge, which is being carried out now. It will prove a difficult operation if the enemy remains in contact. I remember your precise instructions as to method and direction of retirement if necessity arises.

" I think that immediate attention should be directed to the defence of Havre."

I did not mind it much till I got to Namur. Namur fallen! Namur taken in a single day—although a French brigade had joined the Belgians in its defence. We were evidently in the presence of new facts and of a new standard of values. If strong fortresses were to melt like wisps of vapour in a morning sun, many judgments would have to be revised. The foundations of thought were quaking. As for the strategic position, it was clear that the encircling arm was not going to be hacked off at the shoulder, but would close in a crushing grip. Where would it stop? What of the naked Channel ports? Dunkirk, Calais, Boulogne! " Fortify Havre," said Sir John French. One day's general battle and the sanguine advance and hoped-for counterstroke had been converted into " Fortify Havre." " It will be difficult to withdraw the troops if the enemy remains in contact "—a disquieting observation. I forget much of what passed between us. But the apparition of Kitchener *Agonistes* in my doorway will dwell with me as long as I live. It was like seeing old John Bull on the rack!

THE BATTLE OF THE MARNE
September 1914

This battle, which lasted for four days, was the greatest of the war. The Germans aimed not at the capture of Paris or Verdun or Nancy, but at the final destruction of the French military power. Had they succeeded in breaking the French front between Paris and Verdun or in falling upon its rear from the direction of Nancy, nearly half the French Army, certainly more than a million men, would have been cut off in the Verdun angle. The rest, whatever happened in the neighbourhood of Paris, would have had to retreat to the southward and would never again have been numerous enough to form a complete front. Compared with stakes like these, the entry into Paris by the German right flank or the capture of the Channel Ports by a couple of German corps were insignificant and rightly discarded by the German Headquarters. Once the French Army was cut in half and finally beaten, everything would fall into their hands. They therefore directed all their available troops to the battlefield, ignored the Channel Ports, and compelled von Kluck, commanding their right army, to skirt Paris and close in to their main battle front. How near they were to success will long be debated and never decided. But certainly they were within an ace. No military reproach lies upon their disregard of other objectives : but only upon any failure to disregard them. It is not to their neglect to enter Paris or seize Calais that their fatal defeat was due, but rather to the withdrawal of two German army corps to repel the Russian invasion of East Prussia.

The soul of the French nation triumphed in this death struggle, and their armies, defeated on the frontier, turned after the long marches of retreat, and attacked and fought with glorious and desperate tenacity. British attention has naturally been concentrated upon the intense military situation developed before and around Paris, in which our own army played a decisive part ; and the various pressures which operated upon von Kluck have now been minutely exposed. Attacked on his right flank and rear by Maunoury's army while advancing to the main battle-field, he was compelled to counter-march first two of his corps and then his two remaining corps in order to make head against the new danger. Thus a gap of 30 miles was opened in the German line between von Kluck and von Bülow. Into this gap marched the battered but reanimated British army. The tide had turned. But the whole of this great situation about Paris was itself only complementary to the battle as a whole. The gaze of the military student must range along the whole line of the French armies, the defeat of any one of which would have been fatal. Not least his eye will rest upon the very centre of the Paris-Verdun line, where Foch though driven back maintained his resistance. " My centre cedes. My right recoils. Situation excellent. I attack." But all the four French armies between Paris and Verdun fought with desperate valour, while Dubail and de Castelnau round the corner maintained their superb defence. And thus, weakened by its rapid advance, the whole German line came to a standstill. And as this condition was reached, the penetration by the British and by the Fifth French army on the British right of the gap in the German line between von Bülow and von Kluck determined both these commanders in succession to retreat, and thus imposed a retrograde movement upon the whole of the invading hosts. " The most formidable avalanche of fire and steel ever let loose upon a nation " had spent its force.

From the moment when the German hopes of destroying the French armies by a general battle and thus of ending the war at a single stroke had definitely failed, all the secondary and incidental objectives which hitherto they had rightly discarded became of immense consequence. As passion declined, material things resumed their values. The struggle of *armies* and *nations* having failed to reach a decision, *places* recovered their significance, and geography rather than psychology began to rule the lines of war. Paris now unattainable, the Channel Ports—Dunkirk, Calais and Boulogne—still half naked, and lastly Antwerp, all reappeared in the field of values like submerged rocks when the tidal wave recedes.

BATTLE OF THE
FALKLAND ISLANDS

December 8th 1914

At 5 o'clock that afternoon, I was working in my room at the Admiralty when Admiral Oliver entered with

the following telegram. It was from the Governor of the
Falkland Islands and ran as follows :

" Admiral Spee arrived at daylight this morning with
all his ships and is now in action with Admiral Sturdee's
whole fleet, *which was coaling*."

We had had so many unpleasant surprises that these last
words sent a shiver up my spine. Had we been taken by
surprise and, in spite of all our superiority, mauled, unready, at anchor? " Can it mean that? " I said to the Chief
of the Staff. " I hope not," was all that he said. I could
see that my suggestion, though I hardly meant it seriously,
had disquieted him. Two hours later, however, the door
opened again, and this time the countenance of the stern
and sombre Oliver wore something which closely res-
embled a grin. " It's all right, sir ; they are all at the
bottom." And with one exception so they were.

When the leading German ships were sighted far away
on the distant horizon, Admiral Sturdee and his squadron
were indeed coaling. From the intelligence he had received
he had convinced himself that the Germans were at Val-
paraiso, and he intended to sail the next day in the hope
of doubling the Horn before the enemy could do so. More
than two hours passed after the enemy first came in sight
before he could raise steam and get under way. The first
shots were fired by the 12-inch guns of the *Canopus* from
her stationary position on the mudbanks of the inner harbour. The *Gneisenau* had continued to approach until she
saw the fatal tripods, whereupon she immediately turned
round and, followed by one of her light cruisers, made off
at full speed to join her main body. In a few moments the
whole of the German squadron was steaming off in a
westerly direction with all possible speed. At 10 o'clock,
the *Kent, Carnarvon* and *Glasgow* having already sailed,

Admiral Sturdee came out of the harbour in the *Invincible*, followed by the *Inflexible* and *Cornwall*; while the light cruisers, one of whom (the *Bristol*) had her engines actually opened up, hurried on after as fast as possible.

The whole five ships of the German squadron were now visible, hull down on the horizon about fifteen miles away. The order was given for general chase, but later on, having the day before him, the Admiral regulated the speeds, the battle-cruisers maintaining only about 20 knots. This, however, was quite sufficient to overhaul the Germans, who after their long sojourn in the Pacific without docking were not able to steam more than 18 knots in company. Even so, the *Leipzig* began to lag behind, and shortly before 1 o'clock, the *Inflexible* opened fire upon her at 16,000 yards. Confronted with having his ships devoured one by one, von Spee took a decision which was certainly in accordance with the best traditions of the sea. Signalling to his light cruisers to make their escape to the South American coast, he turned with the *Scharnhorst* and *Gneisenau* to face his pursuers. The action which followed was on the British side uneventful. The German Admiral endeavoured more than once to close the ranges at which his powerful secondary armament of 5.9's could play their part. The British held off just far enough to make this fire ineffective, and pounded the enemy with their 12-inch guns. At this long range, however, it took considerable time and much ammunition to achieve the destruction of the German cruisers. The *Scharnhorst*, with the Admiral and all hands, sank at 4.17 p.m., her last signal to her consort being to save herself. *Gneisenau* continued to fight against hopeless odds with the utmost fortitude until about 6 o'clock when, being in a completely disabled condition, she opened her sea-cocks and vanished, with her flag still flying, beneath the icy waters of the ocean. The British ships rushing to the spot and lowering every available boat were able to save only 200 Germans, many of whom died the next day from the shock of the cold water. When both the *Scharnhorst* and *Gneisenau* had sunk, the *Inflexible* had only thirty and the *Invincible* only twenty-two rounds left for each of their 12-inch guns.

Meanwhile the other British cruisers had each selected one of the flying German light vessels, and a series of chases ensued. The *Kent* (Captain Allen) overtook and sank the *Nürnberg* by an effort of steaming which surpassed all previous records and even, it is stated, her designed speed. The *Nürnberg* refused to surrender, and as she foundered by the head, the victors could see a group of men on her uplifted stern waving to the last the German flag. The *Leipzig* was finished off by the *Glasgow* and the *Cornwall*. The *Dresden* alone for the time made good her escape. She was hunted down and destroyed three months later in the roadstead of Mas-a-Fuera.

Thus came to an end the German cruiser warfare in the outer seas. With the exception of the *Karlsruhe*, of which nothing had been heard for some time and which we now know was sunk by an internal explosion on November 4, and the *Dresden* soon to be hunted down, no German ships of war remained on any of the oceans of the world. It had taken four months from the beginning of the war to achieve this result. Its consequences were far-reaching, and affected simultaneously our position in every part of the globe. The strain was everywhere relaxed. All our enterprises, whether of war or commerce, proceeded in every theatre without the slightest hindrance. Within twenty-four hours orders were sent to a score of British ships to return to Home waters. For the first time we saw ourselves possessed of immense surpluses of ships of certain classes, of trained men and of naval supplies of all kinds, and were in a position to use them to the best advantage. The public, though gratified by the annihilating character of the victory, was quite unconscious of its immense importance to the whole naval situation.

THE YEAR 1915

The year 1915 was fated to be disastrous to the cause of the Allies and to the whole world. By the mistakes of this year the opportunity was lost of confining the conflagration within limits which though enormous were not uncontrolled. Thereafter the fire roared on till it burnt itself out. Thereafter events passed very largely outside the scope of conscious choice. Governments and individuals conformed to the rhythm of the tragedy, and swayed and staggered forward in helpless violence, slaughtering and squandering on ever-increasing scales, till injuries were wrought to the structure of human society which a century will not efface, and which may conceivably prove fatal to the present civilization. But in January, 1915, the terrific affair was still not unmanageable. It could have been grasped in human hands and brought to rest in righteous and fruitful victory before the world was exhausted, before the nations were broken, before the empires were shattered to pieces, before Europe was ruined.

It was not to be. Mankind was not to escape so easily from the catastrophe in which it had involved itself. Pride was everywhere to be humbled, and nowhere to receive its satisfaction. No splendid harmony was to crown the wonderful achievements. No prize was to reward the sacrifices of the combatants. Victory was to be bought so dear as to be almost indistinguishable from defeat. It was not to give even security to the victors. There never was to be "The silence following great words of Peace". To the convulsions of the struggle must succeed the impotent turmoil of the aftermath. Noble hopes, high comradeship and glorious daring were in every nation to lead only to disappointment, disillusion and prostration. The sufferings and impoverishment of peoples might arrest their warfare, the collapse of the defeated might still the cannonade, but their hatreds continue unappeased and their quarrels are still unsettled. The most complete victory ever gained in arms has failed to solve the European problem or remove the dangers which produced the war.

DEADLOCK AND FRONTAL ATTACK

When the old year closed a complete deadlock existed between the great combatants in the West by land and by sea. The German fleet remained sheltered in its fortified harbours, and the British Admiralty had discovered no way of drawing it out. The trench lines ran continuously from the Alps to the sea, and there was no possibility of manoeuvre. The Admirals pinned their faith to the blockade ; the Generals turned to a war of exhaustion and to still more dire attempts to pierce the enemy's front. All the wars of the world could show nothing to compare with the continuous front which had now been established. Ramparts more than 350 miles long, ceaselessly guarded by millions of men, sustained by thousands of cannon, stretched from the Swiss frontier to the North Sea. The Germans had tried in October and November to break through while these lines were still weak and thin. They had failed with heavy losses. The French and British Headquarters had still to be instructed in the defensive power of barbed wire and entrenched machine guns. . . .

Battles are won by slaughter and manoeuvre. The greater the general, the more he contributes in manoeuvre, the less he demands in slaughter. The theory which has exalted the " bataille d'usure " or " battle of wearing down " into a foremost position, is contradicted by history and would be repulsed by the greatest captains of the past. Nearly all the battles which are regarded as masterpieces of the military art, from which have been derived the foundation of states and the fame of commanders, have been battles of manoeuvre in which very often the enemy has found himself defeated by some novel expedient or device, some queer, swift, unexpected thrust or stratagem. In many such battles the losses of the victors have been small. There is required for the composition of a great commander not only massive common sense and reasoning power, not only imagination, but also an element of leger-demain, an original and sinister touch, which leaves the enemy puzzled as well as beaten. It is because military leaders are credited with gifts of this order which enable them to ensure victory and save slaughter that their pro-fession is held in such high honour. For if their art were nothing more than a dreary process of exchanging lives, and counting heads at the end, they would rank much lower in the scale of human esteem.

There are many kinds of manoeuvres in war, some only of which take place upon the battlefield. There are manoeuvres far to the flank or rear. There are manoeuvres in time, in diplomacy, in mechanics, in psychology ; all of which are removed from the battlefield, but react very decisively upon it, and the object of all is to find easier ways, other than sheer slaughter, of achieving the main purpose. The distinction between politics and strategy diminishes as the point of view is raised. At the summit true politics and strategy are one. The manoeuvre which brings an ally into the field is as serviceable as that which wins a great battle. The manoeuvre which gains an important strategic point may be less valuable than that which placates or overawes a dangerous neutral. We suffered grievously at the beginning of the war from the want of a common clearing house where these different relative values could be established and exchanged.

DEADLOCK AT SEA

German naval chroniclers are accustomed to dwell in biting terms upon the failure of the British Fleet to attack them at the beginning of the war. They describe the martial ardour which inspired the German Navy, and their constant and instant expectation of battle. Admiral Scheer relates how as early as August 2, 1914, his colleague commanding the 1st German Squadron urged him to come through the Kiel Canal that very night to join the rest of the Fleet at Wilhelmshaven lest if he waited till daylight he should be too late. He describes the feverish energy with which every scrap of woodwork and paint was stripped from the interiors of German ships the better to prepare them for action. He professes astonishment, not unmingled with derision, that the British disappointed his hope. Considering that the German Fleet remained for the first four months of the war absolutely motionless in its strongly fortified river mouths and harbours protected by its minefields and its submarines, this attitude of mind on the part of a skilful sailor appears to be somwhat forced.

If the Germans really believed that the Grand Fleet would be sent through their minefields to give them battle in their war harbours, they must have rated our intelligence very low. Such a course could only have cast away the British Fleet and achieved our ruin in a few hours. Nor would empty demonstrations off Heligoland, Sylt or Borkum have achieved any useful object. Both Scheer and Tirpitz write as if we had only to appear off these islands to compel the German High Seas Fleet to put to sea for the decisive battle. Yet at the same time we are told that the orders to the German Navy were not to fight a general battle until the British Fleet had been worn down by minor losses to a condition of equality. Why then should the Germans come out and fight a battle at heavy odds because British warships were exchanging shells with the batteries on the German islands? A much more sensible course for the Germans would be to send submarines by day and destroyers by night to torpedo the demonstrators and to sow the area with mines in case they should return. In this way the German equalization policy would have had a very good chance; and one can believe that such action by the British Fleet would have been very agreeable to German wishes. What more, indeed, could they want than that the British Fleet should be swiftly worn down in patrolling boastfully and idiotically outside the German harbours?

We also were anxious for a battle; but not a fool's

ORIGIN OF THE TANKS

There was no novelty about the idea of an armoured vehicle to travel across country and pass over trenches and other natural obstacles while carrying guns and fighting men. Mr. H. G. Wells, in an article written in 1903, had practically exhausted the possibilities of imagination in this sphere. Moreover, from very early times the history of war is filled with devices of this character for use in the attack of fortresses and fortified positions. The general principles of applying the idea were also fairly obvious. Bullet-proof armour had been carried to a high point of perfection by various hardening processes. The internal-combustion engine supplied the motive power. The Pedrail and Caterpillar systems were both well known, and had been widely applied in many parts of the world. Thus the three elements out of which tanks have been principally constituted were at hand to give effect to the idea.

There are, however, two things to be kept distinct :

(*a*) The responsibility for initiating and sustaining the action which led to the tanks being produced, and

(*b*) the credit for solving the extremely difficult problems connected with design apart from main principles.

These services were entirely separate. There never was a moment when it was possible to say that a tank had been " invented ". There was never a person about whom it could be said : " This man invented the tank ". But there was a moment when the actual manufacture of the first tanks was definitely ordered, and there was a moment when an effective machine was designed as the direct outcome of this authorization.

I consider that the responsibility for the mechanical execution of the project was borne by Mr. Tennyson-d'Eyncourt. Without his high authority and immense expert knowledge the project could not have been carried to success. Under his guidance, invaluable services in the sphere of adaptation and manufacture were rendered by Sir William Tritton and Major Wilson. But I sanctioned the expenditure of public money in reliance upon Mr. Tennyson-d'Eyncourt's gifts and knowledge, and his assurances that the mechanical difficulties could be solved. I trusted him, as I would have trusted Admiral Bacon in the earlier project, to say whether the thing could be done or not and to find a way round and through the technical difficulties. And once he said it could be done, I was prepared to incur both risk and responsibility in providing the necessary funds and in issuing the necessary authority. It was with him alone that I dealt, and it was from me alone that he received his orders.

Others, such as Colonel Swinton and Captain T. G. Tulloch, had seized the idea and had even laid specific proposals before the War Office in January, 1915. These officers had not, however, the executive authority which alone could ensure progress and their efforts were brought to nothing by the obstruction of some of their superiors. They were unfortunate in not being able to command the resources necessary for action, or to convince those who had the power to act.

After I left the Admiralty at the end of May, 1915, another moment of extreme peril threatened the enterprise. The new Board of Admiralty included three out of the four naval members of the old Board. Reinforced by Sir Henry Jackson, the new First Sea Lord, they appear to have viewed the financial commitments which had already been incurred to an extent of about £45,000 as either undesirable or wholly beyond the sphere of Admiralty interests.

They, therefore, in the general disfavour in which my affairs were at this time involved, proposed to terminate the contracts and scrap the whole project. However, Mr. Tennyson-d'Eyncourt remained faithful to the charge I had laid upon him. He warned me of the decisions which were impending, or which had perhaps been taken, and I thereupon as a Member of the War Committee of the Cabinet appealed personally to Mr. Balfour, the new First Lord. After consideration, Mr. Balfour decided that the construction of one experimental machine should be proceeded with. One alone survived. But this proved to be the " Mother Tank " which, displayed in Hatfield Park in January, 1916, became the exact model of the tanks which fought on the Somme in August, 1916, and was the parent and in principle the prototype of all the heavy tanks that fought in the Great War.

ACTION OF THE DOGGER BANK— DAYBREAK AT THE ADMIRALTY

January 24th 1915

There can be few purely mental experiences more charged with cold excitement than to follow, almost from minute to minute, the phases of a great naval action from the silent rooms of the Admiralty. Out on blue water in the fighting ships amid the stunning detonations of the cannonade, fractions of the event unfold themselves to the corporeal eye. There is the scene of action at its highest ; there is the wrath of battle ; there is the intense, self-effacing, physical or mental toil. But in Whitehall only the clock ticks, and quiet men enter with quiet steps laying

D

slips of pencilled paper before other men equally silent who draw lines and scribble calculations, and point with the finger or make brief subdued comments. Telegram succeeds telegram at a few minutes' interval as they are picked up and decoded, often in the wrong sequence, frequently of dubious import ; and out of these a picture always flickering and changing rises in the mind, and imagination strikes out around it at every stage flashes of hope or fear.

NO SECOND CHANCE
IN NAVAL COMBAT

There are a hundred ways of explaining a defeat on land and of obscuring the consequences of any mistake. Of these the simplest is to continue the attack next day in a different direction or under different conditions. But on the sea no chance returns. The enemy disappears for months and the battle is over. The Admiral's orders uttered from minute to minute are recorded for ever in the log-book of every vessel engaged. The great ships, unless their mechanism ceases to function, obey punctually and inexorably the directions they receive from the human will. The course and speed of every vessel at every moment are recorded. The value of every vessel sunk is known. Their names are published. The charts and compasses are produced, and with almost exact accuracy the position and movement of every ship can be fixed in relation to every other. The battle-field is flat and almost unvarying. Exact explanations can be required at every point, and the whole intense scene can be reconstructed and analysed in the glare of history. This should always be borne in mind in forming judgments.

THE GALLIPOLI PENINSULA

April 25th 1915

The Gallipoli Peninsula stretches into the Ægean Sea for 52 miles and is at its broadest 12 miles across. But its *ankle*, the Isthmus which joins it to the Mainland, is only 3½ miles wide near the village of Bulair ; and at its *neck* opposite Maidos at the south-western end the width is scarcely 6 miles. This very considerable area is mountainous, rugged, and broken by ravines. Four main hill features dominate the ground : the semi-circular chain of hills surrounding Suvla Bay rising to 600 or 700 feet ; the Sari Bair mountain just over 1,000 feet high ; the Kilid Bahr Plateau opposite the Narrows between 600 and 700 feet high ; and about 6 miles from the south-western tip the peak of Achi Baba, also 700 feet high.

Outside the Straits the landing-places are comparatively few. The cliffs fall precipitously to the sea and are pierced only by occasional narrow gullies. The surface of the Peninsula is covered for the most part with scrub, interspersed with patches of cultivation. A considerable supply of water in springs and wells exists throughout the region, particularly in the neighbourhood of Suvla Bay. One other feature of practical significance requires to be noted. The tip of the Peninsula from Achi Baba to Cape Helles has the appearance from the sea of being a gradual slope, but in fact this all-important tip is spoon-shaped and thus to a very large extent protected by its rim from direct naval fire.

The operations which were now to take place presented to both sides the most incalculable and uncertain problems of war. To land a large army in the face of a long-warned and carefully prepared defence by brave troops and modern weapons was to attempt what had never yet been dared and what might well prove impossible. On the other hand, the mysterious mobility of amphibious power imposed equal perils and embarrassments upon the defenders. General Liman von Sanders knew, as we have seen, that an army estimated at between 80,000 and 90,000 men was being concentrated at Mudros, in Egypt or close at hand. Where and when would they strike? There were obviously three main alternatives, any one of which might lead to fatal consequences—the Asiatic shore, the Bulair Isthmus and the southern end of the Peninsula. Of these the Asiatic shore gave the best prospects for the landing and manoeuvring of a large army. The Bulair Isthmus, if taken, cut the communications of all the troops on the Peninsula both by land and sea, and thus in von Sanders' words, " afforded the prospects of a strategic decision." Thirdly, to quote von Sanders, " The strip of coast on each side of Gaba Tebe was the landing-place best suited to obtaining a quick decision, as a broad depression inter-rupted by only one gentle rise led straight from it to Maidos ". There were also at the southern end of the Peninsula the landing-places in the neighbourhood of Cape Helles giving access to the peak of Achi Baba whence the forts on the Narrows were directly commanded. The enemy had no means of knowing which of these widely separated and potentially decisive objectives would receive the impending attack. To meet this uncertain, unknown, unknowable and yet vital situation the German Com-mander was forced to divide the 5th Turkish Army into three equal parts, each containing about 20,000 men and 50 guns. Whichever part was attacked first must hold out for two or three days against superior numbers until help could come. To minimize this perilous interval the com-

munications between the three parts had been, as we have
seen, improved as far as possible. Roads had been made
and boats and shipping accumulated at suitable points in
the Straits. Nevertheless the fact remained that Liman
von Sanders must resign himself to meet in the first instance the whole of the Allied Army with one third of his
own already equal forces, and nearly three days must
elapse after battle was thus joined before any substantial
Turkish reinforcements could arrive.

THE BATTLE OF SUVLA BAY
August 6th 1915

The long and varied annals of the British Army contain
no more heart-breaking episode than the Battle of
Suvla Bay. The greatness of the prize in view, the narrowness by which it was missed, the extremes of valiant skill
and of incompetence, of effort and inertia, which were
equally presented, the malevolent fortune which played
about the field, are features not easily to be matched in
our history. The tale has often been told, and no more
than a general survey can here be attempted.

Sir Ian Hamilton's plan had for its supreme object the
capture of Hill 971 (Koja Chemen Tepe), the dominating
point of the Sari Bair Ridge, and working from there, to
grip the neck of the Peninsula from Gaba Tepe to Maidos.
This conception was elaborated as follows :

(1) To break out with a rush from Anzac and cut off the
bulk of the Turkish Army from land communication with
Constantinople.

(2) To gain artillery positions which would cut off the bulk of the Turkish Army from sea traffic whether with Constantinople or with Asia.

(3) To secure Suvla Bay as a winter base for Anzac and all the troops operating in that neighbourhood.

For this purpose three separate attacks were prepared in extreme detail by the Army Staff during the month of July : first, a holding attack by two of the six divisions at Helles to prevent the Turks from removing any troops from this sector of the front ; secondly, a great attack from Anzac on the main and dominating ridge of Sari Bair by the two Australasian divisions, reinforced by the 13th New Army Division and one British and one Indian brigade ; and thirdly a landing by two divisions (the 10th and 11th) forming the IXth Corps at Suvla Bay to secure the Anafarta Ridge and join their right hands to the Anzac attack and help it as it progressed.

The Helles sector was held by 35,000 men under General Davies. To the Anzac attack were assigned 37,000 under General Birdwood ; and to the Suvla attack, 25,000 under General Stopford ; the whole aggregating, with a reserve on the islands or approaching on the sea of 20,000 to 25,000, about 120,000 fighting men.

The Turks believed that the British had received reinforcements amounting perhaps to 100,000 men, and they expected a general attack, together with a landing, early in August. They realized that the Sari Bair Ridge was the key to the Narrows ; they were apprehensive of landings near Kum Tepe or near Bulair, and in addition they had to guard the Asiatic shore. They knew that Suvla and Ejelmer Bays were possible landing-places, but they did not regard landings there as sufficiently probable to warrant further dissipation of their strength. On the evening of

August 6 their dispositions were as follows : at Helles, 40,000 rifles with 94 guns : opposite Anzac and between Anzac and Helles, 30,000 rifles, supported by 76 guns ; at Bulair, 20,000 rifles and 80 guns ; on the Asiatic coast, 20,000 rifles with about 60 guns. In all, including detachments of troops guarding the coast at various points, the Turks had been able to marshal 20 divisions, comprising about 120,000 rifles with 330 guns, and of these 90,000 to 100,000 men and 270 guns were actually on the Gallipoli Peninsula.

The forces on both sides available for the battle are thus seen to be approximately equal. The British did not possess any of the preponderance necessary for an offensive. Once their attack was fully disclosed and battle was joined along the whole front, there was no reasonable expectation of their being able to defeat the Turkish Army. There was, however, a chance of seizing vital positions by surprise before the Turks could bring up all their forces. The situation, in fact, exactly reproduces that of April 25, but on a larger scale. Once again the advantages of sea power have been neutralized by delay and the enemy given time to gather forces equal to our own ; once again a frightful and dubious ordeal has taken the place of a sound and reasonably sure operation ; once again the only hope lies in the devotion of the troops and the skill of the leaders ; once again all is at the mercy of time and chance. . . .

The closing event of the battle has now to be recorded. When daylight broke on the morning of the 10th the British from Anzac still held their hard-won positions on Chunuk Bair. Two battalions of the 13th Division—the 6th North Lancashires and the 5th Wiltshires—had relieved the worn-out troops who had stormed the hill. They had barely settled down in their new position when they were exposed to a tremendous attack. After his succesful action at Suvla Bay on the 9th, Mustapha Kemal passed the night in preparing a supreme effort to regain this priceless ridge. The whole of the Turkish 8th Division brought from the Asiatic shore with three additional battalions and aided by a powerful and converging artillery were led forward to the assault by Mustapha Kemal in person. The thousand British rifles—all for whom room could be found on the narrow summit—were engulfed and overwhelmed in this fierce flood. Very few of the Lancashire men escaped, and the Wiltshire battalion was literally annihilated. Flushed with victory the Turks pressed over the summit and poured down the steep face of the mountain in dense waves of men intent on driving the invaders into the sea. But here they encountered the whole blast of fire from the Fleet and from every gun and machine gun in the Anzac-British line. Under this storm the advancing Turkish masses were effectually crushed. Of three or four thousand men who descended the seaward slopes of the hill, only a few hundred regained the crest. But there they stayed—and stayed till the end of the story. Thus by the 10th the whole of the second great effort to win the Straits had ended at all points without decisive gains.

EVACUATION OF GALLIPOLI

December 1915

General Monro was an officer of swift decision. He came, he saw, he capitulated. He reached the Dardanelles on October 28 ; and already on the 29th he and his staff were discussing nothing but evacuation. On the 30th he landed on the Peninsula. Without going beyond the Beaches, he familiarized himself in the space of six hours with the conditions prevailing on the 15-mile front of Anzac, Suvla and Helles, and spoke a few discouraging words to the principal officers at each point. To the Divisional Commanders summoned to meet him at their respective Corps Headquarters, he put separately and in turn a question in the following sense : " On the supposition that you are going to get no more drafts can you maintain your position in spite of the arrival of strong reinforcements with heavy guns and limitless German ammunition? " He thus collected a number of dubious answers, armed with which he returned to Imbros. He never again set foot on the Peninsula during the tenure of his command. His Chief-of-the-Staff, also an enthusiast for evacuation, never visited it at all. On October 31 General Monro despatched his telegram recommending the total evacuation of the Gallipoli Peninsula and the final abandonment of the campaign. According to his own statements he contemplated, in addition to the ruin of the whole enterprise, a loss of from thirty to forty per cent. of the Army, i.e. about forty thousand officers and men. This he was prepared to accept. Two days later he left for Egypt, leaving the command of the Dardanelles Army temporarily in the hands of General Birdwood.

General Monro's telegram of " Evacuation " fell like a thunderbolt upon Lord Kitchener ; and for a moment and under the shock he rose in all the strength which he commanded when he represented the indomitable core of our national character.

Lord Kitchener to General Birdwood.

November 3, 1915.

" Very secret.

" You know the report sent in by Monro. I shall come out to you ; am leaving to-morrow night. I have seen Captain Keyes, and I believe the Admiralty will agree to making naval attempt to force the passage of the Straits. We must do what we can to assist them, and I think that as soon as our ships are in the Sea of Marmora we should seize the Bulair isthmus and hold it so as to supply the Navy if the Turks still hold out.

" Examine very carefully the best position for landing near the marsh at the head of the Gulf of Xeros, so that we could get a line across the isthmus, with ships at both sides. In order to find the troops for this undertaking we should have to reduce the numbers in the trenches to the lowest possible, and perhaps evacuate positions at Suvla. All the best fighting men that could be spared, including your boys from Anzac and every one I can sweep up in Egypt, might be concentrated at Mudros ready for this enterprise.

" There will probably be a change in the naval command, Wemyss being appointed in command to carry through the naval part of the work.

" As regards the military command, you would have the whole force, and should carefully select your commanders and troops. I would suggest Maude, Fanshawe, Marshall, Peyton, Godley, Cox, leaving others to hold the lines. Please work out plans for this, or alternative plans as you may think best. We must do it right this time.

" I absolutely refuse to sign orders for evacuation, which I think would be the gravest disaster and would condemn a large percentage of our men to death or imprisonment.

" Monro will be appointed to the command of the Salonika force."

Here was the true Kitchener. Here in this flaming telegram—whether Bulair was the best place or not—was the Man the British Empire believed him to be, in whom millions set their faith—resolute, self-reliant, creative, lionhearted.

Unhappily the next day :

Lord Kitchener to General Birdwood.
November 4, 1915.

" I am coming as arranged. . . . The more I look at the problem the less I see my way through, so you had better work out very quietly and secretly any scheme for getting the troops off the peninsula."

It was with melancholy but intense relief that I learned in France of the successful and bloodless execution of this critical operation which was accomplished on the night of December 19. The utmost credit belongs to the naval and military officers who perfected in exact detail the arrangements, and to the Admirals and Generals by whom they were so successfully carried out. The weather, on which all depended, was favourable for exactly the vital forty-eight hours, and the Turks were utterly unsuspecting. Indeed, when dawn broke on empty trenches and famous positions, bought at so terrible a cost, now silent as the graves with which they were surrounded, the haggard Turkish soldiers and their undaunted chiefs could hardly believe their eyes. Their position, and that of their country whose capital they had defended with soldierly tenacity, were now translated at a stroke from extreme jeopardy into renewed and resuscitated power. Conviction, determination and the will to win, steadfastly maintained by their High Command, had brought victory to the defence in spite of their inferiority in numbers and in resources of all kinds and of the inherent strategic perils of their position. The lack of these qualities on our side at the summit of power had defrauded the attackers of the reward, pregnant in its consequences to the whole world, to which their overwhelming potential strength and resources, their actual numbers and apparatus, their daring, their devotion and their fearful sacrifices had given them the right.

The evacuation of Helles was performed with equal skill and with equal good fortune on January 8, and the story of the Dardanelles came finally to an end. This consummation was acclaimed by the shallow and the uninstructed as if it had been a victory.

VERDUN

At four o'clock in the morning of February 21, 1916, the explosion of a fourteen-inch shell in the Archbishop's Palace at Verdun gave signal of battle, and after a brief but most powerful bombardment three German Army Corps advanced upon the apex of the French front, their right hand on the Meuse. The troops in the forward positions attacked were, except towards the eastern flank, driven backwards towards the fortress line. The battle was continued on the 22nd and the 23rd. The brave Colonel Driant was killed in the woodlands covering the retreat of his Chasseurs. The line was reformed on the ridges near Douaumont : but the German six-inch artillery, dragged forward by tractors, hurled upon the new position so terrific a fire-storm that the French Division chiefly concerned collapsed entirely. During the afternoon of the 24th, both the General commanding the Verdun area and the Commander of the Group of Armies in which it lay (Langle de Cary), telegraphed to Chantilly, advising an immediate withdrawal to the left bank of the Meuse, and the consequent abandonment of the town and fortress of Verdun.

General Joffre was by no means disconcerted by these unexpected and untoward events. He preserved throughout that admirable serenity for which he was noted, which no doubt would have equally distinguished him on the flaming crests of Douaumont. He assented on the 22nd to the movement of the Ist and XXth Corps, and to a request to Sir Douglas Haig to relieve in the line with British troops the Tenth French Army to reinforce Verdun. For the rest he remained in Olympian tranquillity, inspiring by his unaffected calm, regular meals and peaceful slumbers confidence in all about him. A less detached view was necessarily taken by Castelnau. The Second French Army had been relieved in the line some time before by the increasing British forces. This army was in the best order, rested and trained. Its staff had not been affected by the new French rule obliging every Staff Officer to do a spell of duty with the fighting troops. Its Commander, Pétain, had gained already in the war one of the highest reputations. On the evening of February 24, General de Castelnau presented himself to General Joffre and proposed to move the whole of the Second French Army to Verdun. The Commander-in-Chief assented to this. At eleven o'clock on the same night Castelnau, having received further reports of the most serious character, requested by telephone permission to proceed personally to Verdun with

plenary powers. Pierrefeu has described the incident
which followed. The Commander-in-Chief was already
asleep. Following his almost invariable custom he had
retired to rest at ten o'clock. The orderly officer on duty
declared it impossible to disturb him. At first Castelnau
submitted. But a few minutes later a further message
from Verdun foreshadowing the immediate evacuation of
the whole of the right bank of the Meuse arrived, and on
this Castelnau would brook no further obstruction. He
went in person to the Villa Poiret in which the great soldier
was reposing. Upon the express order of the Major-General
an aide-de-camp took the responsibility of knocking
at the formidable double-locked door. The supreme Chief,
after perusing the telegrams, gave at once the authorization
for General de Castelnau to proceed with full powers,
declared there must be no retreat, and then returned to his
rest.

Castelnau started forthwith a little after midnight. At
Avize, Headquarters of Langle de Cary and the centre
group of armies, he quelled the pessimism that existed,
and from there telephoned to Verdun announcing his
impending arrival and calling upon General Herr " on the
order of the Commander-in-Chief not to yield ground but
to defend it step by step," and warning him that if this
order was not executed, " the consequences would be most
grave for him (Herr)." By daylight of the 25th Castelnau
reached Verdun and found himself confronted with the
tragic scenes of confusion and disorder which haunt the
immediate rear of a defeated battle-front. All accounts
agree that the influence and authority of Castelnau on the
25th reanimated the defence and for the moment restored
the situation. Wherever he went, decision and order followed him. He reiterated the command at all costs to

hold the heights of the Meuse and to stop the enemy on the right bank. The Xth and Ist Army Corps now arriving on the scene were thrown into the battle with this intention. While taking these emergency measures, Castelnau had already telegraphed to Pétain ordering him to take command, not only of the Second French Army, which was now moving, but also of all the troops in the fortified region of Verdun.

On the morning of the 26th Pétain received from Castelnau the direction of the battle, which he continued to conduct, while at the same time mastering the local situation. The neglect of the field and permanent defences of a fortress which it was decided to defend to the death, now bequeathed a cruel legacy to the French troops. In advance of the permanent forts there were neither continuous lines of trenches nor the efficient organization of strong points. Telephone systems and communication trenches were scarce or non-existent. The forts themselves were all empty and dismantled. Even their machine guns and cupolas had been extracted and their flanking batteries disarmed. All these deficiencies had now to be repaired in full conflict and under tremendous fire. Besides the direction of the battle and the organization of his forces and rapidly growing artillery, Pétain took a number of general decisions. Four successive lines of defence were immediately set in hand. In full accord with the views of the much-chastised General Coutanceau, Pétain directed the immediate re-occupation and re-arming of all the forts. To each he assigned a garrison with fourteen days' food and water, and solemn orders never to capitulate. The immense value of the large subterranean galleries of these forts, in which a whole battalion could live in absolute security till the moment of counter-attack, was now to be proved. Lastly, the new commander instituted the marvellous system of motor-lorries between Verdun and Bar le Duc. No less than three thousand of these passed up and down this road every twenty-four hours, and conveyed each week during seven months of conflict an average of 90,000 men and 50,000 tons of material. Along this "Sacred Way", as it was rightly called, no less than sixty-six divisions of the French Army were to pass on their journey to the anvil and the furnace fires.

JUTLAND—THE BATTLE CRUISER ACTION

May 31st 1916

Both sides deliberately converged to effective striking distance. Fire was opened by the *Lützow* and answered by the *Lion* a little after a quarter to four. Each ship engaged its respective antagonist. As there were six British to five German battle-cruisers, the *Lion* and the *Princess Royal* were able to concentrate on the enemy's flagship *Lützow*. The chances of the battle on either side led to discrepancies in the selection of targets, and sometimes two British ships were firing at one German, while another was ignored, or vice versa. Two minutes after the great guns had opened fire at about 14,000 yards, the *Lion* was hit twice ; and the third salvo of the *Princess Royal* struck the *Lützow*. On both sides four guns at a time were fired, and at every discharge four shells each weighing about half a ton smote target or water in a volley. In the first thirty-seven minutes of an action which lasted above two hours,

one-third of the British force was destroyed. At four
o'clock the *Indefatigable*, after twelve minutes at battery
with the *Von der Tann*, hit by three simultaneous shells
from a salvo of four, blew up and sank almost without
survivors. Twenty-six minutes later the *Queen Mary*,
smitten amidships by a plunging salvo from the *Derfflinger*,
burst into flame, capsized, and after thirty seconds exploded
into a pillar of smoke which rose 800 feet in the air, bearing
with it for 200 feet such items as a 50-foot steamboat. The
Tiger and the *New Zealand*, following her at the speed of
an ordinary train, and with only 500 yards between them,
had barely time to sheer off port and starboard to avoid her
wreck. The *Tiger* passed through the smoke cloud black
as night, and her gunnery officer, unable to fire, took
advantage of the pitch-darkness to reset to zero the director
controls of his four turrets. Meanwhile the *Lion*, after
being eight minutes in action, was hit on her midship
turret (Q) by a shell which, but for a sublime act of personal devotion and comprehension, would have been fatal.

All the crew of the turret except its commanding officer,
Major Hervey (Royal Marine Artillery), and his sergeant
were instantly killed ; and Major Hervey had both his legs
shattered or torn off. Each turret in a capital ship is a self-
contained organism. It is seated in the hull of the vessel
like a fort ; it reaches from the armoured gun-house visible
to all, 50 feet downwards to the very keel. Its intricate
hydraulic machinery, its ammunition trunk communi-
cating with the shell-rooms and magazines—all turn
together in whatever direction its twin guns may point.
The shell of the *Lützow* wrecked the turret and set the
wreckage on fire. The shock flung and jammed one of
the guns upward, and twenty minutes later the cartridge
which was in its breech slid out. It caught fire and ignited

the other charges in the gun-cages. The flash from these passed down the trunk to the charges at the bottom. None but dead and dying remained in the turret. All had been finished by the original shell-burst. The men in the switch-board department and the handling parties of the shell-room were instantly killed by the flash of the cordite fire. The blast passed through and through the turret in all its passages and foundations, and rose 200 feet above its gaping roof. But the doors of the magazines were closed. Major Hervey, shattered, weltering, stifled, seared, had found it possible to give the order down the voice tube : " Close magazine doors and flood magazines." So the *Lion* drove on her course unconscious of her peril, or by what expiring breath it had been effectually averted. In the long, rough, glorious history of the Royal Marines there is no name and no deed which in its character and its consequences ranks above this.

Meanwhile the Vice-Admiral, pacing the bridge among the shell fragments rebounding from the water, and like Nelson of old in the brunt of the enemy's fire, has learned that the *Indefatigable* and the *Queen Mary* have been destroyed, and that his own magazines are menaced by fire. It is difficult to compare sea with land war. But each battle-cruiser was a unit comparable at least to a complete infantry division. Two divisions out of his six have been annihilated in the twinkling of an eye. The enemy, whom he could not defeat with six ships to five, are now five ships to four. Far away all five German battle-cruisers—grey smudges changing momentarily into " rippling sheets of flame "—are still intact and seemingly invulnerable. " Nevertheless," proceeds the official narrative, " the squadron continued its course undismayed " But the movement of these blind, inanimate castles of steel was governed at this moment entirely by the spirit of a single man. Had he faltered, had he taken less than a conqueror's view of the British fighting chances, all these great engines of sea power and war power would have wobbled off in meaningless disarray. This is a moment on which British naval historians will be glad to dwell; and the actual facts deserve to be recorded. The *Indefatigable* had disappeared beneath the waves. The *Queen Mary* had towered up to heaven in a pillar of fire. The *Lion* was in flames. A tremendous salvo struck upon or about her following ship, the *Princess Royal*, which vanished in a cloud of spray and smoke. A signalman sprang on to the *Lion's* bridge with the words: " *Princess Royal* blown up, sir ". On this the Vice-Admiral said to his Flag Captain, " Chatfield, there seems to be something wrong with our —— ships today. Turn two points to port," i.e., two points nearer the enemy.

THE ENCOUNTER

At 11.30 the High Sea Fleet, after some minor alterations in course, crashed into the 4th British Flotilla, and a fierce brief conflict followed. The destroyers *Tipperary* and *Broke* were disabled. The *Spitfire* collided with the battleship *Nassau*, and the *Sparrowhawk* collided with the injured *Broke*. The German cruiser *Elbing* was rammed and disabled by the *Posen*. The *Rostock* was torpedoed. The rest of the British flotilla made off into the night, and turning again on their course, ran a second time into the enemy, when the destroyers *Fortune* and *Ardent* were both sunk by gunfire. A little after midnight the armoured cruiser *Black Prince*, which had become detached

from the Fleet and was endeavouring to rejoin, found
herself within 1,600 yards of the German super-Dread-
nought Squadron, and was instantly blown to pieces; and
her crew of 750 men perished without survivors. At 12.25
the head of the German line, which was by now on the port
quarter of the British Fleet, cut into the 9th, 10th and 13th
British Flotillas and sank the destroyer *Turbulent*. In these
unexpected clashes the British flotillas following dutifully
in the wake of the Grand Fleet suffered as severely as if
they had been launched in an actual attack. The last contact was at 2.10, when the 12th Flotilla sighting the enemy
who had now worked right round to port, and led by
Captain Stirling with an aggressive intention and definite
plan of attack, destroyed the *Pommern* with her entire crew
of 700 men, and sank the German destroyer V4. This was
the end of the fighting.

Up till half an hour after midnight there was still time
for Jellicoe to reach the Horn Reef in time for a daylight
battle. Even after that hour the German rear and stragglers
could have been cut off. The repeated bursts of heavy
firing, the flash of great explosions, the beams of search-
lights—all taking place in succession from west to east—
were not readily capable of more than one interpretation.
But the Grand Fleet continued steadily on its course to the
south; and when it turned northward at 2.30 a.m., the
Germans were for ever beyond its reach. The northern
course also carried the British Fleet away from the retreating enemy; and it is clear that from this time onward the
Commander-in-Chief had definitely abandoned all expectation of renewing the action. It remained only to collect
all forces, to sweep the battle area on the chance of stragglers, and to return to harbour. This was accordingly
done.

So ended the Battle of Jutland. The Germans loudly proclaimed a victory. There was no victory for anyone ; but they had good reason to be content with their young Navy. It had fought skilfully and well. It had made its escape from the grip of overwhelming forces, and in so doing had inflicted heavier loss in ships and men than it had itself received. The British Battle Fleet was never seriously in action. Only one ship, the *Colossus*, was struck by an enemy shell, and out of more than 20,000 men in the battleships only two were killed and five wounded. To this supreme instrument had been devoted the best of all that Britain could give for many years. It was vastly superior to its opponent in numbers, tonnage, speed, and above all gun power, and was at least its equal in discipline, individual skill and courage. The disappointment of all ranks was deep ; and immediately there arose reproaches and recriminations, continued to this day, through which this account has sought to steer a faithful and impartial passage. All hoped that another opportunity would be granted them, and eagerly sought to profit by the lessons of the battle. The chance of an annihilating victory had been perhaps offered at the moment of deployment, had been offered again an hour later when Scheer made his great miscalculation, and for the third time when a little before midnight the Commander-in Chief decided to reject the evidence of the Admiralty message. Three times is a lot. . . .

The ponderous, poignant responsibilities borne successfully, if not triumphantly, by Sir John Jellicoe during two years of faithful command, constitute unanswerable claims to the lasting respect of the nation. But the Royal Navy must find in other personalities and other episodes the golden links which carried forward through the Great War

the audacious and conquering traditions of the past ; and
it is to Beatty and the battle-cruisers, to Keyes at Zee-
brugge, to Tyrwhitt and his Harwich striking force, to the
destroyer and submarine flotillas out in all weathers and
against all foes, to the wild adventures of the Q-ships, to
the steadfast resolution of the British Merchant Service,
that the eyes of rising generations will turn.

BATTLE OF THE SOMME
July 1916

Let us descend from a general viewpoint into closer
contact with a single Division. The 8th Division, with
all its three brigades in line, was to assault the Ovillers
spur : the centre brigade up the ridge ; the others through
the valleys on each side. Both the valleys were enfiladed
from the German positions at La Boiselle and in front of
Thiepval. Against these three brigades stood the German
180th Infantry Regiment with two battalions holding the
front defences, and the third battalion in reserve north of
Pozières. After allowing for battalion reserves, there were
ten Companies comprising about 1,800 men to oppose the
three brigades, together about 8,500 bayonets, of the 8th
Division.

At 7.30 the British artillery barrage lifted. The trench
mortars ceased fire, and the leading battalions of all three
brigades rose and moved forward, each battalion extended
on a frontage of 400 yards. A violent machine-gun and
rifle fire opened immediately along the whole front of the
German position, particularly from the machine-gun nests
of La Boiselle and Ovillers ; and almost simultaneously

the German batteries behind Ovillers placed a barrage in No Man's Land and along the British front line and support trenches. Here let the German eye-witness speak :

" The intense bombardment was realized by all to be a prelude to the infantry assault at last. The men in the dugouts therefore waited ready, a belt full of hand-grenades around them, gripping their rifles and listening for the bombardment to lift from the front defence zone on to the rear defences. It was of vital importance to lose not a second in taking up position in the open to meet the British infantry who would be advancing immediately behind the artillery barrage. Looking towards the British trenches through the long trench periscopes held up out of the dugout entrances, there could be seen a mass of steel helmets above their parapet showing that their storm-troops were ready for the assault. At 7.30 a.m. the hurricane of shells ceased as suddenly as it had begun. Our men at once clambered up the steep shafts leading from the dugouts to daylight and ran singly or in groups to the nearest shell craters. The machine guns were pulled out of the dugouts and hurriedly placed into position, their crews dragging the heavy ammunition boxes up the steps and out to the guns. A rough firing line was thus rapidly established. As soon as in position, a series of extended lines of British infantry were seen moving forward from the British trenches. The first line appeared to continue without end to right and left. It was quickly followed by a second line, then a third and a fourth. They came on at a steady easy pace as if expecting to find nothing alive in our front trenches. . . . The front line, preceded by a thin line of skirmishers and bombers, was now half-way across No Man's Land. " Get ready! " was passed along our front from crater to crater, and heads appeared over the crater edges as final positions were taken up for the best view and machine guns mounted firmly in place. A few minutes later, when the leading British line was within 100 yards, the rattle of machine-gun and rifle fire broke out from along the whole line of craters. Some fired kneeling so as to get a better target over the broken ground, while others in the excitement of the moment stood up regardless of their own safety to fire into the crowd of men in front of them. Red rockets sped up into the blue sky as a signal to the artillery, and immediately afterwards a mass of shells from the German batteries in rear tore through the air and burst among the advancing lines. Whole sections seemed to fall, and the rear formations, moving in closer order, quickly scattered. The advance rapidly crumpled under this hail of shells and bullets. All along the line men could be seen throwing their arms into the air and collapsing never to move again. Badly wounded rolled about in their agony, and others less severely injured crawled to the nearest shell-hole for shelter. The British soldier, however, has no lack of courage, and once his hand is set to the plough he is not easily turned from his purpose. The extended lines, though badly shaken and with many gaps, now came on all the faster. Instead of a leisurely walk they covered the ground in short rushes at the double. Within a few minutes the leading troops had reached within a stone's throw of our front trench, and while some of us continued to fire at point-blank range, others threw hand-grenades among them. The British bombers answered back, while the infantry rushed forward with fixed bayonets. The noise of battle became indescribable. The shouting of orders and the shrill British cheers as they charged forward could be heard above the violent and intense fusillade of machine guns and rifles and the bursting bombs, and above the deep thunderings of the artillery and the shell explosions. With all this were mingled the moans and groans of the wounded, the cries for help and the last screams of death. Again and again the extended lines of British infantry broke against the German defence like waves against a cliff, only to be beaten back.

It was an amazing spectacle of unexampled gallantry, courage and bull-dog determination on both sides."

At several points the British who had survived the awful fire-storm broke into the German trenches. They were nowhere strong enough to maintain their position ; and by nine o'clock the whole of the troops who were still alive and unwounded were either back in their own front-line trenches, or sheltering in the shell-holes of No Man's Land, or cut off and desperately defending themselves in the captured German trenches. A renewed attack was immediately ordered by Divisional Headquarters. But the Brigadiers reported that they had no longer the force to attempt it. A fresh brigade was sent from the IIIrd Corps Headquarters. But before it could share the fate of the others, all signs of fighting inside the German trenches by the British who had entered them had been extinguished ; and the orders to renew the assault were cancelled. Here are some of the losses :

2/Middlesex	. .	22 officers ;	592	other ranks
2/Devons .	. .	16 ,,	418	,, ,,
2/West Yorks	. .	16 ,,	490	,, ,,
2/Berkshire	. .	20 ,,	414	,, ,,
2/Lincoln .	. .	20 ,,	434	,, ,,
1/Irish Rifles	. .	17 ,,	411	,, ,,
8/K.O.Y.L.I.	. .	25 (all),,	522	,, ,,
8/York and Lancaster		23 ,,	613	,, ,,
9/York and Lancaster		23 ,,	517	,, ,,
11/Sherwood Foresters		20 ,,	488	,, ,,

In all, the Division lost in little more than two hours 218 out of 300 officers and 5,274 other ranks out of 8,500 who had gone into action. By the evening of July 1, the German 180th Infantry Regiment was again in possession of the whole of its trenches. Its losses during the day's fighting had been 8 officers and 273 soldiers killed, wounded and missing. Only two of its three battalions had been engaged. It had not been necessary to call the reserve battalion to their aid.

Night closed over the still-thundering battlefield. Nearly 60,000 British soldiers had fallen, killed or wounded, or were prisoners in the hands of the enemy. This was the greatest loss and slaughter sustained in a single day in the whole history of the British Army. Of the infantry who advanced to the attack, nearly half had been overtaken by death, wounds or capture. Against this, apart from territory, we had gained 4,000 prisoners and a score of cannon.

FALL OF ROUMANIA

November 1916

Roumania had now been at war for two months, and by the beginning of November five additional German divisions and two cavalry divisions had joined Falkenhayn's army. Thus powerfully reinforced, he attacked the Vulkan Pass in earnest. By November 26 he had forced his way through and entered the Roumanian plain, descending the valley of the Jiu and incidentally cutting off the Roumanian forces holding the tip of the tongue near Orsova. This movement compromised in succession the defence of the other passes. By the end of November, Falkenhayn had joined hands with Mackensen from across the Danube ; and on December 6, after a well-contested three-days' battle between Falkenhayn's and Mackensen's armies, together amounting to fifteen divisions, and what was left of the Roumanian forces, he entered Bucharest in triumph. The Roumanians, defending themselves stubbornly, retreated eastward towards the considerable Russian Army which had now at last arrived. Notwithstanding torrential rains and winter conditions, Falkenhayn and Mackensen followed apace. The roads ceased to exist. The troops were short of food and every necessity. Ludendorff, according to Falkenhayn, sent " floods of telegrams, as superfluous as they were unpleasant ", but neither winter clothing nor supplies. Still the Germans persevered, and after a series of stern battles mainly against Russian forces, reached the Sereth River on January 7. Here their advance ended. The tongue of Roumania had been torn out by its roots. There remained of that unhappy kingdom only the northern province. In this narrow region around the town of Jassy what remained of the armies which four months before had entered the war so full of hope endured for many months privation and even famine, from which not only thousands of soldiers but far larger numbers of refugees perished lamentably. Thus did Roumania share in the end the hideous miseries of all the Balkan peoples.

How unteachable, how blinded by their passions are the races of men! The First Great War, bringing tribulation to so many, offered to the Christian peoples of the Balkans their supreme opportunity. Others had to toil and dare and suffer. They had only to forgive and to unite. By a single spontaneous realization of their common interests the Confederation of the Balkans would have become one of the Great Powers of Europe, with Constantinople, under some international instrument, as its combined capital. A concerted armed neutrality followed by decisive intervention at the chosen moment against their chosen enemies, Turkey and Austria, could easily have given each individual state the major part of its legitimate ambitions, and would have given to all safety, prosperity and power. They chose instead to drink in company the corrosive cup of internecine vengeance. And the cup is not yet drained.

U-BOAT WARFARE

However long the controversy may last, there will never be any agreement between the belligerent nations on the rights and wrongs of the U-boat warfare. The Germans never understood, and never will understand, the horror and indignation with which their opponents and the neutral world regarded their attack. They believed sincerely that the outcry was only hypocrisy and propaganda. The law and custom of the sea were very old. They had grown up in the course of centuries, and, although frequently broken in the instance, had in the main stood the stress of many bitter conflicts between nations. To seize even an enemy merchant ship at sea was an act which imposed strict obligations on the captor. To make a neutral ship a prize of war stirred whole histories of international law. But between taking a ship and sinking a ship was a gulf. The captor of a neutral ship at sea had by long tradition been bound to bring his prize into harbour and judge her before the Prize Courts. To sink her incontinently was odious ; to sink her without providing for the safety of the crew, to leave that crew to perish in open boats or drown amid the waves was in the eyes of all sea-faring peoples a grisly act, which hitherto had never been practised deliberately except by pirates. Thus old sea-going nations, particularly Britain, France, Holland, Nor-way and the United States, saw in the U-boat war against merchant ships, and particularly neutral merchant ships, depth beyond depth of enormity. And indeed the spec-tacle of helpless merchant seamen, their barque shattered and foundering, left with hard intention by fellow-mariners to perish in the cruel sea, was hideous.

But the Germans were newcomers on salt water. They cared little for all these ancient traditions of seafaring folk. Death for them was the same in whatever form it came to men. It ended in a more or less painful manner their mortal span. Why was it more horrible to be choked with salt water than with poison gas, or to starve in an open boat than to rot wounded but alive in No Man's Land? The British blockade treated the whole of Germany as if it were a beleaguered fortress, and avowedly sought to starve the whole population—men, women and children, old and young, wounded and sound into submission. Suppose the issues had arisen on land instead of at sea ; suppose large numbers of Americans and neutrals had carried food or shell into the zone of the armies under the fire of the German artillery ; suppose their convoys were known to be travelling certain roads towards the front : who would have hesitated for a moment to overwhelm them with drum-fire and blast them from the face of the earth? Who ever hesitated to fire on towns and villages because helpless and inoffensive non-combatants were gathered there? If they came within reach of the guns, they had to take their chance, and why should not this apply to the torpedoes too? Why should it be legitimate to slay a neutral or a non-combatant on land by cannon if he got in the way, and a hideous atrocity to slay the same neutral or non-combatant by torpedo on the seas? Where was the sense in drawing distinctions between the two processes? Policy might spread its web of calculation, but in logic the path was clear. Yes, we will if necesary kill everyone of every condition who comes within our power and hinders us from winning the war, and we draw no distinction between land and sea. Thus the German Naval Staff. But the neutrals took a different view.

THE RUSSIAN COLLAPSE

March 1917

Many streams had flowed together to bring the deluge. The Russian revolution was begun by social, military and political forces which within a week were left aghast behind it. In its opening paroxysm all conscious Russia participated. It was primarily a patriotic revolt against the misfortunes and mismanagement of the War. Defeats and disasters, want of food and prohibition of alcohol, the slaughter of millions of men, joined with inefficiency and corruption to produce a state of exasperation among all classes which had no outlet but revolt, could find no scapegoat but the Sovereign. For a year past the Czar and his wife had been the objects of growing universal resentment. The fond, obstinate husband and father, the absolute monarch obviously devoid of all the qualities of a national ruler in times of crisis, bore the burden of all the sufferings which the German Armies had inflicted on the Russian State. Behind him the Empress, a still more hated figure, dwelt in her tiny circle listening only to her cronies—her lady companion Madame Virubova, her spiritual adviser the sensual mystic Rasputin—and presumed thence and on such promptings to sway the policy and fortunes of the tormented Empire.

In vain the Imperial family, deeply concerned for their own existence—apart from all other issues—approached their Head. In vain the leaders of the Duma and every independent figure in Russia made their protests. In vain the Ambassadors of the Allied Powers dropped their elaborate hints, or even uttered solemn and formal warnings under the direction of their Governments. Nicholas II, distressed, remained immovable. He saw as clearly as they did the increasing peril. He knew of no means by which it could be averted. In his view nothing but autocracy established through centuries had enabled the Russians to proceed thus far in the teeth of calamity. No people had suffered and sacrificed like the Russians. No State, no nation, had ever gone through trials on such a scale and retained its coherent structure. The vast machine creaked and groaned. But it still worked. One more effort and victory would come. To change the system, to open the gate to intruders, to part with any portion of the despotic power, was in the eyes of the Czar to bring about a total collapse. Therefore, though plunged daily deeper in anxiety and perplexity, he was held alike by all his instincts and his reasoning faculties in a fixed position. He stood like a baited animal tied to a stake and feebly at bay. . . .

All sorts of Russians made the revolution. No sort of Russian reaped its profit. Among the crowds who thronged the turbulent streets and ante-rooms of Petrograd in these March days with resolve for " Change at all costs " in their hearts, were found Grand Dukes, fine ladies, the bitterest

die-hards and absolutists like Purishkevitch and Yusupov ;
resolute, patriotic politicians like Rodzianko and Guchkov ;
experienced Generals ; diplomatists and financiers of the
old régime ; Liberals and Democrats ; Socialists like
Kerenski ; sturdy citizens and tradesfolk ; faithful soldiers
seeking to free their Prince from bad advisers ; ardent
nationalists resolved to purge Russia from secret German
influence ; multitudes of loyal peasants and workmen ;
and behind all, cold, calculating, ruthless, patient, stirring
all, demanding all, awaiting all, the world-wide organization of International Communism.

Actually the deposition of the Czar was effected by the
Chiefs of his Army. Nicholas was at his Headquarters at
Mohilev when on the afternoon of March 11 the first telegrams about the disorders in Petrograd began to flow in.
It was reported at first that they were of no great consequence. Had he been in his Capital accessible to all the
moderate forces now inflamed, there might still have been
time, not indeed as we hold to avert disaster, but to lessen
its shock. But he was at Mohilev, and the Grand Duke
Nicholas who should have ruled the Armies was far off in
the half-banishment of Tiflis. On the morning of the 11th
Rodzianko, President of the Duma, confronted with a
swiftly mounting crisis, sent the following telegram to his
Master :

" Position serious. Anarchy in the capital. Government
paralysed. Arrangements for transport, supply and fuel in
complete disorder. General discontent is increasing. Dis-
orderly firing on the streets. Part of the troops are firing
on one another. Essential to entrust some individual who
possesses the confidence of the country with the formation
of a new government. There must be no delay. Any

procrastination fatal. I pray to God that in this hour responsibility fall not on the wearer of the crown!"

He repeated this to the Commanders-in-Chief on all the Army-group " Fronts ", and to Alexeiev at the Stavka, with a request for their support ; and next day, the 12th, he telegraphed again to the Czar :

" The situation is growing worse. Immediate steps must be taken, for tomorrow will be too late. The final hour has come when the fate of the country and the dynasty must be decided."

To such grave tidings were added scarcely less disturbing news from Tsarskoe Selo. The Royal children had sickened of the measles. The Czar replied to his counsellors with hard defiance, and to his wife with overflowing sympathy.

As the day wore on Alexeiev took to his bed with anxiety and fever. The Czar called for the Imperial train. His duties as a Sovereign and as a father equally demanded his return to the seat of Government. The train was ready at midnight ; but it took six hours more to clear the line. The Dowager-Empress had arrived. Mother and son travelled together. The next afternoon the train stopped at Dno. Impossible to proceed! A bridge had been, it was said, blown up or damaged. The Czar indicated an alternative route, and for the first time came in contact with naked resistance. Such authority as now reigned in Petrograd refused to permit his further approach. Where to turn? Some hours passed. Back to Mohilev? We do not know how far he tested this possibility. Perhaps he had been conscious of the unspoken reproach with which the atmosphere of the Stavka was loaded. To the Northern Front then—to General Ruzski. Here at least he would

E

find a trusty commander, whose armies lay nearest to the rebellious capital.

The train reached Pskov. Ruzski was there with grave salutes. But with him also very soon were Guchkov and Shulguin as a deputation from the Duma. Here were able, determined public men with plain advice : immediate abdication in favour of his son, and the Regency of his brother, the Grand Duke Michael Alexandrovich. The Czar appealed to Ruzski. Ruzski, anticipating his responsibilities, had felt that the matter was too serious for him. Already before the Czar's arrival he had consulted the Stavka and the other commanders. Accordingly fateful telegrams had been dispatched through the Stavka along the whole length of the Russian front. All the Army Group Commanders, Brusilov, Ewarth, the Grand Duke, and finally, with many reservations, Sakharov from distant Roumania, declared in favour of abdication. The document was drawn. Guchkov presented the pen. Nicholas was about to sign. Suddenly he asked whether he and his family could reside in the Crimea, in that palace of Livadia whose sunlit gardens seemed green and calm and tranquil. Bluntly he was told he must leave Russia forthwith, and that the new sovereign must remain among his people. On this his fatherly love triumphed over his public duty and indeed over his coronation oath. Rather than be separated from his son, he disinherited that son. The paper was redrafted and Nicholas II abdicated in favour of his brother. Thus all claim of legitimacy was shivered ; and everything in a second stage was thrown into redoubled confusion.

However, it is over now. The Czar has ceased to reign. The brother, around whom everything is melting, fears to seize the abandoned reins of power without the vote of a

National Assembly, impossible to obtain. Nothing could ever bring stabilizing ideas together again. We cannot here follow the long, swift, splintering, crashing descent which ended, as it could only end, in the abyss. The dynasty was gone. Vainly did leaders of the Duma and the Zemstvos strive to clutch at hand-holds. In their turn they broke. Vainly did Kerenski with his nationalist democracy try to stop the fall a long leap lower down. Vainly did the great men of action, Kornilov the warrior, Savinkov the terrorist-patriot, strive to marshal the social-revolutionary forces in defence of Russia. All fell headlong into the depths where Lenin, Trotski, Zinoviev and other unnatural spirits awaited their prey.

INTERVENTION OF THE UNITED STATES
April 6th 1917

Of all the grand miscalculations of the German High Command none is more remarkable than their inability to comprehend the meaning of war with the American Union. It is perhaps the crowning example of the unwisdom of basing a war policy upon the computation of material factors alone. The war effort of 120,000,000 educated people, equipped with science, and possessed of the resources of an unattackable continent, nay, of a New World, could not be measured by the number of drilled soldiers, of trained officers, of forged cannon, of ships of war they happened to have at their disposal. It betokens ignorance of the elemental forces resident in such a community to suppose they could be permanently frustrated by a mechanical instrument called the U-boat. How rash to balance the hostile exertions of the largest, if not the leading, civilized nation in the world against the chance that they would not arrive in time upon the field of battle! How hard to condemn the war-worn, wearied, already out-numbered heroic German people to mortal conflict with this fresh, mighty, and once aroused, implacable antagonist!

There is no need to exaggerate the material assistance given by the United States to the Allies. All that could be sent was given as fast and as freely as possible, whether in manhood, in ships or in money. But the war ended long before the material power of the United States could be brought to bear as a decisive or even as a principal factor. It ended with over 2,000,000 American soldiers on the soil of France. A campaign in 1919 would have seen very large American armies continually engaged, and these by 1920 might well have amounted to 5,000,000 of men. Compared to potentialities of this kind, what would have been the value of, let us say, the capture of Paris? As for the 200 U-boats, the mechanical hope, there was still the British Navy, which at this period, under the ægis of an over-whelming battle-fleet, maintained upwards of 3,000 armed vessels on the seas.

But if the physical power of the United States was not in fact applied in any serious degree to the beating down of Germany ; if for instance only a few score thousand Germans fell by American hands ; the moral consequence of the United States joining the Allies was indeed the deciding cause in the conflict.

The war had lasted nearly three years ; all the original combatants were at extreme tension ; on both sides the dangers of the front were matched by other dangers far

behind the throbbing lines of contact. Russia has suc-
cumbed to these new dangers ; Austria is breaking up ;
Turkey and Bulgaria are wearing thin ; Germany herself
is forced even in full battle to concede far-reaching Constitutional rights and franchise to her people ; France is
desperate ; Italy is about to pass within an ace of destruction ; and even in stolid Britain there is a different light in
the eyes of men. Suddenly a nation of one hundred and
twenty millions unfurls her standard on what is already
the stronger side ; suddenly the most numerous democracy
in the world, long posing as a judge, is hurled, nay, hurls
itself into the conflict. The loss of Russia was forgotten in
this new reinforcement. Defeatist movements were
strangled on the one side and on the other inflamed. Far
and wide through every warring nation spread these two
opposite impressions—" The whole world is against us "
—" The whole world is on our side ".

POLITICIANS *v.* GENERALS

A series of absurd conventions became established,
perhaps inevitably, in the public mind. The first and
most monstrous of these was that the Generals and Admirals were more competent to deal with the broad issues of the
war than abler men in other spheres of life. The General
no doubt was an expert on how to move his troops, and the
Admiral upon how to fight his ships, though even in this
restricted field the limitations of their scientific knowledge
when confronted with unforeseen conditions and un-
dreamed-of scales became immediately apparent. But
outside this technical aspect they were helpless and mis-

leading arbiters in problems in whose solution the aid of the statesman, the financier, the manufacturer, the inventor, the psychologist, was equally required. The foolish doctrine was preached to the public through innumerable agencies that Generals and Admirals must be right on war matters, and civilians of all kinds must be wrong. These erroneous conceptions were inculcated billion-fold by the newspapers under the crudest forms. The feeble or presumptuous politician is portrayed cowering in his office, intent in the crash of the world on Party intrigues or personal glorification, fearful of responsibility, incapable of aught save shallow phrase-making. To him enters the calm, noble, resolute figure of the great Commander by land or sea, resplendent in uniform, glittering with decorations, irradiated with the lustre of the hero, shod with the science and armed with the panoply of war. This stately figure, devoid of the slightest thought of self, offers his clear far-sighted guidance and counsel for vehement action or artifice or wise delay. But his advice is rejected ; his sound plans put aside ; his courageous initiative baffled by political chatterboxes and incompetents. As well, it was suggested, might a great surgeon, about to operate with sure science and the study of a lifetime upon a desperate case, have his arm jogged or his hand impeded, or even the lancet snatched from him, by some agitated relation of the patient. Such was the picture presented to the public, and such was the mood which ruled. It was not, however, entirely in accordance with the facts ; and facts, especially in war, are stubborn things.

THE TWENTY-FIRST OF MARCH,
1918

Before I went to my bed in the ruins of Nurlu, Tudor said to me : " It is certainly coming now. Trench raids this evening have identified no less than eight enemy battalions on a single half-mile of the front ". The night was quiet except for the rumble of artillery fire, mostly distant, and the thudding explosions of occasional aeroplane raids. I woke up in a complete silence at a few minutes past four and lay musing. Suddenly, after what seemed about half an hour, the silence was broken by six or seven very loud and very heavy explosions several miles away. I thought they were our 12-inch guns, but they were probably mines. And then, exactly as a pianist runs his hands across the keyboard from treble to bass, there rose in less than one minute the most tremendous cannonade I shall ever hear. " At 4.30 a.m.," says Ludendorff in his account, " our barrage came down with a crash." Far away, both to the north and to the south, the intense roar and reverberation rolled upwards to us, while through the chinks in the carefully papered window the flame of the bombardment lit like flickering firelight my tiny cabin.

I dressed and went out. On the duckboards outside the Mess I met Tudor. " This is *it*," he said. " I have ordered all our batteries to open. You will hear them in a minute." But the crash of the German shells bursting on our trench lines eight thousand yards away was so overpowering that the accession to the tumult of nearly two hundred guns firing from much nearer to us could not be even distinguished. From the Divisional Headquarters on the high ground of Nurlu one could see the front line for many miles. It swept round us in a wide curve of red leaping flame stretching to the north far along the front of the Third Army, as well as of the Fifth Army on the south, and quite unending in either direction. There were still two hours to daylight, and the enormous explosions of shells upon our trenches seemed almost to touch each other, with hardly an interval in space or time. Among the bursting shells there rose at intervals, but almost continually, the much larger flames of exploding magazines. The weight and intensity of the bombardment surpassed anything which anyone had ever known before.

Only one gun was firing at the Headquarters. He belonged to the variety called " Percy ", and all his shells fell harmlessly a hundred yards away. A quarter of a mile to the south along the Péronne road a much heavier gun was demolishing the divisional canteen. Daylight supervened on pandemonium, and the flame picture pulsated under a pall of smoke from which great fountains of the exploding " dumps " rose mushroom-headed. It was my duty to leave these scenes ; and at ten o'clock, with mingled emotions, I bade my friends farewell and motored without misadventure along the road to Péronne. The impression I had of Tudor was of an iron peg hammered in to the frozen ground, immovable. And so indeed it proved. The 9th Division held not only its Battle but its Forward Zone at the junction of the Third and Fifth Armies against every assault, and only retired when ordered to do so in consequence of the general movement of the line.

ENDURANCE

Before the war it had seemed incredible that such terrors and slaughters, even if they began, could last more than a few months. After the first two years it was difficult to believe that they would ever end. We seemed separated from the old life by a measureless gulf. The adaptive genius of man had almost habituated him to the horrors of his new environment. Far away shone a pale star of home and peace ; but all around the storm roared with unabated and indeed increasing fury. Year after year every optimist had been discredited, every sober hope cast down, and the British nation had doggedly resigned itself to pursue its task without inquiry when the end would come. In the circles of Government, where so many plans had to be made for more than a year ahead, this mood formed the subconscious foundation of our thoughts. Ultimate victory seemed certain. But how it would come, and whether it would come in 1919 or in 1920, or later, were inquiries too speculative to pursue amid the imperious needs of each day. Still less would anyone dare to hope for peace in 1918. Nevertheless, when from time to time the mental eye fell upon these puzzles, this question immediately presented itself : Would Germany collapse all of a sudden as she had done after Jena, or would she fight it out to the bitter end like the French under Napoleon or the Confederates under Lee? The Great War came when both sides were confident of victory. Would it continue after one side was sure it had no hope? Was it in the German nature, so valiant yet at the same time so logical, to fight on in revengeful despair? Should we have a year of battle on the Rhine, the march to Berlin, the breaking up of the armies in the open field, the subjugation of the inhabitants ; or would there be some intense nervous spasm, some overwhelming and almost universal acceptance of defeat and all that defeat involved? We had always fancied it would be Jena. But all our plans were for a long-drawn alternative.

CULMINATION

The war was now entered upon its final phase. During the year 1918, the effort of Britain and of the British Empire reached its highest pitch. The Imperial forces in the field against the enemy in all theatres amounted to four and a half million men, and those under arms to nearly six millions. The strength of the Grand Fleet in vessels of every kind reached its maximum, and the Germans were no longer in a condition even to put to sea. The U-boat warfare was defeated and kept down by the operations of nearly 4,000 armed vessels flying the White Ensign. Under the protection of these agencies upwards of two million United States troops were transported across the Atlantic, of which more than half were carried in British ships, and landed in France during the year with hardly any loss of life by enemy action. The British Mercantile Marine of 20,000 vessels maintained the supply of all the British armies and carried without appreciable hindrance all the food and materials needed for the life of the British islands, for their war industries and for any commerce not required for war production. The control of the seas against the enemy in every quarter of the globe was absolute, and this result was obtained by the employment in the fighting fleets and flotillas, in the Mercantile

Marine, in the Naval arsenals and dockyards, and in the shipbuilding yards of over 1,200,000 men. The British munition plants absorbing the labours of nearly two and a half million persons produced all the shell and artillery that the British armies could use, together with every requisite in increasing abundance. In addition Britain furnished steel, coal, and other war materials in immense quantities to France and Italy, and was preparing, without prejudice to any other obligation, to supply the United States with the whole of the medium artillery required for an Army of eighty divisions for a campaign in 1919. All the preparations had been made, and the process was far advanced of fitting the British armies with technical equipment of every kind for 1919 on a scale in quality and in novelty far superior to any outputs yet achieved. In all there were actually employed under the Crown in the armies, in the fleets and in the war factories, excluding those engaged in the production of food, coal and civil necessaries, nearly eight million men and three-quarters of a million women. The financial measures needed to develop and sustain this prodigious manifestation had required in 1918 alone over three thousand million pounds sterling, of which one thousand millions were raised by the taxation of forty-five million persons in the British Isles and sixteen hundred millions were borrowed at home from the same persons and four hundred millions borrowed abroad mainly from the United States on the credit of the British Government.

But it is with the final effort of the British Army that this chapter is chiefly concerned. From the opening of the campaign of 1918 on March 21 down to the Armistice on November 11 the British armies in France suffered 830,000 casualties, and inflicted on the Germans in killed, wounded

VICTORY 1918
November 11th 1918

Those who choose the moment for beginning wars do not always fix the moment for ending them. To ask for an armistice is one thing, to obtain it is another. The new Chancellor—Prince Max of Baden—sent his note to President Wilson on the 5th. He based himself on the "Fourteen Points," which in the name of Germany he accepted. The President replied on the 8th, asking questions and demanding a German withdrawal from invaded territory as a guarantee of good faith. On the 12th Germany and Austria declared themselves willing to evacuate all invaded territory as a preliminary to an armistice. On the 14th the President indicated that there could be no negotiations with the Emperor. As for an armistice, the conditions must be left to the Commanders in the field, but absolute safeguards must be provided for the maintenance of " the present military supremacy of the armies of the United States and of the Allies in the field ". . . .

The armistice for which Hindenburg and Ludendorff had argued wore by now the aspect of an unconditional surrender. Ludendorff thereupon wished to fight on, declaring with truth that nothing could worsen the terms which Germany would receive. On the 27th the German Government, being resolved on total submission, moved the Emperor to dismiss him from his post. Hindenburg remained " greatly falling with a falling State ". To him and to the German machine-gunners belong the honours of the final agony.

When the great organizations of this world are strained beyond breaking point, their structure often collapses at all points simultaneously. There is nothing on which policy, however wise, can build ; no foothold can be found for virtue or valour, no authority or impetus for a rescuing genius. The mighty framework of German Imperial Power, which a few days before had overshadowed the nations, shivered suddenly into a thousand individually disintegrating fragments. All her Allies whom she had so long sustained, fell down broken and ruined, begging separately for peace. The faithful armies were beaten at the front and demoralized from the rear. The proud, efficient Navy mutinied. Revolution exploded in the most disciplined and docile of States. The Supreme War Lord fled.

Such a spectacle appals mankind ; and a knell rang in the ear of the victors, even in their hour of triumph.

It was a few minutes before the eleventh hour of the eleventh day of the eleventh month. I stood at the window of my room looking up Northumberland Avenue towards Trafalgar Square, waiting for Big Ben to tell that the War was over. My mind strayed back across the scarring years to the scenes and emotions of the night at the Admiralty when I listened for these same chimes in order to give the signal of war against Germany to our Fleets and squadrons across the world. And now all was over! The unarmed and untrained island nation, who with no defence but its Navy had faced unquestioningly the strongest manifestation of military power in human record, had completed its task. Our country had emerged from the ordeal alive and safe, its vast possessions intact, its war effort still waxing, its institutions unshaken, its people and Empire united as never before. Victory had come after all the hazards and heartbreaks in an absolute and unlimited form.

All the Kings and Emperors with whom we had warred were in flight or in exile. All their Armies and Fleets were destroyed or subdued. In this Britain had borne a notable part, and done her best from first to last.

The minutes passed. I was conscious of reaction rather than elation. The material purposes on which one's work had been centred, every process of thought on which one had lived, crumbled into nothing. The whole vast business of supply, the growing outputs, the careful hoards, the secret future plans—but yesterday the whole duty of life —all at a stroke vanished like a nightmare dream, leaving a void behind. My mind mechanically persisted in exploring the problems of demobilization. What was to happen to our three million Munition workers? What would they make now? How would the roaring factories be converted? How in fact are swords beaten into ploughshares? How long would it take to bring the Armies home? What would they do when they get home? We had of course a demobilization plan for the Ministry of Munitions. It had been carefully worked out, but it had played no part in our thoughts. Now it must be put into operation. The levers must be pulled—*Full Steam Astern*. The Munitions Council must meet without delay.

And then suddenly the first stroke of the chime. I looked again at the broad street beneath me. It was deserted. From the portals of one of the large hotels absorbed by Government Departments darted the slight figure of a girl clerk, distractedly gesticulating while another stroke resounded. Then from all sides men and women came scurrying into the street. Streams of people poured out of all the buildings. The bells of London began to clash. Northumberland Avenue was now crowded with people in hundreds, nay, thousands, rushing hither and thither in a frantic manner, shouting and screaming with joy. I could see that Trafalgar Square was already swarming. Around me in our very headquarters, in the Hotel Metropole, disorder had broken out. Doors banged. Feet clattered down corridors. Everyone rose from the desk and cast aside pen and paper. All bounds were broken. The tumult grew. It grew like a gale, but from all sides simultaneously. The street was now a seething mass of humanity. Flags appeared as if by magic. Streams of men and women flowed from the Embankment. They mingled with torrents pouring down the Strand on their way to acclaim the King. Almost before the the last stroke of the clock had died away, the strict, war-straitened, regulated streets of London had become a triumphant pandemonium. At any rate it was clear that no more work would be done that day. Yes, the chains which had held the world were broken. Links of imperative need, links of discipline, links of brute force, links of self-sacrifice, links of terror, links of honour which had held our nation, nay, the greater part of mankind, to grinding toil, to a compulsive cause—every one had snapped upon a few strokes of the clock. Safety, freedom, peace, home, the dear one back at the fireside—all after fifty-two months of gaunt distortion. After fifty-two months of making burdens grievous to be borne, and binding them on men's backs, at last, all at once, suddenly and everywhere the burdens were cast down. At least so for the moment it seemed.

My wife arrived, and we decided to go and offer our congratulations to the Prime Minister, on whom the central impact of the home struggle had fallen, in his hour of recompense. But no sooner had we entered our car than twenty people mounted upon it, and in the midst of a wildly cheering multitude we were impelled slowly forward through Whitehall. We had driven together the opposite way along the same road on the afternoon of the ultimatum. There had been the same crowd and almost the same enthusiasm. It was with feelings which do not lend themselves to words that I heard the cheers of the brave people who had borne so much and given all, who had never wavered, who had never lost faith in their country or its destiny, and who could be indulgent to the faults of their servants when the hour of deliverance had come.

GERMANY'S CARDINAL MISTAKES

The total defeat of Germany was due to three cardinal mistakes : the decision to march through Belgium regardless of bringing Britain into the war ; the decision to begin the unrestricted U-boat warfare regardless of bringing the United States into the war ; and thirdly, the decision to use the German forces liberated from Russia in 1918 for a final onslaught in France. But for the first mistake they would have beaten France and Russia easily in a year ; but for the second mistake they would have been able to make a satisfactory peace in 1917 ; but for the third mistake they would have been able to confront the Allies with an unbreakable front on the Meuse or on the Rhine, and to have made self-respecting terms as a price for abridging the slaughter. All these three errors were committed by the same forces, and by the very forces that made the military strength of the German Empire. The German General Staff, which sustained the German cause with such wonderful power, was responsible for all these three fatal decisions. Thus nations as well as individuals come to ruin through the over-exercise of those very qualities and faculties on which their dominion has been founded.

REJOICING AND REACTION

The conclusion of the [First] Great War raised England to the highest position she has yet attained. For the fourth time in four successive centuries she had headed and sustained the resistance of Europe to a military tyranny; and for the fourth time the war had ended leaving the group of small States of the Low Countries, for whose protection England had declared war, in full independence. Spain, the French Monarchy, the French Empire and the German Empire had overrun and sought to possess or dominate these regions. During 400 years England had withstood them all by war and policy, and all had been defeated and driven out. To that list of mighty Sovereigns and supreme military Lords which already included Philip II, Louis XIV and Napoleon, there could now be added the name of William II of Germany. These four great series of events, directed unswervingly to the same end through so many generations and all crowned with success, constitute a record of persistency and achievement without parallel in the history of ancient or modern times.

But other substantial advantages had been obtained. The menace of the German navy was destroyed and the overweening power of Germany had been for many years definitely set back. The Russian Empire which had been our Ally had been succeeded by a revolutionary government which had renounced all claims to Constantinople, and which by its inherent vices and inefficiency could not soon be a serious military danger to India. On the other hand, England was united with her nearest neighbour and oldest enemy—France—by ties of comradeship in suffering and in victory which promised to be both strong and durable. British and United States troops had fought for the first time side by side, and the two great branches of the English-speaking world had begun again to write their history in common. Lastly, the British Empire had stood every shock and strain during the long and frightful world convulsion. The parliamentary institutions by which the life of the Mother Country and the self-governing Dominions found expression had proved themselves as serviceable for waging war as for maintaining freedom and progress in time of peace. The invisible ties of interest, sentiment and tradition which across all the waters of the world united the Empire had proved more effective than the most binding formal guarantees, and armies of half a million Canadians, Australians and New Zealanders had been drawn by these indefinable and often imperceptible attractions across greater distances than any armies had travelled before, to die and conquer for a cause and quarrel which only remotely affected their immediate material safety. All the peoples and all the creeds of India during the years of crisis had made in their own way a spontaneous demonstration of loyalty, and sustained the war by arms and money on a scale till then unknown. The rebellion in South Africa in 1914 had been repressed by the very Boer generals who had been our most dangerous antagonists in the South African War, and who had signed with us the liberating treaty of Vereeniging. Only in parts of Ireland had there been a failure and a repudiation, and about that there was a lengthy tale to tell.

The pageant of victory unrolled itself before the eyes of the British nation. All the Emperors and Kings with whom we had warred had been dethroned, and all their valiant armies were shattered to pieces. The terrible enemy whose might and craft had so long threatened our existence, whose force had destroyed the flower of the British nation, annihilated the Russian Empire and left all our Allies except the United States at the last gasp, lay prostrate at the mercy of the conquerors. The ordeal was over. The peril had been warded off. The slaughter and the sacrifices had not been in vain and were at an end ; and the over-strained people in the hour of deliverance gave themselves up for a space to the sensations of triumph. Church and State united in solemn thanksgiving. The whole land made holiday. Triple avenues of captured cannon lined the Mall. Every street was thronged with jubilant men and women. All classes were mingled in universal re-joicing. Feasting, music and illuminations turned the shrouded nights of war into a blazing day. The vast crowds were convulsed with emotions beyond expression ; and in Trafalgar Square the joy of the London revellers left enduring marks upon the granite plinth of Nelson's column.

Who shall grudge or mock these overpowering entrance-ments? Every Allied nation shared them. Every victori-ous capital or city in the five continents reproduced in its own fashion the scenes and sounds of London. These hours were brief, their memory fleeting ; they passed as suddenly as they had begun. Too much blood had been spilt. Too much life-essence had been consumed. The gaps in every home were too wide and empty. The shock of an awakening and the sense of disillusion followed swiftly upon the poor rejoicings with which hundreds of millions saluted the achievement of their hearts' desire. There still remained the satisfaction of safety assured, of peace restored, of honour preserved, of the comforts of fruitful industry, of the home-coming of the soldiers ; but these were in the background ; and with them all there mingled the ache for those who would never come home.

Along the British lines in France and Belgium eleven o'clock had produced a reaction revealing the mysterious nature of man. The cannonade was stilled ; the armies halted where they stood. Motionless in the silence the soldiers looked at each other with vacant eyes. A sense of awe, of perplexity, and even of melancholy stole coldly upon men who a few minutes before had been striding forward in the ardour of hot pursuit. It was as though an abyss had opened before the conquerors' feet.

" Unarm, Eros ; the long day's task is done."

The fighting troops seemed for a time incapable of adjusting themselves to the abrupt relaxation of strain. So quiet were the forward camps on the night of victory that one would have thought they belonged to brave men after doing their best at last defeated. This wave of psychological depression passed as quickly as the opposite mood in Britain ; and in a few days Home had become the foundation of all desires. But here again were disillusion and hope deferred.

ABNORMAL CONDITIONS

Great allowances must be made for the behaviour of all the peoples and of all their governments—victors and vanquished alike—as they emerged from the furnace of fifty-two months' world war. The conditions were outside all previous experience. At the outbreak with all its unknown and measureless possibilities the flood of crisis flowed along channels which for some distance had already been prepared. The naval and military leaders and the staffs behind them assumed the immediate direction ; and they had plans which, whether good or bad, were certainly worked out in the utmost detail. These plans of scientific havoc were put into execution ; and the second series of events arose out of their clashings. Every War Office and every Admiralty emitted laconic orders, and for a while the consequences followed almost automatically. The immense forces of destruction, long gathered and stored, were released. When a battleship is launched the operation is short and simple. A few speeches are made ; a few prayers are said ; a bottle of champagne is broken ; a few wedges are knocked away ; and thousands of tons of steel swiftly gathering momentum glide irrevocably into the water. Very different are the problems of bringing that same ship, shattered in action, ripped by torpedoes, crowded with wounded, half full of water, safely back to harbour through storm and mist and adverse tides.

Of course, for more than a year before the war ended plans had been prepared for demobilization and for reconstruction. Men had been withdrawn from the conduct of the war to study and elaborate the measures consequent upon an assumed successful peace. But they were not in any sphere the dominant figures. All other eyes were riveted on the war. The whole mind of the state, every energy which it could command, were concentrated on victory and self-preservation. This other field of interest —hypothetical, contingent, remote—was but dimly lighted. What had we to do with peace while we did not know whether we should not be destroyed? Who could think of reconstruction while the whole world was being hammered to pieces, or of demobilization when the sole aim was to hurl every man and every shell into the battle?

Moreover the governing minds among the Allies never expected the war to end in 1918. Behind the advancing armies all thought and preparation were concentrated upon the spring campaign on the Meuse or on the Rhine. It was to be the greatest campaign of all. More millions of men, more thousands of cannons, more tens of thousands of shells a week ; aeroplanes by the hundred thousand and tanks by the ten thousand : new deadly engines, inventions and poisons of diabolical quality applied upon a gigantic scale : all were moving forward under the ceaseless impulse of the whole effective manhood and womanhood of every warring state. And then suddenly peace! The ramparts against which the united battering-rams of the strongest part of mankind were thundering disintegrated, leaving behind them only a cloud of dust into which the Allies and all their apparatus toppled headlong forward and lay sprawling.

LENIN

1870–1924

In the middle of April 1917 the Germans took a sombre decision. Ludendorff refers to it with bated breath. Full allowance must be made for the desperate stakes to which the German war leaders were already committed. They were in the mood which had opened unlimited submarine warfare with the certainty of bringing the United

States into the war against them. Upon the Western front they had from the beginning used the most terrible means of offence at their disposal. They had employed poison gas on the largest scale and had invented the " Flammen-werfer." Nevertheless it was with a sense of awe that they turned upon Russia the most grisly of all weapons. They transferred Lenin in a sealed truck like a plague bacillus from Switzerland into Russia. Lenin arrived at Petrograd on April 16. Who was this being in whom there resided these dire potentialities? Lenin was to Karl Marx what Omar was to Mahomet. He translated faith into acts. He devised the practical methods by which the Marxian theories could be applied in his own time. He invented the Communist plan of campaign. He issued the orders, he prescribed the watchwords, he gave the signal and he led the attack.

Lenin was also Vengeance. Child of the bureaucracy, by birth a petty noble, reared by a locally much respected Government School Inspector, his early ideas turned by not unusual contradictions through pity to revolt extinguishing pity. Lenin had an unimpeachable father and a rebellious elder brother. This dearly loved companion meddled in assassination. He was hanged in 1894. Lenin was then sixteen. He was at the age to feel. His mind was a remarkable instrument. When its light shone it revealed the whole world, its history, its sorrows, its stupidities, its shams, and above all its wrongs. It revealed all facts in its focus—the most unwelcome, the most inspiring—with an equal ray. The intellect was capacious and in some phases superb. It was capable of universal comprehension in a degree rarely reached among men. The execution of the elder brother deflected this broad white light through a prism : and the prism was red.

But the mind of Lenin was used and driven by a will not less exceptional. The body, tough, square and vigorous in spite of disease, was well fitted to harbour till middle age these incandescent agencies. Before they burnt out his work was done, and a thousand years will not forget it. Men's thoughts and systems in these ages are moving forward. The solutions which Lenin adopted for their troubles are already falling behind the requirements and information of our day. Science irresistible leaps off at irrelevant and henceforth dominating tangents. Social life flows through broadening and multiplying channels. The tomb of the most audacious experimentalist might already bear the placard " Out of date ". An easier generation lightly turns the pages which record the Russian Terror. Youth momentarily interested asks whether it was before or after the Great War; and turns ardent to a thousand new possibilities. The educated nations are absorbed in practical affairs. Socialists and Populists are fast trooping back from the blind alleys of thought and scrambling out of the pits of action into which the Russians have blundered. But Lenin has left his mark. He has won his place. And in the cutting off of the lives of men and women no Asiatic conqueror, not Tamerlane, not Jenghiz Khan can match his fame.

Implacable vengeance, rising from a frozen pity in a tranquil, sensible, matter-of-fact, good-humoured integument! His weapon logic; his mood opportunist. His sympathies cold and wide as the Arctic Ocean ; his hatreds tight as the hangman's noose. His purpose to save the world : his method to blow it up. Absolute principles, but readiness to change them. Apt at once to kill or learn : dooms and afterthoughts : ruffianism and philanthropy : But a good husband ; a gentle guest ; happy, his biographers assure us, to wash up the dishes or dandle the baby ; as mildly amused to stalk a capercailzie as to butcher an Emperor. The quality of Lenin's revenge was impersonal. Confronted with the need of killing any particular person he showed reluctance—even distress. But to blot out a million, to proscribe entire classes, to light the flames of intestine war in every land with the inevitable destruction of the well-being of whole nations—these were sublime abstractions.

" A Russian statistical investigation ", writes Professor Sarolea, " estimates that the dictators killed 28 bishops, 1,219 priests, 6,000 professors and teachers, 9,000 doctors, 12,950 landowners, 54,000 officers, 70,000 policemen, 193,290 workmen, 260,000 soldiers, 355,250 intellectuals and professional men, and 815,000 peasants." These figures do not of course include the vast abridgements of the Russian population which followed from famine.

Lenin was the Grand Repudiator. He repudiated everything. He repudiated God, King, Country, morals, treaties, debts, rents, interest, the laws and customs of centuries, all contracts written or implied, the whole structure—such as it is—of human society. In the end he repudiated himself. He repudiated the Communist system. He confessed its failure in an all-important sphere. He proclaimed the New Economic Policy and recognized private trade. He repudiated what he had slaughtered so many for not believing. They were right it seemed after all. They were unlucky that he did not find it out before. But these things happen sometimes : and how great is the man who acknowledges his mistakes! Back again to wash the dishes and give the child a sweetmeat. Thence once more to the rescue of mankind. This time perhaps the shot will be better aimed. It may kill those who are wrong :

not those who are right. But what after all are men? If Imperialism had its cannon food, should the Communist laboratory be denied the raw material for sociological experiment?

When the subtle acids he had secreted ate through the physical texture of his brain Lenin mowed the ground. The Walls of the Kremlin were not the only witnesses of a strange decay. It was reported that for several months before his death he mumbled old prayers to the deposed gods with ceaseless iteration. If it be true, it shows that Irony is not unknown on Mount Olympus. But this gibbering creature was no longer Lenin. He had already gone. His body lingered for a space to mock the vanished soul. It is still preserved in pickle for the curiosity of the Moscow public, and for the consolation of the faithful.

Lenin's intellect failed at the moment when its destructive force was exhausted, and when sovereign remedial functions were its quest. He alone could have led Russia into the enchanted quagmire ; he alone could have found the way back to the causeway. He saw ; he turned ; he perished. The strong illuminant that guided him was cut off at the moment when he turned resolutely for home. The Russian people were left floundering in the bog. Their worst misfortune was his birth : their next worst— his death.

THE RUSSIAN CIVIL WAR

1919

During the year 1919 there was fought over the whole of Russia a strange war ; a war in areas so vast that considerable armies, armies indeed of hundreds of thousands of men, were lost—dispersed, melted, evaporated ; a war in which there were no real battles, only raids and affrays and massacres, as the result of which countries as large as England or France changed hands to and fro ; a war of flags on the map, of picket lines, of cavalry screens advancing or receding by hundreds of miles without solid cause or durable consequence ; a war with little valour and no mercy. Whoever could advance found it easy to continue ; whoever was forced to retire found it difficult to stop. On paper it looked like the Great War on the Western and Eastern fronts. In fact it was only its ghost : a thin, cold, unsubstantial conflict in the Realms of Dis. Koltchak first and then Denikin advanced in what were called offensives over enormous territories. As they advanced they spread their lines ever wider and ever thinner. It seemed that they would go on till they had scarcely one man to the mile. When the moment came the Bolsheviks lying in the centre, equally feeble but at any rate tending willy-nilly constantly towards compression, gave a prick or a punch at this point or that. Thereupon the balloon burst and all the flags moved back and the cities changed hands and found it convenient to change opinions, and horrible vengeances were wreaked on helpless people, vengeances perseveringly paid over months of fine-spun inquisition. Mighty natural or strategic barriers, like the line of the Volga River or the line of the Ural Mountains, were found to be no resting-places ; no strategic consequences followed from their loss or gain. A war of few casualties and unnumbered executions! The tragedy of each Russian city, of loyal families, of countless humble households might fill libraries of dreary volumes.

But the population of Russia is a village population. The peasant millions dwell in scores of thousands of villages. There was always the land, and Nature brought forth her fruits. What was the life of these villages in this period? Savinkov gave a convincing account of it when we lunched together one day with Lloyd George. It was in some ways the story of the Indian villages over whose heads the waves of conquest swept and recoiled in bygone ages. They had the land. They had murdered or chased away its former owners. The village society had flowed over into new and well-cultivated fields. They now had these long-coveted domains for themselves. No more landlords : no more rent. The earth and its fullness—no more—no less. They did not yet understand that under Communism they would have a new landlord, the Soviet State—a landlord who would demand a higher rent to feed his hungry cities. A collective landlord who could not be killed but who could and would without compunction kill them.

Meanwhile they were self-supporting. Their rude existence could be maintained apart altogether from the outer world or modern apparatus. From the skins of beasts they made garments and footwear. The bees gave them honey in place of sugar. They gave them also wax for such lights as might be needed after sundown. There was bread ; there was meat ; there were roots. They ate and drank and squatted on the land. Not for them the causes of men. Communism, Czarism ; the World Revolution, Holy Russia ; Empire or Proletariat, civilization or barbarism, tyranny or freedom—these were all the same to them in theory ; but also—whoever won—much the same in fact. There they were and there they stayed ; and with hard toil, there they gained their daily bread. One morning arrives a Cossack patrol. " Christ is risen ; the Allies are advancing ; Russia is saved ; you are free.

The Soviet is no more." And the peasants grunted, and duly elected their Council of Elders, and the Cossack patrol rode off, taking with it what it might require up to the limit of what it could carry. On an afternoon a few weeks later, or it may be a few days later, arrived a Bolshevik in a battered motor-car with half-a-dozen gunmen, also saying, " You are free ; your chains are broken ; Christ is a fraud ; religion is the opiate of democracy ; Brothers, Comrades, rejoice for the great days that have dawned." And the peasants grunted. And the Bolshevik said, " Away with this Council of Elders, exploiters of the poor, the base tools of reaction. Elect in their place your village Soviet, henceforward the sickle and hammer of your Proletarian rights ". So the peasants swept away the Council of Elders and re-elected with rude ceremony the village Soviet. But they chose exactly the same people who had hitherto formed the Council of Elders and the land also remained in their possession. And presently the Bolshevik and his gunmen got their motor-car to start and throbbed off into the distance, or perhaps into the Cossack patrol.

Moscow held the controls of Russia ; and when the cause of the Allies burnt itself out in victory, there were no other controls ; just chatter and slaughter on a background of Robinson Crusoe toil. The ancient capital lay at the centre of a web of railroads radiating to every point of the compass. And in the midst a spider! Vain hope to crush the spider by the advance of lines of encircling flies! Still I suppose that twenty or thirty thousand resolute, comprehending, well-armed Europeans could, without any serious difficulty or loss, have made their way very swiftly along any of the great railroads which converged on Moscow ; and have brought to the hard ordeal of battle any force that stood against them. But twenty or thirty thousand resolute men did not exist or could not be brought together. Denikin's forces foraged over enormous areas. They boasted a superficial political sway. They lived on the country and by doing so soon alienated the rural population which at first had welcomed them. Had he collected the necessary supplies at one spot in the south for a direct dash to Moscow, and had he seized the psychological moment just before the Siberian armies began to fade away, he would have had a good chance of success. Master of Moscow and its unequalled railway centre with a corps of trustworthy troops, his power and prestige might have been unshakable. But there never was a thrust ; no Napoleon eagle-swoop at the mysterious capital ; only the long thin lines wending on ever thinner, weaker and more weary. And then finally when the Bolsheviks in the centre of the circle were sufficiently concentrated by the mere fact of retirement, they in their turn advanced and found in front of them—nothing!—nothing but helpless populations and scores of thousands of compromised families and individuals.

The fitful and fluid operations of the Russian armies found a counterpart in the policy, or want of policy, of the Allies. Were they at war with Soviet Russia? Certainly not ; but they shot Soviet Russians at sight. They stood as invaders on Russian soil. They armed the enemies of the Soviet Government. They blockaded its ports, and sunk its battleships. They earnestly desired and schemed its downfall. But war—shocking! Interference—shame! It was, they repeated, a matter of indifference to them how Russians settled their own internal affairs. They were impartial—Bang! And then—at the same time—parley and try to trade.

THE REFUGEES

As Denikin's failure became pronounced, the fitful countenance which the Great Powers had given him was swiftly withdrawn. On February 3, 1920, it became my duty to instruct General Holman to put the facts plainly before the Russian leader. " I cannot hold out any expectation that the British Government will give any further aid beyond what has already been promised in the final packet. Neither will they use their influence to make an aggressive combination between the Poles, the Baltic States, Finland, etc., with Denikin against Soviet Russia. Their reason is that they do not possess the resources in men or money sufficient to carry any such enterprise to success, and they do not wish to encourage others without having the power to sustain them. . . . The British Government in general agreement with the French Government are disposed to offer to the Border States a measure of support in case they are attacked by the Soviet Government. . . . It is no good arguing whether this is a wise or a right policy : it is what I believe is going to happen. It is said the Border States are only fighting for their independence, while Denikin is fighting for the control of Russia. We cannot undertake to make further exertions in support of this last objective, although we sympathize with it. . . . The question which must now be faced is how to save as much as possible from the wreck."

I now pinned my hopes to finding some asylum, however temporary, for the mass of refugees who fled southward from Red vengeance. The Cossack territories of the Don and the Kuban, where the whole population was passionately anti-Bolshevik, might perhaps be constituted an independent or autonomous region. Failing this, there was the Crimea. Into this fertile peninsula the broken fragments of Denikin's armies and several hundred thousand civilian fugitives were soon crowded in every circumstance of misery and want. Their defence was maintained for a few more months after Denikin's supersession, by General Wrangel, a new figure of unusual energy and quality, who thus too late reached the first place in White Russian counsels. Some moral assistance—in the form of gun-fire—was given by the British fleet, officially engaged in rescue work, in preventing the Bolsheviks from invading the Crimea by sea. But in July the marsh defences broke down, the Crimea was overrun, and a hideous flight of refugees to Constantinople ensued. There were not enough ships for half of the panic-stricken multitudes. The savage enemy bore down exultingly their last despairing defenders. Smallpox and typhus epidemics made new alliances with sword and famine. Shiploads of destitute and infected persons—sometimes all dead or moribund—arrived continuously in the already overcrowded, impoverished and straitened Turkish capital. A veil has been drawn over the horrors of this final phase. The British troops and sailors, and some British and American philanthropic agencies in Constantinople gave almost all they possessed in local aid ; but the " Allied and Associated Powers " averted their gaze and stopped their ears. They did not wish to know too much, and like Napoleon at the Beresina could only reply " Voulez-vous ôter mon calme? " After all Death is merciful : it was certainly busy.

Such were the solutions which the victors in the Great War were able to afford to Russian affairs.

THE IRISH TRUCE
July 11th 1921

No act of British state policy in which I have been concerned aroused more violently conflicting emotions than the Irish Settlement. For a system of human government so vast and so variously composed as the British Empire to compact with open rebellion in the peculiar form in which it was developed in Ireland, was an event which might well have shaken to its foundations that authority upon which the peace and order of hundreds of millions of people of many races and communities were erected. Servants of the Crown in the faithful performance of their duty had been and were being cruelly murdered as a feature in a deliberately adopted method of warfare. It was only possible to say of those responsible for these acts that they were not actuated by selfish or sordid motives; that they were ready to lay down their own lives; and that in the main they were supported by the sentiment of their fellow-countrymen. To receive the leaders of such men at the Council Board, and to attempt to form through their agency the government of a civilized state, must be regarded as one of the most questionable and hazardous experiments upon which a great Empire in the plenitude of its power had ever embarked.

On the other hand stood the history of Ireland—an unending quarrel and mutual injuries done to each other by sister countries and close neighbours, generation after generation; and the earnest desire in Britain was to end this hateful feud. During the nineteenth century both England and Ireland had re-stated their cases in forms far superior to those of the dark times of the past. England had lavished remedial measures and conciliatory procedures upon Ireland ; Ireland in the main had rested herself upon constitutional action to support her claim. It would have been possible in 1886 to have reached a solution on a basis infinitely less perilous both to Ireland and to Great Britain than that to which we were ultimately drawn. Said Mr. Gladstone in the House of Commons before the fateful division on the Home Rule Bill, " Ireland stands at your bar expectant, hopeful, almost suppliant. Her words are words of truth and soberness. She asks a blessed oblivion of the past, and in that oblivion our interest is deeper even than hers. . . . Think, I beseech you —think well, think wisely ; think not for the moment but for the years that are to come, before you reject this Bill."

And, after all, we were the victors in the greatest struggle of all time. We did not claim more than our true share in those supreme events, but it was sufficient to make us easy in our own minds about a matter so comparatively small in a material sense as Ireland. No one, for instance, could say that the life of the Empire was in danger when every hostile force in the world, including armies of millions of soldiers, had passed out of existence, when the German fleet lay at the bottom of Scapa Flow, and when every armed opponent was prostrate. No one could say we were a cowardly or decadent race. There may be no logical relevance for such thoughts, but they contributed an important factor to the national decision. And what was the alternative? It was to plunge one small corner of the Empire into an iron repression, which could not be carried through without an admixture of murder and counter-murder, terror and counter-terror. Only national self-preservation could have excused such a policy, and no reasonable man could allege that self-preservation was involved.

However, the die was now cast. A truce had been proclaimed. The gunmen emerged from their hiding-places and strode the streets of Dublin as the leaders of a nation as old and as proud as our own. The troops and police and Black and Tans, but yesterday urged on to extirpate the murder gang, now stood relaxed and embarrassed while parleys on equal terms were in full swing. Impossible thereafter to resume the same kind of war! Impossible to refill or heat up again those cauldrons of hatred and contempt on which such quarrels are fed! Other courses remained at our disposal as a last resort. Ports and cities could be held ; Dublin could be held ; Ulster could be defended ; all communications between Sinn Fein Ireland and the outer world could be severed ; all trade between the two islands, that is to say the whole of Irish trade except from Ulster, could be stopped—at a price. But from the moment of the truce, the attempt to govern Southern Ireland upon the authority of the Imperial Parliament had come to an end.

THE IRISH SETTLEMENT

December 6th 1921

From the outset it became of the utmost importance to convince those who were now accepted as the Irish leaders, of the sincerity and good will of the Imperial Government. The issue was too grave for bargaining and haggling. We stated from the very beginning all that we were prepared to give, and that in no circumstances could we go any further. We also made it clear that if our offer were accepted, we would without hesitation carry it through without regard to any political misfortune which might in consequence fall upon the Government or upon its leading members. On this basis, therefore, and in this spirit the long and critical negotiations were conducted.

We found ourselves confronted in the early days not only with the unpractical and visionary fanaticism and romanticism of the extreme Irish secret societies, but also with those tides of distrust and hatred which had flowed between the two countries for so many centuries. An essential element in dynamite and every other high explosive is some intense acid. These terrible liquids slowly and elaborately prepared unite with perfectly innocent carbon compounds to give that pent-up, concentrated blasting power which shatters the structures and the lives of men. Hatred plays the same part in Governments as acids in chemistry. And here in Ireland were hatreds which in Mr. Kipling's phrase would " eat the live steel from the rifle butt ", hatreds such as, thank God, in Great Britain had not existed for a hundred years. All this we had to overcome.

Mr. Griffith was a writer who had studied deeply European history and the polity of States. He was a man of great firmness of character and of high integrity. He was that unusual figure—a silent Irishman ; he hardly ever said a word. But no word that ever issued from his lips in my presence did he ever unsay. Michael Collins had not enjoyed the same advantages in education as his elder colleague. But he had elemental qualities and mother wit which were in many ways remarkable. He stood far nearer to the terrible incidents of the conflict than his leader. His prestige and influence with the extreme parties in Ireland for that reason were far higher, his difficulties in his own heart and with his associates were far greater. The other delegates were overshadowed by the two leaders. Mr Duggan, however, was a sober-minded, resolute man. In the background Mr. Erskine Childers, though not a delegate, pressed extreme counsels.

In the end, after two months of futilities and rigmarole, scarred by outrages in Ireland in breach of the truce, unutterably wearied Ministers faced the Irish Delegates themselves in actual desperation and knowing well that death stood at their elbows. When we met on the afternoon of December 5, the Prime Minister stated bluntly that we could concede no more and debate no further. They must settle now ; they must sign the agreement for a Treaty in the form to which after all these weeks it had attained, or else quit ; and further, that both sides would be free to resume whatever warfare they could wage against each other. This was an ultimatum delivered, not through diplomatic channels, but face to face, and all present knew and understood that nothing else was possible. Stiff as our personal relations had been, there was by now a mutual respect between the principals and a very deep comprehension of each other's difficulties.

The Irishmen gulped down the ultimatum phlegmatically. Mr. Griffith said, speaking in his soft voice and with his modest manner, " I will give the answer of the Irish Delegates at nine tonight ; but, Mr. Prime Minister, I personally will sign this agreement and will recommend it to my countrymen ". " Do I understand, Mr. Griffith," said Mr. Lloyd George, " that though everyone else refuses you will nevertheless agree to sign? " " Yes, that is so, Mr. Prime Minister ", replied this quiet little man of great heart and of great purpose. Michael Collins rose looking as if he was going to shoot someone, preferably himself. In all my life I have never seen so much passion and suffering in restraint.

We then went off and drummed our heels and had some food and smoked, and discussed plans of campaign. No one expected that anyone but Mr. Griffith would agree, and what validity would his solitary signature possess? As for ourselves, we had already ruptured the loyalties of our friends and supporters.

The British representatives were in their places at nine, but it was not until long after midnight that the Irish Delegation appeared. As before, they were superficially calm and very quiet. There was a long pause, or there seemed to be. Then Mr. Griffith said, " Mr. Prime Minister, the Delegation is willing to sign the agreement, but there are a few points of drafting which perhaps it would be convenient if I mentioned at once " Thus, by the easiest of gestures, he carried the whole matter into the region of minor detail, and everyone concentrated upon these points with overstrained interest so as to drive the main issue into the background for ever.

Soon we were talking busily about technicalities and verbal corrections, and holding firmly to all these lest worse should befall. But underneath this protective chatter a profound change had taken place in the spirit and atmosphere. We had become allies and associates in a common cause—the cause of the Irish Treaty and of peace between two races and two islands. It was nearly three o'clock in the morning before we separated. But agreement was signed by all. As the Irishmen rose to leave, the British Ministers upon a strong impulse walked round and for the first time shook hands. . . . Many toils and vexations lay in the path of the Irish Settlement, and many disappointments and anxieties were in store for both sides. But this was the moment, not soon to be forgotten, when the waters were parted and the streams of destiny began to flow down new valleys towards new seas.

The event was fatal to the Prime Minister. Within a year he had been driven from power. Many other causes, some at least of which could have been avoided, contributed to his fall ; but the Irish Treaty and its circumstances were unforgivable by the most tenacious elements in the Conservative Party. Even among those who steadfastly supported it there were many who said, " It must needs be that offences come, but woe to that man by whom the offence cometh ". Yet in so far as Mr. Lloyd George can link his political misfortunes with this Irish story, he may be content. In falling through Irish difficulties he may fall with Essex and with Strafford, with Pitt and with Gladstone ; and with a line of sovereigns and statesmen great or small spread across the English history books of 700 years. But Lloyd George falls with this mighty difference, that whereas all these others, however great their efforts and sacrifices, left behind them only a problem, he has achieved—must we not hope it?—a solution.

LAWRENCE OF ARABIA
1888–1935

In principle the structure of the story [of Lawrence's *Seven Pillars of Wisdom*] is simple. The Turkish armies operating against Egypt depended upon the desert railway. This slender steel track ran through hundreds of miles of blistering desert. If it were permanently cut the Turkish armies must perish : the ruin of Turkey must follow, and with it the downfall of the mighty Teutonic power which hurled its hate from ten thousand cannons on the plains of Flanders. Here was the Achilles' heel, and it was upon this that this man in his twenties directed his audacious, desperate, romantic assaults. We read of them in numerous succession. Grim camel-rides through sun-scorched, blasted lands, where the extreme desolation of nature appals the traveller. With a motor-car or aeroplane we may now inspect these forbidding solitudes, their endless sands, the hot savage wind-whipped rocks, the mountain gorges of a red-hot noon. Through these with infinite privation men on camels with shattering toil carried dynamite to destroy railway bridges and win the war, and, as we then hoped, free the world.

Here we see Lawrence the soldier. Not only the soldier but the statesman ; rousing the fierce peoples of the desert, penetrating the mysteries of their thought, leading them to the selected points of action and as often as not firing the mine himself. Detailed accounts are given of ferocious battles with thousands of men and little quarter fought under his command on these lava landscapes of hell. There are no mass-effects. All is intense, individual, sentient— and yet cast in conditions which seemed to forbid human existence. Through all, one mind, one soul, one will-power. An epic, a prodigy, a tale of torment, and in the heart of it—a Man.

The impression of the personality of Lawrence remains living and vivid upon the minds of his friends, and the sense of his loss is in no way dimmed among his countrymen. All feel the poorer that he has gone from us. In these days dangers and difficulties gather upon Britain and her Empire, and we are also conscious of a lack of outstanding figures with which to overcome them. Here was a man in whom there existed not only an immense capacity for service, but that touch of genius which everyone recognizes and no one can define. Alike in his great period of adventure and command or in these later years of self-suppression and self-imposed eclipse, he always reigned over those with whom he came in contact. They felt themselves in the presence of an extraordinary being. They felt that his latent reserves of force and will-power were beyond measurement. If he roused himself to action, who should say what crisis he could not surmount or quell? If things were going very badly, how glad one would be to see him come round the corner.

Part of the secret of this stimulating ascendancy lay of course in his disdain for most of the prizes, the pleasures and comforts of life. The world naturally looks with some awe upon a man who appears unconcernedly indifferent to home, money, comfort, rank or even power and fame. The world feels, not without a certain apprehension, that here is someone outside its jurisdiction ; someone before whom its allurements may be spread in vain ; someone strangely enfranchised, untamed, untrammelled by convention, moving independently of the ordinary currents of human action ; a being readily capable of violent revolt or supreme sacrifice, a man, solitary, austere, to whom existence is no more than a duty, yet a duty to be faithfully discharged. He was indeed a dweller upon the mountain tops where the air is cold, crisp and rarefied, and where the view on clear days commands all the kingdoms of the world and the glory of them.

Lawrence was one of those beings whose pace of life was faster and more intense than the ordinary. Just as an aeroplane only flies by its speed and pressure against the air, so he flew best and easiest in the hurricane. He was not in complete harmony with the normal. The fury of the Great War raised the pitch of life to the Lawrence standard. The multitudes were swept forward till their pace was the same as his. In this heroic period he found himself in perfect relation to both men and events.

I have often wondered what would have happened to Lawrence if the Great War had continued for several more years. His fame was spreading fast and with the momentum of the fabulous throughout Asia. The earth trembled with the wrath of the warring nations. All the metals were molten. Everything was in motion. No one could say what was impossible. Lawrence might have realized Napoleon's young dream of conquering the East ; he might have arrived at Constantinople in 1919 or 1920 with many of the tribes and races of Asia Minor and Arabia at his back. But the storm wind ceased as suddenly as it had arisen. The skies became clear ; the bells of Armistice rang out. Mankind returned with indescribable relief to its long-interrupted, fondly-cherished ordinary life, and Lawrence was left once more moving alone on a different plane and at a different speed.

When his literary masterpiece was written, lost and written again ; when every illustration had been profoundly considered and every incident of typography and paragraphing settled with meticulous care ; when Lawrence on his bicycle had carried the precious volumes to the few—the very few—he deemed worthy to read them, happily he found another task which cheered and comforted his soul. He saw as clearly as anyone the vision of Air power and all that it would mean in traffic and war. He found in the life of an aircraftsman that balm of peace and equipoise which no great station or command could have bestowed upon him. He felt that in living the life of a private in the Royal Air Force he would dignify that honourable calling and help to attract all that is keenest in our youthful manhood to the sphere where it is most urgently needed. For this service and example, to which he devoted the last twelve years of his life, we owe him a separate debt. It was in itself a princely gift.

Lawrence had a full measure of the versatility of genius. He held one of those master keys which unlock the doors of many kinds of treasure-houses. He was a savant as well as a soldier. He was an archaeologist as well as a man of action. He was an accomplished scholar as well as an Arab partisan. He was a mechanic as well as a philosopher. His background of sombre experience and reflection only seemed to set forth more brightly the charm and gaiety of his companionship, and the generous majesty of his nature. Those who knew him best miss him most; but our country misses him most of all; and misses him most of all now. For this is a time when the great problems upon which his thought and work had been so long centred, problems of aerial defence, problems of our relations with the Arab peoples, fill an ever larger space in our affairs. For all his reiterated renunciations I always felt that he was a man who held himself ready for a new call. While Lawrence lived one always felt—I certainly felt it strongly —that some overpowering need would draw him from the modest path he chose to tread and set him once again in full action at the centre of memorable events.

It was not to be. The summons which reached him, and for which he was equally prepared, was of a different order. It came as he would have wished it, swift and sudden on the wings of Speed. He had reached the last leap in his gallant course through life.

All is over ! Fleet career,
  Dash of greyhound slipping thongs,
Flight of falcon, bound of deer,
Mad hoof-thunder in our rear,
  Cold air rushing up our lungs,
  Din of many tongues.

King George the Fifth wrote to Lawrence's brother, " His name will live in history ". That is true. It will live in English letters ; it will live in the traditions of the Royal Air Force ; it will live in the annals of war and in the legends of Arabia.

THE MUNICH AGREEMENT

October 1938

All is over. Silent, mournful, abandoned, broken, Czechoslovakia recedes into the darkness. She has suffered in every respect by her association with the Western democracies and with the League of Nations, of which she has always been an obedient servant. She has suffered in particular from her association with France, under whose guidance and policy she has been actuated for so long. The very measures taken by His Majesty's Government in the Anglo-French Agreement to give her the best chance possible, namely, the 50 per cent. clean cut in certain districts instead of a plebiscite, have turned to her detriment, because there is to be a plebiscite too in wide areas, and those other Powers who had claims have also come down upon the helpless victim. Those municipal elections upon whose voting the basis is taken for the

50 per cent. cut were held on issues which had nothing to do with joining Germany. When I saw Herr Henlein over here he assured me that was not the desire of his people. Positive statements were made that it was only a question of home rule, of having a position of their own in the Czechoslovakian State. No one has a right to say that the plebiscite which is to be taken in areas under Saar conditions, and the clean-cut of the 50 per cent. areas—that those two operations together amount in the slightest degree to a verdict of self-determination. It is a fraud and a farce to invoke that name.

In my holiday I thought it was a chance to study the reign of King Ethelred the Unready. The House will remember that that was a period of great misfortune, in which, from the strong position which we had gained under the descendants of King Alfred, we fell very swiftly into chaos. It was the period of Danegeld and of foreign pressure. I must say that the rugged words of the Anglo-Saxon Chronicle, written a thousand years ago, seem to me apposite, at least as apposite as those quotations from Shakespeare with which we have been regaled by the last speaker from the Opposition Bench. Here is what the Anglo-Saxon Chronicle said, and I think the words apply very much to our treatment of Germany and our relations with her. " All these calamities fell upon us because of evil counsel, because tribute was not offered to them at the right time nor yet were they resisted ; but when they had done the most evil, then was peace made with them." That is the wisdom of the past, for all wisdom is not new wisdom.

What I find unendurable is the sense of our country falling into the power, into the orbit and influence of Nazi Germany, and of our existence becoming dependent upon their good will or pleasure. It is to prevent that that I have tried my best to urge the maintenance of every bulwark of defence—first, the timely creation of an Air Force superior to anything within striking distance of our shores ; secondly, the gathering together of the collective strength of many nations ; and thirdly, the making of alliances and military conventions, all within the Covenant, in order to gather together forces at any rate to restrain the onward movement of this power. It has all been in vain. Every position has been successively undermined and abandoned on specious and plausible excuses.

I do not grudge our loyal, brave people, who were ready to do their duty no matter what the cost, who never flinched under the strain of last week—I do not grudge them the natural, spontaneous outburst of joy and relief when they learned that the hard ordeal would no longer be required of them at the moment ; but they should know the truth. They should know that there has been gross neglect and deficiency in our defences ; they should know that we have sustained a defeat without a war, the consequences of which will travel far with us along our road ; they should know that we have passed an awful milestone in our history, when the whole equilibrium of Europe has been deranged, and that the terrible words have for the time being been pronounced against the Western democracies : " Thou art weighed in the balance and found wanting." And do not suppose that this is the end. This is only the beginning of the reckoning. This is only the first sip, the first foretaste of a bitter cup which will be proffered to us year by year unless by a supreme recovery of moral health and martial vigour, we arise again and take our stand for freedom as in the olden time.

WAR THE SECOND

September 1939

In this solemn hour it is a consolation to recall and to dwell upon our repeated efforts for peace. All have been ill-starred, but all have been faithful and sincere. This is of the highest moral value—and not only moral value, but practical value—at the present time, because the wholehearted concurrence of scores of millions of men and women, whose co-operation is indispensable and whose comradeship and brotherhood are indispensable, is the only foundation upon which the trial and tribulation of modern war can be endured and surmounted. This moral conviction alone affords that ever-fresh resilience which renews the strength and energy of people in long, doubtful and dark days. Outside, the storms of war may blow and the lands may be lashed with the fury of its gales, but in our own hearts this Sunday morning there is peace. Our hands may be active, but our consciences are at rest.

We must not underrate the gravity of the task which lies before us or the temerity of the ordeal, to which we shall not be found unequal. We must expect many disappointments, and many unpleasant surprises, but we may be sure that the task which we have freely accepted is one not beyond the compass and the strength of the British Empire and the French Republic. The Prime Minister said it was a sad day, and that is indeed true, but at the present time there is another note which may be present, and that is a feeling of thankfulness that, if these great trials were to come upon our Island, there is a generation of Britons here now ready to prove itself not unworthy of the days of yore and not unworthy of those great men, the fathers of our land, who laid the foundations of our laws and shaped the greatness of our country.

This is not a question of fighting for Danzig or fighting for Poland. We are fighting to save the whole world from the pestilence of Nazi tyranny and in defence of all that is most sacred to man. This is no war of domination or imperial aggrandisement or material gain ; no war to shut any country out of its sunlight and means of progress. It is a war, viewed in its inherent quality, to establish, on impregnable rocks, the rights of the individual, and it is a war to establish and revive the stature of man. Perhaps it might seem a paradox that a war undertaken in the name of liberty and right should require, as a necessary part of its processes, the surrender for the time being of so many of the dearly valued liberties and rights. In these last few days the House of Commons has been voting dozens of Bills which hand over to the executive our most dearly valued traditional liberties. We are sure that these will be in hands which will not abuse them, which will use them for no class or party interests, which will cherish and guard them, and we look forward to the day, surely and confidently we look forward to the day, when our liberties and rights will be restored to us, and when we shall be able to share them with the peoples to whom such blessings are unknown.

BACK TO THE ADMIRALTY
October 1939

Here I am in the same post as I was twenty-five years ago. Rough times lie ahead ; but how different is the scene from that of October, 1914! Then the French front, with its British army fighting in the line, seemed to be about to break under the terrible impact of German Imperialism. Then Russia had been laid low at Tannenberg ; then the whole might of the Austro-Hungarian Empire was in battle against us ; then the brave, warlike Turks were about to join our enemies. Then we had to be ready night and day to fight a decisive sea battle with a formidable German fleet almost, in many respects, the equal of our own. We faced these adverse conditions then ; we have nothing worse to face to-night. . . .

I do not underrate what lies before us, but I must say this : I cannot doubt we have the strength to carry a good cause forward, and to break down the barriers which stand between the wage-earning masses of every land and that freer and more abundant daily life which science is ready to afford. That is my conviction, and I look back upon the history of the past to find many sources of encouragement. Of all the wars that men have fought in their hard pilgrimage, none was more noble than the great Civil War in America nearly eighty years ago. Both sides fought with high conviction, and the war was long and hard. All the heroism of the South could not redeem their cause from the stain of slavery, just as all the courage and skill which the Germans always show in war will not free them from the reproach of Nazism, with its intolerance and its brutality. We may take good heart from what happened in America in those famous days of the nineteenth century. We may be sure that the world will roll forward into broader destinies. We may remember the words of old John Bright after the American Civil War was over, when he said to an audience of English working folk : " At last after the smoke of the battlefield had cleared away, the horrid shape which had cast its shadow over the whole continent had vanished and was gone for ever."

PRIME MINISTER
May 10th 1940

The morning of the tenth of May dawned, and with it came tremendous news. Boxes with telegrams poured in from the Admiralty, the War Office and the Foreign Office. The Germans had struck their long-awaited blow. Holland and Belgium were both invaded. Their frontiers had been crossed at numerous points. The whole movement of the German Army upon the invasion of the Low Countries and of France had begun.

At about 10 o'clock Sir Kingsley Wood came to see me, having just been with the Prime Minister. He told me that Mr. Chamberlain was inclined to feel that the great battle which had broken upon us made it necessary for him to remain at his post. Kingsley Wood had told him that, on the contrary, the new crisis made it all the more necessary to have a National Government, which alone could confront it, and he added that Mr. Chamberlain had accepted this view. At 11 o'clock I was again summoned to Downing Street by the Prime Minister. There once more I found Lord Halifax. We took our seats at the table opposite Mr. Chamberlain. He told us that he was satisfied that it was beyond his power to form a National Government. The response he had received from the Labour leaders left him in no doubt of this. The question therefore was whom he should advise the King to send for after his own resignation had been accepted. His demeanour was cool, unruffled, and seemingly quite detached from the personal aspects of the affair. He looked at us both across the table.

I have had many important interviews in my public life,

and this was certainly the most important. Usually I talk a great deal, but on this occasion I was silent. Mr. Chamberlain evidently had in his mind the stormy scene in the House of Commons two nights before, when I had seemed to be in such heated controversy with the Labour Party. Although this had been in his support and defence, he nevertheless felt that it might be an obstacle to my obtaining their adherence at this juncture. I do not recall the actual words he used, but this was the implication. His biographer, Mr. Feiling, states definitely that he preferred Lord Halifax. As I remained silent, a very long pause ensued. It certainly seemed longer than the two minutes which one observes in the commemorations of Armistice Day. Then at length Halifax spoke. He said he felt that his position as a Peer, out of the House of Commons, would make it very difficult for him to discharge the duties of Prime Minister in a war like this. He would be held responsible for everything, but would not have the power to guide the Assembly upon whose confidence the life of every Government depended. He spoke for some minutes in this sense, and by the time he had finished it was clear that the duty would fall upon me—had in fact fallen upon me. Then, for the first time, I spoke. I said I would have no communication with either of the Opposition Parties until I had the King's commission to form a Government. On this the momentous conversation came to an end, and we reverted to our ordinary easy and familiar manners of men who had worked for years together and whose lives in and out of office had been spent in all the friendliness of British politics. I then went back to the Admiralty where, as may well be imagined, much awaited me.

The Dutch Ministers were in my room. Haggard and

worn, with horror in their eyes, they had just flown over from Amsterdam. Their country had been attacked without the slightest pretext or warning. The avalanche of fire and steel had rolled across the frontiers, and when resistance broke out and the Dutch frontier guards fired, an overwhelming onslaught was made from the air. The whole country was in a state of wild confusion ; the long-prepared defence scheme had been put into operation ; the dykes were opened ; the waters spread far and wide. But the Germans had already crossed the outer lines, and were now streaming across the causeway which enclosed the Zuyder Zee. Could we do anything to prevent this? Luckily we had a flotilla not far away, and this was immediately ordered to sweep the causeway with fire, and take the heaviest toll possible of the swarming invaders. The Queen was still in Holland, but it did not seem she could remain there long.

As a consequence of these discussions, a large number of orders were dispatched by the Admiralty to all our ships in the neighbourhood, and close relations were established with the Royal Dutch Navy. Even with the recent over-running of Norway and Denmark in their minds, the Dutch Ministers seemed unable to understand how the great German nation, which, up to the night before, had professed nothing but friendship, should suddenly have made this frightful and brutal onslaught. Upon these proceedings and other affairs an hour or two passed. A spate of telegrams pressed in from all the frontiers affected by the forward heave of the German armies. It seemed that the old Schlieffen plan, brought up to date with its Dutch extension, was already in full operation. In 1914 the swinging right arm of the German invasion had swept through Belgium but had stopped short of Holland. It was well known then that had war been delayed for three or four years, the extra army group would have been ready, and the railway terminals and communications adapted, for a movement through Holland. Now the famous movement had been launched with all these facilities and with every circumstance of surprise and treachery. But other developments lay ahead. The decisive stroke of the enemy was not to be a turning movement on the flank, but a break through the main front. This none of us or the French, who were in responsible command, foresaw. Earlier in the year I had, in a published interview, warned these neutral countries of the fate which was impending upon them and which was evident from the troop dispositions and road and rail development, as well as from the captured German plans. My words had been resented.

In the splintering crash of this vast battle the quiet conversations we had had in Downing Street faded or fell back in one's mind. However, I remember being told that Mr. Chamberlain had gone, or was going, to see the King, and this was naturally to be expected. Presently a message arrived summoning me to the Palace at 6 o'clock. It only takes two minutes to drive there from the Admiralty along the Mall. Although I suppose the evening newspapers must have been full of the terrific news from the Continent, nothing had been mentioned about the Cabinet crisis. The public had not had time to take in what was happening either abroad or at home, and there was no crowd about the Palace gates.

I was taken immediately to the King. His Majesty received me most graciously and bade me sit down. He looked at me searchingly and quizzically for some moments, and then said : " I suppose you don't know why I have sent for you?" Adopting his mood, I replied : " Sir, I simply couldn't imagine why." He laughed and said : " I want to ask you to form a Government." I said I would certainly do so.

The King had made no stipulation about the Government being National in character, and I felt that my commission was in no formal way dependent upon this point. But in view of what had happened, and the conditions which had led to Mr. Chamberlain's resignation, a Government of National character was obviously inherent in the situation. If I found it impossible to come to terms with the Opposition Parties, I should not have been constitutionally debarred from trying to form the strongest Government possible of all who would stand by the country in the hour of peril, provided that such a Government could command a majority in the House of Commons. I told the King that I would immediately send for the leaders of the Labour and Liberal Parties, that I proposed to form a War Cabinet of five or six Ministers, and that I hoped to let him have at least five names before midnight. On this I took my leave and returned to the Admiralty.

Between seven and eight, at my request, Mr. Attlee called upon me. He brought with him Mr. Greenwood. I told him of the authority I had to form a Government and asked if the Labour Party would join. He said they would. I proposed that they should take rather more than a third of the places, having two seats in the War Cabinet of five, or it might be six, and I asked Mr. Attlee to let me have a list of men so that we could discuss particular offices. I mentioned Mr. Bevin, Mr. Alexander, Mr. Morrison and Mr. Dalton as men whose services in high office were immediately required. I had, of course, known both Attlee and Greenwood for a long time in the House of Commons. During the eleven years before the outbreak of war, I had in my more or less independent position come far more often into collision with the Conservative and National Governments than with the Labour and Liberal Oppositions. We had a pleasant talk for a little while, and they went off to report by telephone to their friends and followers at Bournemouth, with whom of course they had been in the closest contact during the previous forty-eight hours.

I invited Mr. Chamberlain to lead the House of Commons as Lord President of the Council, and he replied by telephone that he accepted and had arranged to broadcast at 9 that night, stating that he had resigned, and urging everyone to support and aid his successor. This he did in magnanimous terms. I asked Lord Halifax to join the War Cabinet while remaining Foreign Secretary. At about 10, I sent the King a list of the five names, as I had promised. I had already made up my mind who they should be. Mr. Eden should go to the War Office ; Mr. Alexander should come to the Admiralty ; and Sir Archibald Sinclair, Leader of the Liberal Party, should take the Air Ministry. At the same time I assumed the office of Minister of Defence, without, however, attempting to define its scope and powers.

Thus, then, on the night of the tenth of May, at the outset of this mighty battle, I acquired the chief power in the State, which henceforth I wielded in ever-growing measure for five years and three months of world war, at the end of which time, all our enemies having surrendered unconditionally or being about to do so, I was immediately dismissed by the British electorate from all further conduct of their affairs.

During these last crowded days of the political crisis my pulse had not quickened at any moment. I took it all as it came. But I cannot conceal from the reader of this truthful account that as I went to bed at about 3 a.m., I was conscious of a profound sense of relief. At last I had the authority to give directions over the whole scene. I felt as if I were walking with destiny, and that all my past life had been but a preparation for this hour and for this trial. Eleven years in the political wilderness had freed me from ordinary Party antagonisms. My warnings over the last six years had been so numerous, so detailed, and were now so terribly vindicated, that no one could gainsay me. I could not be reproached either for making the war or with want of preparation for it. I thought I knew a good deal about it all, and I was sure I should not fail. Therefore, although impatient for the morning, I slept soundly and had no need for cheering dreams. Facts are better than dreams.

BLOOD, TOIL, TEARS, AND SWEAT
May 13th 1940

On Friday evening last I received His Majesty's Commission to form a new Administration. It was the evident wish and will of Parliament and the nation that this should be conceived on the broadest possible basis and that it should include all parties, both those who supported the late Government and also the parties of the Opposition. I have completed the most important part of this task. A War Cabinet has been formed of five Members, representing, with the Opposition Liberals, the unity of the nation. The three party Leaders have agreed to serve, either in the War Cabinet or in high executive office. The three Fighting Services have been filled. It was necessary that this should be done in one single day, on account of the extreme urgency and rigour of events. A number of other key positions were filled yesterday, and I am submitting a further list to His Majesty to-night. I hope to complete the appointment of the principal Ministers during tomorrow. The appointment of the other Ministers usually takes a little longer, but I trust that, when Parliament meets again, this part of my task will be completed, and that the Administration will be complete in all respects.

I considered it in the public interest to suggest that the House should be summoned to meet today. Mr. Speaker agreed, and took the necessary steps, in accordance with the powers conferred upon him by the Resolution of the House. At the end of the proceedings to-day, the Adjournment of the House will be proposed until Tuesday, 21st May, with, of course, provision for earlier meeting if need be. The business to be considered during that week will be notified to Members at the earliest opportunity. I now invite the House, by the Resolution which stands in my name, to record its approval of the steps taken and to declare its confidence in the new Government.

To form an Administration of this scale and complexity is a serious undertaking in itself, but it must be remembered that we are in the preliminary stage of one of the greatest battles in history, that we are in action at many points in Norway and in Holland, that we have to be prepared in the Mediterranean, that the air battle is continuous and that many preparations have to be made here at home. In this crisis I hope I may be pardoned if I do not address the House at any length to-day. I hope that any of my friends and colleagues, or former colleagues, who are affected by the political reconstruction, will make all allowance for any lack of ceremony with which it has been necessary to act. I would say to the House, as I said to those who have joined this Government : " I have nothing to offer but blood, toil, tears and sweat."

We have before us an ordeal of the most grievous kind. We have before us many, many long months of struggle and of suffering. You ask, what is our policy? I will say : It is to wage war, by sea, land and air, with all our might and with all the strength that God can give us : to wage war against a monstrous tyranny, never surpassed in the dark, lamentable catalogue of human crime. That is our policy. You ask, What is our aim? I can answer in one word : Victory—victory at all costs, victory in spite of all terror, victory, however long and hard the road may be; for without victory, there is no survival. Let that be realised ; no survival for the British Empire ; no survival for all that the British Empire has stood for, no survival for the urge and impulse of the ages that mankind will move forward towards its goal. But I take up my task with buoyancy and hope. I feel sure that our cause will not be suffered to fail among men. At this time I feel entitled to claim the aid of all, and I say, " Come, then, let us go forward together with our united strength."

"BE YE MEN OF VALOUR"
May 19th 1940

We must expect that as soon as stability is reached on the Western Front, the bulk of that hideous apparatus of aggression which gashed Holland into ruin and slavery in a few days, will be turned upon us. I am sure I speak for all when I say we are ready to face it; to endure it ; and to retaliate against it—to any extent that the unwritten laws of war permit. There will be many men, and many women, in this island who when the ordeal comes upon them, as come it will, will feel comfort, and even a pride, that they are sharing the perils of our lads at the Front—soldiers, sailors and airmen, God bless them—and are drawing away from them a part at least of the onslaught they have to bear. Is not this the appointed time for all to make the utmost exertions in their power? If the battle is to be won, we must provide our men with ever-increasing quantities of the weapons and ammunition they need. We must have, and have quickly, more aeroplanes, more tanks, more shells, more guns. There is imperious need for these vital munitions. They increase our strength against the powerfully armed enemy. They replace the wastage of the obstinate struggle ; and the knowledge that wastage will speedily be replaced enables us to draw more readily upon our reserves and throw them in now that everything counts so much.

Our task is not only to win the battle—but to win the War. After this battle in France abates its force, there will come the battle for our island—for all that Britain is, and all that Britain means. That will be the struggle. In that supreme emergency we shall not hesitate to take every step, even the most drastic, to call forth from our people the last ounce and the last inch of effort of which they are capable. The interests of property, the hours of labour, are nothing compared with the struggle for life and honour, for right and freedom, to which we have vowed ourselves.

I have received from the Chiefs of the French Republic, and in particular from its indomitable Prime Minister, M. Reynaud, the most sacred pledges that whatever happens they will fight to the end, be it bitter or be it glorious. Nay, if we fight to the end, it can only be glorious.

Having received His Majesty's commission, I have formed an administration of men and women of every party and of almost every point of view. We have differed and quarrelled in the past; but now one bond unites us all—to wage war until victory is won, and never to surrender ourselves to servitude and shame, whatever the cost and the agony may be. This is one of the most awe-striking periods in the long history of France and Britain. It is also beyond doubt the most sublime. Side by side, unaided except by their kith and kin in the great Dominions and by the wide Empires which rest beneath their shield—side by side, the British and French peoples have advanced to rescue not only Europe but mankind from the foulest and most soul-destroying tyranny which has ever darkened and stained the pages of history. Behind them— behind us—behind the armies and fleets of Britain and France—gather a group of shattered States and bludgeoned races: the Czechs, the Poles, the Norwegians, the Danes, the Dutch, the Belgians—upon all of whom the long night of barbarism will descend, unbroken even by a star of hope, unless we conquer, as conquer we must ; as conquer we shall.

Today is Trinity Sunday. Centuries ago words were written to be a call and a spur to the faithful servants of Truth and Justice : " Arm yourselves, and be ye men of valour, and be in readiness for the conflict ; for it is better for us to perish in battle than to look upon the outrage of our nation and our altar. As the Will of God is in Heaven, even so let it be ".

CAPITULATION OF BELGIUM
May 28th 1940

The situation of the British and French Armies now engaged in a most severe battle and beset on three sides and from the air, is evidently extremely grave. The surrender of the Belgian Army in this manner adds appreciably to their grievous peril. But the troops are in good heart, and are fighting with the utmost discipline and tenacity, and I shall, of course, abstain from giving any particulars of what, with the powerful assistance of the Royal Navy and the Royal Air Force, they are doing or hope to do. I expect to make a statement to the House on the general position when the result of the intense struggle now going on can be known and measured. This will not, perhaps, be until the beginning of next week.

Meanwhile, the House should prepare itself for hard and heavy tidings. I have only to add that nothing which may happen in this battle can in any way relieve us of our duty to defend the world cause to which we have vowed

ourselves ; nor should it destroy our confidence in our
power to make our way, as on former occasions in our
history, through disaster and through grief to the ultimate
defeat of our enemies.

DUNKIRK

June 4th 1940

The German eruption swept like a sharp scythe around
the right and rear of the Armies of the north. Eight
or nine armoured divisions, each of about four hundred
armoured vehicles of different kinds, but carefully assorted
to be complementary and divisible into small self-contained
units, cut off all communications between us and the main
French Armies. It severed our own communications for
food and ammunition, which ran first to Amiens and afterwards through Abbeville, and it shore its way up the coast
to Boulogne and Calais, and almost to Dunkirk. Behind
this armoured and mechanised onslaught came a number
of German divisions in lorries, and behind them again
there plodded comparatively slowly the dull brute mass of
the ordinary German Army and German people, always
so ready to be led to the trampling down in other lands of
liberties and comforts which they have never known in
their own.

I have said this armoured scythe-stroke almost reached
Dunkirk—almost but not quite. Boulogne and Calais
were the scenes of desperate fighting. The Guards defended Boulogne for a while and were then withdrawn by
orders from this country. The Rifle Brigade, the 60th
Rifles, and the Queen Victoria's Rifles, with a battalion of

British tanks and 1,000 Frenchmen, in all about four thousand strong, defended Calais to the last. The British Brigadier was given an hour to surrender. He spurned the offer, and four days of intense street fighting passed before silence reigned over Calais, which marked the end of a memorable resistance. Only 30 unwounded survivors were brought off by the Navy and we do not know the fate of their comrades. Their sacrifice, however, was not in vain. At least two armoured divisions, which otherwise would have been turned against the British Expeditionary Force, had to be sent to overcome them. They have added another page to the glories of the light divisions, and the time gained enabled the Gravelines waterlines to be flooded and to be held by the French troops.

Thus it was that the port of Dunkirk was kept open. When it was found impossible for the Armies of the north to reopen their communications to Amiens with the main French Armies, only one choice remained. It seemed, indeed, forlorn. The Belgian, British and French Armies were almost surrounded. Their sole line of retreat was to a single port and to its neighbouring beaches. They were pressed on every side by heavy attacks and far outnumbered in the air.

The enemy attacked on all sides with great strength and fierceness, and their main power, the power of their far more numerous air force, was thrown into the battle or else concentrated upon Dunkirk and the beaches. Pressing in upon the narrow exit, both from the east and from the west, the enemy began to fire with cannon upon the beaches by which alone the shipping could approach or depart. They sowed magnetic mines in the channels and seas ; they sent repeated waves of hostile aircraft, sometimes more than a hundred strong in one formation, to cast their bombs upon the single pier that remained, and upon the sand dunes upon which the troops had their eyes for shelter. Their U-boats, one of which was sunk, and their motor launches took their toll of the vast traffic which now began. For four or five days an intense struggle reigned. All their armoured divisions—or what was left of them—together with great masses of infantry and artillery, hurled themselves in vain upon the ever-narrowing, ever-contracting appendix within which the British and French Armies fought.

Meanwhile, the Royal Navy, with the willing help of countless merchant seamen, strained every nerve to embark the British and Allied troops ; 220 light warships and 650 other vessels were engaged. They had to operate upon the difficult coast, often in adverse weather, under an almost ceaseless hail of bombs and an increasing concentration of artillery fire. Nor were the seas, as I have said, themselves free from mines and torpedoes. It was in conditions such as these that our men carried on, with little or no rest, for days and nights on end, making trip after trip across the dangerous waters, bringing with them always men whom they had rescued. The numbers they have brought back are the measure of their devotion and their courage. The hospital ships, which brought off many thousands of British and French wounded, being so plainly marked were a special target for Nazi bombs ; but the men and women on board them never faltered in their duty.

Meanwhile, the Royal Air Force, which had already been intervening in the battle, so far as its range would allow, from home bases, now used part of its main metropolitan fighter strength, and struck at the German bombers, and at the fighters which in large numbers protected them.

This struggle was protracted and fierce. Suddenly the scene has cleared, the crash and thunder has for the moment—but only for the moment—died away. A miracle of deliverance, achieved by valour, by perseverance, by perfect discipline, by faultless service, by resource, by skill, by unconquerable fidelity, is manifest to us all. The enemy was hurled back by the retreating British and French troops. He was so roughly handled that he did not hurry their departure seriously. The Royal Air Force engaged the main strength of the German Air Force, and inflicted upon them losses of at least four to one; and the Navy, using nearly 1,000 ships of all kinds, carried over 335,000 men, French and British, out of the jaws of death and shame, to their native land and to the tasks which lie immediately ahead. We must be very careful not to assign to this deliverance the attributes of a victory. Wars are not won by evacuations. But there was a victory inside this deliverance, which should be noted. It was gained by the Air Force. Many of our soldiers coming back have not seen the Air Force at work; they saw only the bombers which escaped its protective attack. They underrate its achievements. I have heard much talk of this; that is why I go out of my way to say this. I will tell you about it.

This was a great trial of strength between the British and German Air Forces. Can you conceive a greater objective for the Germans in the air than to make evacuation from these beaches impossible, and to sink all these ships which were displayed, almost to the extent of thousands? Could there have been an objective of greater military importance and significance for the whole purpose of the war than this? They tried hard and they were beaten back; they were frustrated in their task. We got the Army away ; and they have paid fourfold for any losses which they have inflicted. Very large formations of German aeroplanes—and we know that they are a very brave race—have turned on several occasions from the attack of one-quarter of their number of the Royal Air Force, and have dispersed in different directions. Twelve aeroplanes have been hunted by two. One aeroplane was driven into the water and cast away by the mere charge of a British aeroplane which had no more ammunition. All of our types—the Hurricane, the Spitfire and the new Defiant—and all our pilots have been vindicated as superior to what they have at present to face.

When we consider how much greater would be our advantage in defending the air above this island against an overseas attack, I must say that I find in these facts a sure basis upon which practical and reassuring thoughts may rest. I will pay my tribute to these young airmen. The great French Army was very largely, for the time being, cast back and disturbed by the onrush of a few thousand of armoured vehicles. May it not also be that the cause of civilisation itself will be defended by the skill and devotion of a few thousand airmen. There never has been, I suppose, in all the world, in all the history of war, such an opportunity for youth. The Knights of the Round Table, the Crusaders, all fall back into the past : not only distant but prosaic ; these young men, going forth every morn to guard their native land and all that we stand for, holding in their hands these instruments of colossal and shattering power, of whom it may be said that

> " Every morning brought a noble chance
> And every chance brought out a noble knight,"

deserve our gratitude, as do all of the brave men who, in so many ways and on so many occasions, are ready, and continue ready, to give life and all for their native land.

THEIR FINEST HOUR

June 18th 1941

During the great battle in France, we gave very powerful and continuous aid to the French Army, both by fighters and bombers ; but in spite of every kind of pressure we would never allow the entire metropolitan fighter strength of the Air Force to be consumed. The decision was painful, but it was also right, because the fortunes of the battle in France could not have been decisively affected even if we had thrown in our entire fighter force. That battle was lost by the unfortunate strategical opening, by the extraordinary and unforeseen power of the armoured columns and by the great preponderance of the German Army in numbers. Our fighter Air Force might easily have been exhausted as a mere accident in that great struggle, and then we should have found ourselves at the present time in a very serious plight. But as it is, I am happy to inform the House that our fighter strength is stronger at the present time relatively to the Germans, who have suffered terrible losses, than it has ever been ; and consequently we believe ourselves possessed of the capacity to continue the war in the air under better conditions than we have ever experienced before. I look forward confidently to the exploits of our fighter pilots—these splendid men, this brilliant youth—who will have the glory of saving their native land, their island home, and all they love, from the most deadly of all attacks.

There remains, of course, the danger of bombing attacks, which will certainly be made very soon upon us by the bomber forces of the enemy. It is true that the German bomber force is superior in numbers to ours ; but we have a very large bomber force also, which we shall use to strike at military targets in Germany without intermission. I do not at all underrate the severity of the ordeal which lies before us ; but I believe our countrymen will show themselves capable of standing up to it, like the brave men of Barcelona, and will be able to stand up to it, and carry on in spite of it, at least as well as any other people in the world. Much will depend on this ; every man and every woman will have the chance to show the finest qualities of their race, and render the highest service to their cause, For all of us, at this time, whatever our sphere, our station, our occupation or our duties, it will be a help to remember the famous lines :

> " He nothing common did or mean
> Upon that memorable scene."

I have thought it right upon this occasion to give the House and the country some indication of the solid, practical grounds upon which we base our inflexible resolve to continue the war. There are a good many people who say, " Never mind. Win or lose, sink or swim, better die than submit to tyranny—and such a tyranny ". And I do not disassociate myself from them. But I can assure them that our professional advisers of the three Services unitedly advise that we should carry on the war, and that there are good and reasonable hopes of final victory. We have fully informed and consulted all the self-governing Dominions, these great communities far beyond the oceans who have been built up on our laws and on our civilisation, and who are absolutely free to choose their course, but are absolutely devoted to the ancient Motherland, and who feel themselves inspired by the same emotions which lead me to stake our all upon duty and honour. We have fully consulted them, and I have received from their Prime Ministers, Mr. Mackenzie King of Canada, Mr. Menzies of Australia, Mr. Fraser of New Zealand, and General Smuts of South Africa—that wonderful man, with his immense profound mind, and his eye watching from a distance the whole panorama of European affairs—I have received from all those eminent men, who all have Governments behind them elected on wide franchises, who are all there because they represent the will of their people, messages couched in the most moving terms in which they endorse our decision to fight on, and declare themselves ready to share our fortunes and to persevere to the end. That is what we are going to do.

During the first four years of the last war the Allies experienced nothing but disaster and disappointment. That was our constant fear: one blow after another, terrible losses, frightful dangers. Everything miscarried. And yet at the end of those four years the morale of the Allies was higher than that of the Germans, who had moved from one aggressive triumph to another, and who stood everywhere triumphant invaders of the lands into which they had broken. During that war we repeatedly asked ourselves the question: How are we going to win? and no one was able ever to answer it with much precision, until at the end, quite suddenly, quite unexpectedly, our terrible foe collapsed before us, and we were so glutted with victory that in our folly we threw it away.

We do not yet know what will happen in France or whether the French resistance will be prolonged, both in France and in the French Empire overseas. The French Government will be throwing away great opportunities and casting adrift their future if they do not continue the war in accordance with their Treaty obligations, from which we have not felt able to release them. The House will have read the historic declaration in which, at the desire of so many Frenchmen—and of our own hearts—, we have proclaimed our willingness at the darkest hour in French history to conclude a union of common citizenship in this struggle. However matters may go in France or with the French Government, or other French Governments, we in this island and in the British Empire will never lose our sense of comradeship with the French people. If we are now called upon to endure what they have been suffering, we shall emulate their courage, and if final victory rewards our toils they shall share the gains, aye, and freedom shall be restored to all. We abate nothing of our just demands; not one jot or tittle do we recede. Czechs, Poles, Norwegians, Dutch, Belgians have joined their causes to our own. All these shall be restored.

What General Weygand called the Battle of France is over. I expect that the Battle of Britain is about to begin. Upon this battle depends the survival of Christian civilisation. Upon it depends our own British life, and the long continuity of our institutions and our Empire. The whole fury and might of the enemy must very soon be turned on us. Hitler knows that he will have to break us in this island or lose the war. If we can stand up to him, all Europe may be free and the life of the world may move forward into broad, sunlit uplands. But if we fail, then the whole world, including the United States, including all that we

Government at Bordeaux. We shall certainly aid, to the best of our ability and resources, any movement or any action by Frenchmen outside the power of the enemy, to work for the defeat of Nazi German barbarism and for the freedom and restoration of France. What our relations will be with the Bordeaux Government I cannot tell. They have delivered themselves over to the enemy, and lie wholly in his power. He may do much by blandishments or by severities, by propaganda, and by the choosing of pro-German Ministers to make our relations difficult. We do not know whether we shall be allowed to have any British representative in the restricted region called " unoccupied France," because that is entirely surrounded by and under the control of the enemy ; but relying upon the true genius of the French people, and their judgment upon what has happened, when they are allowed to know the facts, we shall endeavour to keep such contacts as are possible through the bars of their prison. Meanwhile we must look to our own salvation and effectual defence, upon which not only British but French, European, and world-wide fortunes depend.

TRAGEDY OF THE FRENCH FLEET

July 4th 1940

Yesterday morning, a carefully chosen British officer, Captain Holland, late Naval Attaché in Paris, was sent on in a destroyer and waited upon the French Admiral Gensoul. After being refused an interview, he presented the following document, which I will read to the House.

The first two paragraphs of the document deal with the general question of the Armistice, which I have already explained in my own words. The fourth paragraph begins as follows : This is the operative paragraph :

" It is impossible for us, your comrades up to now, to allow your fine ships to fall into the power of the German or Italian enemy. We are determined to fight on to the end, and if we win, as we think we shall, we shall never forget that France was our Ally, that our interests are the same as hers and that our common enemy is Germany. Should we conquer, we solemnly declare that we shall restore the greatness and territory of France. For this purpose, we must make sure that the best ships of the French Navy are not used against us by the common foe. In these circumstances, His Majesty's Government have instructed me [that is, the British Admiral] to demand that the French Fleet now at Mers-el-Kebir and Oran shall act in accordance with one of the following alternatives :

(*a*) Sail with us and continue to fight for victory against the Germans and Italians.

(*b*) Sail with reduced crews under our control to a British port. The reduced crews will be repatriated at the earliest moment.

If either of these courses is adopted by you, we will restore your ships to France at the conclusion of the war or pay full compensation if they are damaged meanwhile.

(*c*) Alternatively, if you feel bound to stipulate that your ships should not be used against the Germans or Italians unless these break the Armistice, then sail them with us with reduced crews, to some French port in the West Indies, Martinique, for instance, where they can be demilitarised to our satisfaction or be perhaps entrusted to the United States and remain safe until the end of the war, the crews being repatriated.

If you refuse these fair offers, I must, with profound regret, require you to sink your ships within six hours.

Finally, failing the above, I have the orders of his Majesty's Government to use whatever force may be necessary to prevent your ships from falling into German or Italian hands."

We had hoped that one or other of the alternatives which we presented would have been accepted, without the necessity of using the terrible force of a British battle squadron. Such a squadron arrived before Oran two hours after Captain Holland and his destroyer. This battle squadron was commanded by Vice-Admiral Somerville, an officer who distinguished himself lately in the bringing-off of over 100,000 Frenchmen during the evacuation from Dunkirk. Admiral Somerville was further provided, besides his battleships, with a cruiser force and strong flotillas. All day the parleys continued, and we hoped until the afternoon that our terms would be accepted without bloodshed. However, no doubt in obedience to the orders dictated by the Germans from Wiesbaden, where the Franco-German Armistice Commission is in session, Admiral Gensoul refused to comply and announced his intention of fighting. Admiral Somerville was, therefore, ordered to complete his mission before darkness fell, and at 5.53 p.m. he opened fire upon this powerful French Fleet, which was also protected by its shore batteries. At 6 p.m. he reported that he was heavily engaged. The action lasted for some ten minutes and was followed by heavy attacks from our naval aircraft, carried in the *Ark Royal*. At 7.20 p.m. Admiral Somerville forwarded a further report, which stated that a battle cruiser of the

Strasbourg class was damaged and ashore; that a battle-ship of the *Bretagne* class had been sunk, that another of the same class had been heavily damaged, and that two French destroyers and a seaplane carrier, *Commandant Teste*, were also sunk or burned.

While this melancholy action was being fought either the battle cruiser *Strasbourg* or the *Dunkerque*, one or the other, managed to slip out of harbour in a gallant effort to reach Toulon or a North African port and place herself under German control, in accordance with the Armistice terms of the Bordeaux Government—though all this her crew and captain may not have realised. She was pursued by aircraft of the Fleet Air Arm and hit by at least one torpedo. She may have been joined by other French vessels from Algiers, which were well placed to do so and to reach Toulon before we would overtake them. She will, at any rate, be out of action for many months to come.

I need hardly say that the French ships were fought, albeit in this unnatural cause, with the characteristic courage of the French Navy, and every allowance must be made for Admiral Gensoul and his officers who felt them-selves obliged to obey the orders they received from their Government and could not look behind that Government to see the German dictation. I fear the loss of life among the French and in the harbour must have been very heavy, as we were compelled to use a severe measure of force and several immense explosions were heard. None of the British ships taking part in the action was in any way affected in gun-power or mobility by the heavy fire directed upon them.

WAR SITUATION

August 20th 1940

Hitler is now sprawled over Europe. Our offensive springs are being slowly compressed, and we must resolutely and methodically prepare ourselves for the campaigns of 1941 and 1942. Two or three years are not a long time, even in our short precarious lives. They are nothing in the history of the nation, and when we are doing the finest thing in the world, and have the honour to be the sole champion of the liberties of all Europe, we must not grudge these years or weary as we toil and struggle through them. It does not follow that our energies in future years will be exclusively confined to defending ourselves and our possessions. Many opportunities may lie open to amphibious power, and we must be ready to take advantage of them. One of the ways to bring this war to a speedy end is to convince the enemy, not by words, but by deeds, that we have both the will and the means, not only to go on indefinitely but to strike heavy and unexpected blows. The road to victory may not be so long as we expect. But we have no right to count upon this. Be it long or short, rough or smooth, we mean to reach our journey's end.

The gratitude of every home in our Island, in our Empire, and indeed throughout the world, except in the abodes of the guilty, goes out to the British airmen who, undaunted by odds, unwearied in their constant challenge and mortal danger, are turning the tide of the world war by their prowess and by their devotion. Never in the field of human conflict was so much owed by so many to so few. All hearts go out to the fighter pilots, whose brilliant actions we see with our own eyes day after day ; but we must never forget that all the time, night after night, month after month, our bomber squadrons travel far into Germany, find their targets in the darkness by the highest navigational skill, aim their attacks, often under the heaviest fire, often with serious loss, with deliberate careful discrimination, and inflict shattering blows upon the whole of the technical and war-making structure of the Nazi power.

For the rest, we have to gain the victory. That is our task. There is, however, one direction in which we can see a little more clearly ahead. We have to think not only for ourselves but for the lasting security of the cause and principles for which we are fighting and of the long future of the British Commonwealth of Nations. Some months ago we came to the conclusion that the interests of the United States and of the British Empire both required that the United States should have facilities for the naval and air defence of the Western hemisphere against the attack of a Nazi power which might have acquired temporary but lengthy control of a large part of Western Europe and its formidable resources. We had therefore decided spontaneously, and without being asked or offered any inducement, to inform the Government of the United States that we would be glad to place such defence facilities at their disposal by leasing suitable sites in our Trans-atlantic possessions for their greater security against the unmeasured dangers of the future. The principle of association of interests for common purposes between Great Britain and the United States had developed even before the war. Various agreements had been reached about certain small islands in the Pacific Ocean which had become important as air fuelling points. In all this line of thought we found ourselves in very close harmony with the Government of Canada.

Presently we learned that anxiety was also felt in the United States about the air and naval defence of their Atlantic seaboard, and President Roosevelt has recently made it clear that he would like to discuss with us, and with the Dominion of Canada and with Newfoundland, the development of American naval and air facilities in Newfoundland and in the West Indies. There is, of course, no question of any transference of sovereignty— that has never been suggested—or of any action being taken, without the consent or against the wishes of the various Colonies concerned, but for our part, His Majesty's Government are entirely willing to accord defence facilities to the United States on a 99 years' leasehold basis, and we feel sure that our interests no less than theirs, and the interests of the Colonies themselves and of Canada and Newfoundland will be served thereby. These are important steps. Undoubtedly this process means that these two great organisations of the English-speaking democracies, the British Empire and the United States, will have to be somewhat mixed up together in some of their affairs for mutual and general advantage. For my own part, looking out upon the future, I do not view the process with any misgivings. I could not stop it if I wished ; no one can stop it. Like the Mississippi, it just keeps rolling along. Let it roll. Let it roll on full flood, inexorable, irresistible, benignant, to broader lands and better days.

PROSPECT OF INVASION

September 11th 1940

If this invasion is going to be tried at all, it does not seem that it can be long delayed. The weather may break at any time. Besides this, it is difficult for the enemy to keep these gatherings of ships waiting about indefinitely, while they are bombed every night by our bombers, and very often shelled by our warships which are waiting for them outside.

Therefore we must regard the next week or so as a very important period in our history. It ranks with the days when the Spanish Armada was approaching the Channel, and Drake was finishing his game of bowls; or when Nelson stood between us and Napoleon's Grand Army at Boulogne. We have read all about this in the history books; but what is happening now is on a far greater scale and of far more consequence to the life and future of the world and its civilisation than these brave old days of the past.

Every man and woman will therefore prepare himself to do his duty, whatever it may be, with special pride and care. Our fleets and flotillas are very powerful and numerous; our Air Force is at the highest strength it has ever reached, and it is conscious of its proved superiority, not indeed in numbers, but in men and machines. Our shores are well fortified and strongly manned, and behind them, ready to attack the invaders, we have a far larger and better equipped mobile Army than we have ever had before.

Besides this, we have more than a million and a half men of the Home Guard, who are just as much soldiers of the Regular Army as the Grenadier Guards, and who are determined to fight for every inch of the ground in every village and in every street.

It is with devout and sure confidence that I say : Let God defend the Right.

These cruel, wanton, indiscriminate bombings of London are, of course, a part of Hitler's invasion plans. He hopes, by killing large numbers of civilians, and women and children, that he will terrorise and cow the people of this mighty imperial city, and make them a burden and an anxiety to the Government and thus distract our attention unduly from the ferocious onslaught he is preparing. Little does he know the spirit of the British nation, or the tough fibre of the Londoners, whose forebears played a leading part in the establishment of Parliamentary institutions and who have been bred to value freedom far above their lives. This wicked man, the repository and embodiment of many forms of soul-destroying hatred, this monstrous product of former wrongs and shame, has now resolved to try to break our famous island race by a process of indiscriminate slaughter and destruction. What he has done is to kindle a fire in British hearts, here and all over the world, which will glow long after all traces of the conflagration he has caused in London have been removed. He has lighted a fire which will burn with a steady and consuming flame until the last vestiges of Nazi tyranny have been burnt out of Europe, and until the Old World—and the New—can join hands to rebuild the temples of man's freedom and man's honour, upon foundations which will not soon or easily be overthrown.

This is a time for everyone to stand together, and hold firm, as they are doing. I express my admiration for the exemplary manner in which all the Air Raid Precautions services of London are now being discharged, especially the Fire Brigade, whose work has been so heavy and so dangerous. All the world that is still free marvels at the composure and fortitude with which the citizens of London are facing and surmounting the great ordeal to which they are subjected, the end of which or the severity of which cannot yet be foreseen.

It is a message of good cheer to our fighting Forces on the seas, in the air, and in our waiting Armies in all their posts and stations, that we send them from this capital city. They know that they have behind them a people who will not flinch or weary of the struggle—hard and protracted though it will be ; but that we shall rather draw from the heart of suffering itself the means of inspiration and survival, and of a victory won not only for ourselves but for all ; a victory won not only for our time but for the long and better days that are to come.

THE BATTLE OF BRITAIN

September 15th 1940

We must take September 15 as the culminating date. On this day the Luftwaffe, after two heavy attacks on the 14th, made its greatest concentrated effort in a resumed daylight attack on London.

It was one of the decisive battles of the war, and, like the Battle of Waterloo, it was on a Sunday. I was at Chequers. I had already on several occasions visited the headquarters of No. 11 Fighter Group in order to witness the conduct of an air battle, when not much had happened. However, the weather on this day seemed suitable to the enemy, and accordingly I drove over to Uxbridge and arrived at the Group Headquarters. No. 11 Group comprised no fewer than twenty-five squadrons covering the whole of Essex, Kent, Sussex, and Hampshire, and all the approaches across them to London. Air Vice-Marshal Park had for six months commanded this Group, on which our fate largely depended. From the beginning of Dunkirk all the daylight actions in the South of England had already been conducted by him, and all his arrangements and apparatus had been brought to the highest perfection. My wife and I were taken down to the bomb-proof Operations Room, fifty feet below the ground. All the ascendancy of the Hurricanes and Spitfires would have been fruitless but for this system of underground control centres and telephone cables, which had been devised and built before the war by the Air Ministry under Dowding's advice and impulse. Lasting credit is due to all concerned. In the South of England there were at this time No. 11 Group H.Q. and six subordinate Fighter Station Centres. All these were, as has been described, under heavy stress. The Supreme Command was exercised from the Fighter Headquarters at Stanmore, but the actual handling of the direction of the squadrons was wisely left to No. 11 Group, which controlled the units through its Fighter Stations located in each county.

The Group Operations Room was like a small theatre, about sixty feet across, and with two storeys. We took our seats in the Dress Circle. Below us was the large-scale map-table, around which perhaps twenty highly-trained young men and women, with their telephone assistants, were assembled. Opposite to us, covering the entire wall, where the theatre curtain would be, was a gigantic blackboard divided into six columns with electric bulbs, for the six fighter stations, each of their squadrons having a sub-column of its own, and also divided by lateral lines. Thus the lowest row of bulbs showed as they were lighted the squadrons which were " Standing By " at two minutes' notice, the next row those at " Readiness ", five minutes, then at " Available ", twenty minutes, then those which had taken off, the next row those which had reported having seen the enemy, the next—with red lights—those which were in action, and the top row those which were returning home. On the left-hand side, in a kind of glass stage-box, were the four or five officers whose duty it was to weigh and measure the information received from our Observer Corps, which at this time numbered upwards of fifty thousand men, women, and youths. Radar was still in its infancy, but it gave warning of raids approaching our coast, and the observers, with field-glasses and portable telephones, were our main source of information about raiders flying overland. Thousands of messages were therefore received during an action. Several roomfuls of experienced people in other parts of the underground headquarters sifted them with great rapidity, and transmitted the results from minute to minute directly to the plotters seated around the table on the floor and to the officer supervising from the glass stage-box.

On the right hand was another glass stage-box containing Army officers who reported the action of our anti-aircraft batteries, of which at this time in the Command there were two hundred. At night it was of vital importance to stop these batteries firing over certain areas in which our fighters would be closing with the enemy. I was not unacquainted with the general outlines of this system, having had it explained to me a year before the war by Dowding when I visited him at Stanmore. It had been shaped and refined in constant action, and all was now fused together into a most elaborate instrument of war, the like of which existed nowhere in the world.

" I don't know," said Park, as we went down, " whether anything will happen to-day. At present all is quiet." However, after a quarter of an hour the raid-plotters began to move about. An attack of " 40 plus " was reported to be coming from the German stations in the Dieppe area. The bulbs along the bottom of the wall display-panel began to glow as various squadrons came to " Stand By ". Then in quick succession " 20 plus ", " 40 plus " signals were received, and in another ten minutes it was evident that a serious battle impended. On both sides the air began to fill.

One after another signals came in, " 40 plus ", " 60 plus "; there was even an " 80 plus ". On the floor-table below us the movement of all the waves of attack was marked by pushing discs forward from minute to minute along different lines of approach, while on the blackboard facing us the rising lights showed our fighter squadrons getting into the air, till there were only four or five left " At Readiness ". These air battles, on which so much depended, lasted little more than an hour from the first encounter. The enemy had ample strength to send out new waves of attack, and our squadrons, having gone all out to gain the upper air, would have to refuel after seventy or eighty minutes, or land to rearm after a five-minute engagement. If at this moment of refuelling or rearming the enemy were able to arrive with fresh unchallenged squadrons some of our fighters could be destroyed on the ground. It was therefore one of our principal objects to direct our squadrons so as not to have too many on the ground refuelling or rearming simultaneously during daylight.

Presently the red bulbs showed that the majority of our

squadrons were engaged. A subdued hum arose from the floor, where the busy plotters pushed their discs to and fro in accordance with the swiftly-changing situation. Air Vice-Marshal Park gave general directions for the disposition of his fighter force, which were translated into detailed orders to each Fighter Station by a youngish officer in the centre of the Dress Circle, at whose side I sat. Some years after I asked his name. He was Lord Willoughby de Broke. (I met him next in 1947, when the Jockey Club, of which he was a Steward, invited me to see the Derby. He was surprised that I remembered the occasion.) He now gave the orders for the individual squadrons to ascend and patrol as the result of the final information which appeared on the map-table. The Air Marshal himself walked up and down behind, watching with vigilant eye every move in the game, supervising his junior executive hand, and only occasionally intervening with some decisive order, usually to reinforce a threatened area. In a little while all our squadrons were fighting, and some had already begun to return for fuel. All were in the air. The lower line of bulbs was out. There was not one squadron left in reserve. At this moment Park spoke to Dowding at Stanmore, asking for three squadrons from No. 12 Group to be put at his disposal in case of another major attack while his squadrons were rearming and refuelling. This was done. They were specially needed to cover London and our fighter aerodromes, because No. 11 Group had already shot their bolt.

The young officer, to whom this seemed a matter of routine, continued to give his orders, in accordance with the general directions of his Group Commander, in a calm, low monotone, and the three reinforcing squadrons were soon absorbed. I became conscious of the anxiety of the

Commander, who now stood still behind his subordinate's chair. Hitherto I had watched in silence. I now asked: "What other reserves have we?" "There are none," said Air Vice-Marshal Park. In an account which he wrote about it afterwards he said that at this I "looked grave". Well I might. What losses should we not suffer if our refuelling planes were caught on the ground by further raids of "40 plus" or "50 plus"! The odds were great; our margins small; the stakes infinite.

Another five minutes passed, and most of our squadrons had now descended to refuel. In many cases our resources could not give them overhead protection. Then it appeared that the enemy were going home. The shifting of the discs on the table below showed a continuous eastward movement of German bombers and fighters. No new attack appeared. In another ten minutes the action was ended. We climbed again the stairways which led to the surface, and almost as we emerged the "All Clear" sounded.

"We are very glad, sir, you have seen this," said Park. "Of course, during the last twenty minutes we were so choked with information that we couldn't handle it. This shows you the limitation of our present resources. They have been strained far beyond their limits to-day." I asked whether any results had come to hand, and remarked that the attack appeared to have been repelled satisfactorily. Park replied that he was not satisfied that we had intercepted as many raiders as he had hoped we should. It was evident that the enemy had everywhere pierced our defences. Many scores of German bombers, with their fighter escort, had been reported over London. About a dozen had been brought down while I was below, but no picture of the results of the battle or of the damage or losses could be obtained.

It was 4.30 p.m. before I got back to Chequers, and I immediately went to bed for my afternoon sleep. I must have been tired by the drama of No. 11 Group, for I did not wake until eight. When I rang, John Martin, my Principal Private Secretary, came in with the evening budget of news from all over the world. It was repellent. This had gone wrong here ; that had been delayed there ; an unsatisfactory answer had been received from so-and-so ; there had been bad sinkings in the Atlantic. " However," said Martin, as he finished the account, " all is redeemed by the air. We have shot down one hundred and eighty-three for a loss of under forty ".

Although post-war information has shown that the enemy's losses on this day were only fifty-six, September 15 was the crux of the Battle of Britain. That same night our Bomber Command attacked in strength the shipping in the ports from Boulogne to Antwerp. At Antwerp particularly heavy losses were inflicted. On September 17, as we now know, the Fuehrer decided to postpone " Sea Lion " indefinitely. It was not till October 12 that the invasion was formally called off till the following spring. In July 1941 it was postponed again by Hitler till the spring of 1942, " by which time the Russian campaign will be completed ". This was a vain but an important imagining. On February 13, 1942, Admiral Raeder had his final interview on " Sea Lion " and got Hitler to agree to a complete " stand-down ". Thus perished operation " Sea Lion ". And September 15 may stand as the date of its demise.

CONSTANCY AND VALOUR OUR ONLY SHIELD

October 8th 1940

Because we feel easier in ourselves and see our way more clearly through our difficulties and dangers than we did some months ago, because foreign countries, friends and foes, recognise the giant, enduring, resilient strength of Britain and the British Empire, do not let us dull for one moment the sense of the awful hazards in which we stand. Do not let us lose the conviction that it is only by supreme and superb exertions, unwearying and indomitable, that we shall save our souls alive. No one can predict, no one can even imagine, how this terrible war against German and Nazi aggression will run its course or how far it will spread or how long it will last. Long, dark months of trials and tribulations lie before us. Not only great dangers, but many more misfortunes, many shortcomings, many mistakes, many disappointments will surely be our lot. Death and sorrow will be the companions of our journey ; hardship our garment ; constancy and valour our only shield. We must be united, we must be undaunted, we must be inflexible. Our qualities and deeds must burn and glow through the gloom of Europe until they became the veritable beacon of its salvation.

MESSAGE TO THE FRENCH PEOPLE
October 21st 1940

Français! Armez vos cœurs à neuf avant qu'il ne soit trop tard. Rappelez-vous de quelle façon Napoléon disait avant une de ses victoires : " Ces mêmes Prussiens qui sont aujourd'hui si vantards étaient à 3 contre 1 à Jéna et à 9 contre 1 à Montmirail ". Jamais je ne croirai que l'âme de la France soit morte, ni que sa place parmi les grandes nations du monde puisse être perdue pour toujours.

Tous les complots et tous les crimes de Herr Hitler sont en train d'attirer sur sa tête et sur la tête de ceux qui appartiennent à son régime un châtiment que beaucoup d'entre nous verrons de leur vivant. Il n'y aura pas si longtemps à attendre. L'aventure n'est pas encore finie. Nous sommes sur la piste ; et nos amis de l'autre côté de l'océan Atlantique y sont aussi. Si Herr Hitler ne peut pas nous détruire, nous, nous sommes sûrs de le détruire, avec toute sa clique et tous leurs travaux. Ayez donc espoir et confiance. Tout se rétablira.

Maintenant, nous autres Britanniques, que pouvons-nous vous demander aujourd'hui, dans un moment si âpre et si dur? Ce que nous vous demandons, au milieu de nos efforts pour remporter la victoire que nous partagerons avec vous, c'est que, si vous ne pouvez pas nous aider, au moins vous ne nous fassiez pas obstacle. En effet, vous devez renforcer le bras qui frappe pour vous. Nous croyons que les Français, où qu'ils soient, se sentiront le cœur réchauffé et que la fierté de leur sang tressaillera dans leurs veines chaque fois que nous remporterons un succès dans les airs, sur mer, ou, plus tard—et cela viendra

—sur terre. N'oubliez pas que nous ne nous arrêterons jamais, que nous ne nous lasserons jamais, que jamais nous ne céderons et que notre peuple et notre Empire tout entier se sont voués à la tâche de guérir l'Europe de la pestilence nazie et de sauver le monde d'une nouvelle barbarie. Parmi les Français, ceux qui se trouvent dans l'Empire Colonial et ceux qui habitent la France soi-disant inoccupée peuvent, sans doute, de temps à autre, trouver l'occasion d'agir utilement. Je n'entre pas dans les détails. Les oreilles ennemies nous écoutent. Les autres, vers qui l'affection anglaise se porte d'un seul mouvement, parce qu'ils vivent sous la stricte discipline, l'oppression et l'espionnage des Boches, je leur dis : Quand vous pensez à l'avenir, rappelez-vous les mots de ce grand Français que fut Thiers : il les prononça après 1870, à propos de l'avenir : " Y penser toujours ; n'en parler jamais ".

Allons, bonne nuit, dormez bien, rassemblez vos forces pour l'aube—car l'aube viendra. Elle se lèvera brillante pour les braves, douce pour les fidèles qui auront souffert, glorieuse sur les tombeaux des héros. Vive la France! Et vive aussi la marche en avant des peuples de tous les pays qui veulent reconquérir le patrimoine qui leur appartient de plein droit.

GIVE US THE TOOLS

February 9th 1941

The other day, President Roosevelt gave his opponent in the late Presidential Election a letter of introduction to me, and in it he wrote out a verse, in his own hand-writing, from Longfellow, which he said, " applies to you people as it does to us ". Here is the verse :

> . . . *Sail on, O Ship of State !*
> *Sail on, O Union, strong and great !*
> *Humanity with all its fears,*
> *With all the hopes of future years,*
> *Is hanging breathless on thy fate !*

What is the answer that I shall give, in your name, to this great man, the thrice-chosen head of a nation of a hundred and thirty millions? Here is the answer which I will give to President Roosevelt : Put your confidence in us. Give us your faith and your blessing, and, under Providence, all will be well.

We shall not fail or falter ; we shall not weaken or tire. Neither the sudden shock of battle, nor the long-drawn trials of vigilance and exertion will wear us down. Give us the tools, and we will finish the job.

" BUT WESTWARD, LOOK, THE LAND IS BRIGHT "

April 27th 1941

While therefore we naturally view with sorrow and anxiety much that is happening in Europe and in Africa, and may happen in Asia, we must not lose our sense of proportion and thus become discouraged or alarmed. When we face with a steady eye the difficulties which lie before us, we may derive new confidence from remembering those we have already overcome. Nothing that is happening now is comparable in gravity with the dangers through which we passed last year. Nothing that can happen in the East is comparable with what is happening in the West.

Last time I spoke to you I quoted the lines of Longfellow which President Roosevelt had written out for me in his own hand. I have some other lines which are less well known but which seem apt and appropriate to our fortunes to-night, and I believe they will be so judged wherever the English language is spoken or the flag of freedom flies :

> *For while the tired waves, vainly breaking,*
> *Seem here no painful inch to gain,*
> *Far back, through creeks and inlets making,*
> *Comes silent, flooding in, the main.*

> *And not by eastern windows only,*
> *When daylight comes, comes in the light:*
> *In front the sun climbs slow, how slowly !*
> *But westward, look, the land is bright.*

THE BATTLE OF THE ATLANTIC

June 25th 1941

At the beginning of March there were over 2,600,000 tons of damaged shipping accumulated in our ports, of which about 930,000 tons were ships undergoing repair while working cargo, and nearly 1,700,000 were immobilised by the need of repairs. The tonnage immobilised solely by repairs is the most injurious and obnoxious

feature of the story. In my directive of March 6 I aimed
at beating this down by 400,000 by July 1. But later on
we became more ambitious and we set ourselves as a
target a reduction of 750,000 tons by the same date. We
had a heavy blow as a result of the air attacks made on the
Mersey and the Clyde at the beginning of May. These
added many thousands of tons to the total of ship tonnage
damaged at sea. We also had a windfall which added to
the number of ships to be repaired. A number of ships
given up as hopeless were rescued by our Salvage Service
and added to the repair list. Nevertheless, in spite of these
additions, unwelcome and welcome, the tonnage immobilised by reason of repair on June 12, the latest date for
which I have figures, has been reduced to just under
1,000,000 tons. This represents a gain, not yet indeed of
the 750,000 tons at which we aimed but of 700,000 tons,
which is tolerably near it. Even though we remember,
before we crow too much, that there is always a diminution
in the summer weather of marine casualties, quite apart
from enemy action, the figures I have mentioned should
give rise not only to relief but to satisfaction.

Let us glance for a moment at some of the measures by
which this result has been achieved. The first is, of course,
the steady drive which is being made to increase the labour
force on merchant ship repairs. There are now in the
private shipbuilding yards engaged on hull work, 11,000
more workers than at the end of January. There has also
been a definite transfer from naval to merchant work. My
right hon. friend, the Minister of Labour, has worked very
hard at this.

Another economy in the turn-round has been effected
by a simplification of degaussing. The brilliant and faithful servants who mastered the magnetic mine aspired

naturally towards perfection in the degaussing system beyond what we can afford in these hard times. We have to balance risks against getting the ships quickly to sea. It is now very rare indeed for a ship to be delayed simply on account of degaussing repairs or improvements ; either these are effected while the ship is discharging or loading, or a certain amount of chance is taken. With Mr. Harriman's aid a proportion of the more thorough and more permanent installations is being effected in United States ports. There may well be a saving of two or three days in the turn-round on this process alone. Other savings have been effected by a more close concert of action between the naval and civil port authorities, and though I cannot put a precise figure on the total saving, it is certainly substantial and will be further increased. Never forget that the saving in the turn-round of a single day over the vast field of our traffic is worth a quarter of a million tons in effective imports during a year.

I have never allowed the excuse to be pleaded of congestion at our ports because, in spite of all our difficulties, we are, in fact, only handling and budgeting to handle about half the pre-war traffic. None the less a great effort is being made. Inland sorting depots which enable the goods to be got away quickly from the air-raided quaysides into the country are commended by the Select Committee. Six of these are in process of construction to serve our West Coast ports. The first will come into partial operation in September. To get the best out of the South Wales ports we are quadrupling the railway line from Newport to the Severn Tunnel ; part of the quadrupled line is already in operation. Some of the transport bottlenecks are found at inland junctions on the western side of the island because a greater strain is being cast upon them than they were constructed to bear. These are being opened up. A considerable development of over-side discharge at suitable anchorages has been organised, not only as a relief but as an alternative in case of very heavy attack. A large expansion in our crane facilities is on foot, both to equip new emergency ports and to make existing port facilities more flexible under attack. In May alone 130 mobile cranes were delivered from British factories and from the United States as compared with the previous average of 50 in the last four months. I should trespass unduly upon the House if I were to describe this part of our struggle in any more detail.

I am now able to present some general conclusions. Our losses and those of our Allies by sinking in the last few months have been very heavy. In the last 12 months they amount to 4,600,000 tons. The enemy continually varies his form of attack in order to meet our counter-measures. We give him a hot time in the North Western Approaches, he opens up off the banks of Newfoundland or even nearer to the American coast. We deploy our escorts and our flying-boats more widely, the United States Navy advances into the conflict and the enemy develops heavy and effective U-boat attack off Dakar and in the Cape Verde Islands area. Every move or new device on our side is met by a counter on the other.

It is because it is vital that the enemy should not know how much success attends these moves that we propose in the near future to stop the monthly publication of shipping losses. We have published the very heavy figures for May and also all the arrears which have come in later about the losses for April and March. The April and May figures were swollen by the severe fighting in the Mediterranean; it looks as if the June figures will be better, although, of course, at any moment a flock of U-boats getting into one of our convoys may upset our forecasts. At the present time, June 25, five days before the end of the month, we might hope to be within 300,000 tons. But then again there may be some arrears. Still, June, in the middle of the summer, will certainly show a better figure than February or March, those spring months in which Hitler boasted the fury of his attack would break upon us.

After June we do not propose to publish any more figures. It is giving too much help to the enemy to let him know each month the success or failure of his repeated variants of attack. He knows our figures are true ; they are of the greatest value to him ; I have no doubt the German Admiralty would pay £100,000 a month for the information we so meticulously compile and proclaim. We get nothing in return ; he tells us nothing except extraordinary lies and exaggerations which have long since been discredited. Our task, our effort for survival, is surely hard enough without our becoming an effective branch of the German Intelligence Service. I have no doubt there will be a howl, not only from the Germans, but from some well-meaning patriots of this island. Let them howl. We have got to think of our sailors and merchant seamen, the lives of our countrymen, and of the life of our country, now quivering in the balance of mortal peril.

It would be a great mistake for us to ingeminate and emphasise our woes. I cannot share that sense of detachment which enables some people to feel they are rendering a public service by rubbing-in the most dark and anxious part of our situation. Only the other day our great friend, President Roosevelt, stated some figures about our losses in relation to British and American new building in the

H

most startling and alarming form. There was nothing very new about these figures and facts, and we gave our assent beforehand to the President's use of them. It certainly had a bad effect in all the balancing countries, in Spain, at Vichy, in Turkey and in Japan.

The Japanese Ambassador, in taking leave the other day, a man most friendly to peace between our countries, inquired anxiously of me about Mr. Roosevelt's statement which he evidently felt might be a factor in an adverse decision by Japan, which he hoped to avert. The House must not under-rate the dangers of our plight. We cannot afford to give any advantages to the enemy in naval information nor can we afford to paint our affairs in their darkest colours before the eyes of neutrals and to discourage our friends and encourage our foes all over the world.

I end upon this figure of 31,000,000 tons import in 1941 which I ask shall be kept most strictly secret. If we can bring this in we can carry on our life at home and our war effort in the East without any further serious restrictions. If we fail to do it we shall be definitely weakened in our struggle for existence and for the right to breathe the air of freedom. I believe we shall succeeed, and it may even be there will be some improvement. This would become certain if we obtained more direct assistance from the flotillas and flying-boats of the United States and still more if the United States took the plunge in good time.

On the present showing, if we can resist or deter actual invasion this autumn, we ought to be able, on the present undertakings of the United States, to come through the year 1941. In 1942 we hope to be possessed of very definite air ascendancy and to be able not only to carry our offensive bombing very heavily into Germany, but to redress to some extent the frightful strategic disadvantages we suffer from the present German control of the Atlantic seaports of Europe. If we can deny to the enemy or at least markedly neutralise the enemy-held Atlantic ports and airfields, there is no reason why the year 1942, in which the enormous American new building comes to hand, should not present us with less anxious ordeals than those we must now endure and come through.

I will add only one other word. Let us not forget that the enemy has difficulties of his own ; that some of these difficulties are obvious ; that there may be others which are more apparent to him than to us ; and that all the great struggles of history have been won by superior will-power wresting victory in the teeth of odds or upon the narrowest of margins.

LOSS OF H.M.S. *PRINCE OF WALES* AND *REPULSE*

December 10th 1941

The Japanese onslaught has brought upon the United States and Great Britain very serious injuries to our naval power. In my whole experience I do not remember any naval blow so heavy or so painful as the sinking of the *Prince of Wales* and the *Repulse* on Monday last. These two vast, powerful ships constituted an essential feature in our plans for meeting the new Japanese danger as it loomed against us in the last few months. These ships had reached the right point at the right moment, and were in every respect suited to the task assigned to them. In moving to attack the Japanese transports and landing-craft which were disembarking the invaders of Siam and

Malaya at the Kra Isthmus or thereabouts, Admiral Phillips was undertaking a thoroughly sound, well-considered offensive operation, not indeed free from risk, but not different in principle from many similar operations we have repeatedly carried out in the North Sea and in the Mediterranean. Both ships were sunk in repeated air attacks by bombers and by torpedo-aircraft. These attacks were delivered with skill and determination. There were two high-level attacks, both of which scored hits, and three waves of torpedo-aircraft of nine in each wave which struck each of our ships with several torpedoes. There is no reason to suppose that any new weapons or explosives were employed, or any bombs or torpedoes of exceptional size. The continued waves of attack achieved their purpose, and both ships capsized and sank, having destroyed seven of the attacking aircraft.

The escorting destroyers came immediately to the rescue and have now arrived at Singapore crowded with survivors. There is reason to believe that the loss of life has been less heavy than was at first feared. But I regret that Admiral Sir Tom Phillips is among those reported missing.

" SOME CHICKEN, SOME NECK "

December 30th 1941

The French Army collapsed, and the French nation was dashed into utter and, as it has so far proved, irretrievable confusion. The French Government had at their own suggestion solemnly bound themselves with us not to make a separate peace. It was their duty and it was also their interest to go to North Africa, where they would have been at the head of the French Empire. In Africa, with our aid, they would have had overwhelming sea power. They would have had the recognition of the United States, and the use of all the gold they had lodged beyond the seas. If they had done this Italy might have been driven out of the war before the end of 1940, and France would have held her place as a nation in the counsels of the Allies and at the conference table of the victors. But their generals misled them. When I warned them that Britain would fight on alone whatever they did, their generals told their Prime Minister and his divided Cabinet, " In three weeks England will have her neck wrung like a chicken ". Some chicken ; some neck.

VICTORY AT ALAMEIN

November 11th 1942

I can now read to the House the actual direction which I gave to General Alexander on 10th August, before leaving Cairo for Russia. It has at least the merit of brevity :

" 1. Your prime and main duty will be to take or destroy at the earliest opportunity the German-Italian army commanded by Field-Marshal Rommel, together with all its supplies and establishments in Egypt and Libya.

2. You will discharge, or cause to be discharged, such other duties as appertain to your Command without prejudice to the task described in paragraph 1, which must be considered paramount in His Majesty's interests."

The General may very soon be sending along for further instructions.

In spite of the strain to which General Alexander had been subjected in the hard, adverse campaign in Burma, from which he had emerged with so much credit although he had nothing but retreat and misfortune, he accepted the new duties with ardour. Under him, commanding the Eighth Army, was placed that remarkable soldier, General Montgomery. These two officers set up their headquarters in the desert, and Air Vice-Marshal Coningham, who commands the air forces in the battle there, was in the same little circle of lorries, wagons and tents in which they live. In a very short time an electrifying effect was produced upon the troops, who were also reinforced by every available man and weapon. Meanwhile, in the rearward areas, the intensive training of the formations to be armed with the new American and British weapons proceeded ceaselessly. All these changes had to be made in the face of an imminent attack by Rommel's army, the preparations for which were plainly apparent. In order that the Desert Army should have the fullest freedom of manoeuvre and not have to fall back if its southward flank were turned— because the line did not extend completely to the Qattara Depression ; there was an open flank—every preparation was made to defend Cairo by the assembly of a considerable force, by the mobilising of every man from the rearward Services, exactly as we should do in England in the case of invasion, by the preparations of defence works along the line of the Nile, and by the use of inundations. All this was set in train. The new Command having been installed, my work there was done, and I returned to give my report to the House.

During the night of 30th–31st August, when the moon

was already on the wane, Rommel's threatened attack was delivered. Quite rightly from his point of view, he did not by-pass the army to strike at Cairo, although the road seemed open. We thought he might, but he did not. He did not care to leave behind him the Desert Army now that it was reinforced by the 44th Division, which is commanded with distinction by our Deputy Serjeant-at-Arms (Major-General Hughes) and which was largely reorganised and regrouped. Pivoting on the Italians in the coastal area, he therefore attacked on the southern flank with all his armour and most of his Germans. Then followed the second Battle of Alamein, the first being General Auchinleck's, which stemmed the tide in July. Rommel found himself immediately confronted with stern resistance and with artillery, used on the largest scale and abundantly supplied with ammunition. He did not press the issue to extremes, and, after about three days, he withdrew. Our losses were about 2,000. His were considerably heavier, especially a disproportionate loss in tanks.

The narrowness of the passage between us and the Qattara Depression, which had proved so serviceable to us when we were resisting Rommel's attacks in both the defensive Battles of Alamein, became of course a most serious adverse factor to our advance when we ourselves were ready in our turn to assume the offensive. Our attack had to fit in harmoniously with the great operation in French North Africa to which it was a prelude. We had to wait till our troops were trained in the use of the new weapons which were arriving. We had to have a full moon on account of the method of attack. All these conditions were satisfiable around 23rd October. Meanwhile, however, we knew that the enemy was turning the position in front of us into a veritable fortress, blasting gun-pits and trenches in the solid rock, laying enormous and elaborate minefields, and strengthening himself in every manner both by air and sea transport, in spite of the heavy toll exacted by our Air Force and our submarines. An attack by us round the enemy's southern flank led into difficult country, with no threat to his communications. On the other hand, to blast a hole by a frontal attack in the north by the sea was a most forbidding task. However, when I spent a night on 19th August with Generals Alexander and Montgomery in their desert headquarters, General Montgomery, with General Alexander's full assent, expounded in exact detail the first stages of the plan which has since in fact been carried out. It was an anxious matter. In the last war we devised the tank to clear a way for the infantry, who were otherwise held up by the intensity of machine-gun fire. On this occasion it was the infantry who would have to clear the way for the tanks, to break through the crust and liberate the superior armour. This they could only do in the moonlight, and for this they must be supported with a concentration of artillery more powerful than any used in the present war. On a six-mile front of attack we had a 25-pounder gun, or better, every 23 yards. It is true that in the later barrages of 1918, at the Hindenburg line, and the other long-prepared positions, a concentration of one gun to every 15 yards was attained. But the field guns of those days were 18-pounders. Our 25-pounders are heavier, and we also believe they are the best field guns in the world. It was necessary to effect penetration of about 6,000 yards at the first stroke in order to get through the hostile minefields, trenches and batteries. In the last war it was nearly always possible to make this initial penetration. In those days, the artillery having blasted the gap, the next step was to

gallop the cavalry through what was called the "G in Gap."
But this was never done, as the horsemen were soon
brought to a standstill by the machine-gun posts in the
rear. Horses were shot, and the whole possibility of
exploiting the breach passed away. Times have changed,
however. We have a steel machine cavalry now which,
once a path is cleared through the mines and anti-tank
guns, can certainly go forward against machine-gun
posts to encounter whatever mobile force of the enemy
may be beyond. That is the difference in this matter
between the two wars. I feel sure the House will be glad
that I should put these points to them, because in all that
has been written—and so much has been written—about
this battle, these points which touch the sequence and
articulation of events have not been made very clearly.

For the purpose of turning the breach we made to full
account, an entirely new Corps, the 10th, was formed,
consisting of two British Armoured Divisions and the
New Zealand Division—that "ball of fire" as it was
described to me by those who had seen it work. This very
powerful force of between 40,000 and 50,000 men, including all the best tanks, the Grants and the Shermans, was
withdrawn from the battle front immediately after Rommel's repulse in the second battle of Alamein, and devoted
itself entirely to intensive training, exercises and preparation. It was this thunderbolt hurled through the gap
which finished Rommel and his arrogant army.

The success of all these plans could not have been
achieved without substantial superiority in the air. The
Royal Air Force, which had a substantial proportion of
American-manned squadrons with it, had first to attain
ascendancy over the opposing air force. Having attained
this ascendancy, it was used behind the lines to reduce

the all-important supplies of fuel and ammunition without which the Germans could not effectively resist. It was also used in the battle itself to break up any threatening counter-attacks before they could develop, thus giving the troops time to consolidate the positions won. By reaching out far to the rear of the retreating army, air power completely disorganised the enemy's withdrawal, and once again by the destruction of his mechanised transport prevented the bringing of fuel and ammunition to the front. When we retreated all those hundreds of miles from Tobruk at such speed, what saved us was superior air power. What has consummated Rommel's ruin is that he has had to make this ruinous and speedy retreat with a superior air force hammering him and hampering him at every stage. In Air Marshal Tedder and Air Vice-Marshal Coningham we have two air leaders of the very highest quality, not technicians, but warriors who have worked in perfect harmony with the generals, and the manner in which in this Egyptian campaign the arrangements between the air and the military has been perfected has given a model which should be followed in all combined operations in the future.

It is true we had gathered superior forces, but all this would have been futile but for the masterly military conception of the commanders, the attention to detail which characterised their preparations, and the absolute ruthlessness with which their forces were engaged, not only at the point of rupture, but in gripping the enemy along the entire battle front. This battle is in fact a very fine example of the military art as developed under modern conditions. The skill of the commanders was rivalled by the conduct of their troops. Everyone testifies to the electrifying effect which the new Command had upon the army. This noble Desert Army, which has never doubted its power to beat the enemy, and whose pride had suffered cruelly from retreats and disasters which they could not understand, regained in a week its ardour and self-confidence. Historians may explain Tobruk. The Eighth Army has done better ; it has avenged it.

THE FALL OF SINGAPORE
April 23rd 1942

The House will see that in November and December last year in a few weeks we lost or had put out of action for a long time seven great ships or more than one-third of our battleships and battle-cruisers, and that this happened at a time when we were fully extended and had to meet the attack of a new, fresh and tremendous enemy and while our great ally was temporarily entirely crippled at sea. It is upon this background and with this accompaniment that I will make a very few observations about the tragedy and disaster of Singapore.

On December 7, 1941, there were in Singapore and the Malay Peninsula about 60,000 British, Australian and Indian troops, and immediately after the declaration we set in motion in Malaya, as I have described, between 40,000 and 50,000 others, including a high proportion of technical arms. After a long rearguard action down the Malay Peninsula, there were, according to the War Office figures, about 100,000 men gathered in the island of Singapore by the morning of February 3. On the night of February 8 about 5,000 Japanese made a lodgment on the north-western corner and were gradually reinforced by landings from other points until perhaps 30,000 men had been landed. After five or six days of confused but not very severe fighting the army and fortress surrendered. The Japanese have not stated the number of prisoners they have taken but it does not seem that there was very much bloodshed. This episode and all that led up to it seems to be out of harmony with anything that we have experienced or performed in the present war. Many explanatory factors are mentioned : the absence of the Air Force owing to the enemy's domination of our airfields ; the dispiriting effects of the long retreat upon the troops engaged in it ; the enervating effects of the climate upon all Europeans ; the fact that some of the reinforcements had been a long time on board ship ; and above all the embarrassment to the defence, caused by it being intermingled with a city containing at that time upwards of one million human beings of many races and conditions. In all these circumstances I do not wonder at all that requests should be made for an inquiry by a Royal Commission, not only into what took place upon the spot in the agony of Singapore but into all the arrangements which had been made beforehand. I am convinced, however, that this would not be good for our country, and that it would hamper the prosecution of the war. Australian accounts reflect upon the Indian troops. Other credible witnesses disparage the Australians. The lack of any effective counter-attack by the 18th Division which arrived in such high spirits and good order, and never seem to have had their chance, is criticised. The Generalship is criticised. There is an endless field for recrimination. Most of those concerned are prisoners. General Wavell, who was in charge of the whole ABDA area from January 15 onwards, is far too busy grappling with new perils. We too have enough trouble on our hands to cope with the present and the future, and I could not in any circumstances consent to adding such a burden, for a heavy burden it would be, to those which we have to bear. I must ask the House to support the Government in this decision, which is not taken in any ignoble desire to shield individuals or safeguard the administration but solely in the interests of the State and for the successful prosecution of the war.

THE END OF MUSSOLINI
July 27th 1943

The House will have heard with satisfaction of the downfall of one of the principal criminals of this desolating war. The end of Mussolini's long and severe reign over the Italian people undoubtedly marks the close of an epoch in the life of Italy. The keystone of the Fascist arch has crumbled, and without attempting to prophesy, it does not seem unlikely that the entire Fascist edifice will fall to the ground in ruins, if it has not already so fallen. The totalitarian system of a single party, armed with secret police, engrossing to itself practically all the offices, even the humblest, under the Government, with magistrates and courts under the control of the executive, with the whole network of domestic spies and neighbourly informants—that system, when applied over a long period of time leaves the broad masses without any influence upon their country's destinies and without any independent figures apart from the official classes. That, I think, is a defence for the people of Italy—one defence— although there can be no really valid defence for any country or any people which allows its freedom and inherent rights to pass out of its own hands.

The external shock of war has broken the spell which in Italy held all these masses for so long, in fact for more than twenty years, in physical and even more in moral subjection. We may, therefore, reasonably expect that very great changes will take place in Italy. What their form will be, or how they will impinge upon the forces of German occupation and control, it is too early to forecast. The guilt and folly of Mussolini have cost the Italian people dear. It looked so safe and easy in May, 1940, to stab falling France in the back and advance to appropriate the Mediterranean interests and possessions of what Mussolini no doubt sincerely believed was a decadent and ruined Britain. It looked so safe and easy to fall upon the much smaller State of Greece. However, there have been many undeceptions. Events have taken a different course. By many hazardous turns of fortune and by the long marches of destiny, the British and United States Armies, having occupied the Italian African Empire, the north of Africa, and the bulk of Sicily, now stand at the portals of the Italian mainland armed with the powers of the sea and the air, and with a very large land and amphibious force equipped with every modern weapon and device.

What is it that these masterful forces bring to Italy? They bring, if the Italian people so decide, relief from the war, freedom from servitude, and, after an interval, a respectable place in the new and rescued Europe. When I learn of the scenes enacted in the streets of the fine city of Palermo on the entry of the United States Armies, and review a mass of detailed information with which I have been furnished, I cannot doubt that the main wish of the Italian people is to be quit of their German taskmasters, to be spared a further and perfectly futile ordeal of destruction, and to revive their former democratic and parliamentary institutions. These they can have. The choice is in their hands. As an alternative, the Germans naturally desire that Italy shall become a battle-ground, a preliminary battle-ground, and that by Italian sufferings the ravages of war shall be kept as far away as possible for as long as possible from the German Fatherland. If the Italian Government and people choose that the Germans shall have their way, no choice is left open to us. We shall continue to make war upon Italy from every quarter ; from North and South, from the sea and from the air, and by amphibious descents, we shall endeavour to bring the utmost rigours of war increasingly upon her. Orders to this effect have been given to all the Allied commanders concerned.

A decision by the Italian Government and people to continue under the German yoke will not affect seriously the general course of the war. Still less will it alter its ultimate result. The only consequence will be that in the next few months Italy will be seared and scarred and blackened from one end to the other. I know little or nothing of the new Government. I express no opinion, but it is obvious that so far as their own people are concerned they have a very important decision to take. Meanwhile I am anxious that the various processes by which this decision is reached should be allowed to run their course under no other pressure than that of relentless war. This operation may well take some time. There may be several stages of transition. Past experience shows that when great changes of heart and character take place in the government of a nation, very often one stage is rapidly succeeded by another. I cannot tell. So far, we have had no approaches from the Italian Government, and therefore no new decisions are called upon from us, except those which are connected with the bringing of the maximum avalanche of fire and steel upon all targets of military significance throughout the length and breadth of Italy.

However, I must utter a word of caution. We do not know what is going to happen in Italy, and now that Mussolini has gone, and once the Fascist power is certainly and irretrievably broken, we should be foolish to deprive ourselves of any means of coming to general conclusions with the Italian nation. It would be a grave mistake, when Italian affairs are in this flexible, fluid, formative condition, for the rescuing Powers, Britain and the United States, so to act as to break down the whole structure and expression of the Italian State. We certainly do not seek to reduce Italian life to a condition of chaos and anarchy, and to find ourselves without any authorities with whom to deal. By so doing, we should lay upon our Armies and upon our war effort the burden of occupying, mile after mile, the entire country, and of forcing the individual surrender of every armed or coherent force in every district into which our troops may enter. An immense task of garrisoning, policing and administering would be thrown upon us, involving a grievous expenditure of power, and still more of time.

We must be careful not to get ourselves into the kind of position into which the Germans have blundered in so many countries—that of having to hold down and administer in detail, from day to day, by a system of gauleiters, the entire life of very large populations, thereby becoming responsible under the hard conditions of this present period for the whole of their upkeep and well-being. Such a course might well, in practice, turn the sense of liberation which it may soon be in our power to bestow upon the Italian people, into a sullen discontent against us and all our works. The rescuers might soon, indeed, be regarded as tyrants ; they might even be hated by the Italian people as much or almost as much as their German allies. I certainly do not wish, in the case of Italy, to tread a path which might lead to execution squads and concentration camps, and above all to having to carry on our shoulders a lot of people who ought to be made to carry themselves.

Therefore, my advice to the House of Commons, and to the British nation, and to the Commonwealth and Empire, and to our Allies, may at this juncture be very simply stated. We should let the Italians, to use a homely phrase, stew in their own juice for a bit, and hot up the fire to the utmost in order to accelerate the process, until we obtain from their Government, or whoever possesses the necessary authority, all our indispensable requirements for carrying on the war against our prime and capital foe, which is not Italy but Germany. It is the interest of Italy, and also the interest of the Allies, that the unconditional surrender of Italy should be brought about wholesale and not piecemeal. Whether this can be accomplished or not, I cannot tell, but people in this country and elsewhere who cannot have the necessary knowledge of all the forces at work, or assign true valuations to the various facts and factors, should, I think, at this juncture be restrained in speech and writing, lest they should add to the tasks, the toils and the losses of our Armies, and prolong and darken the miseries which have descended upon the world.

Nevertheless, let us not allow this favourable inclination of our fortunes to blind us to the immensity of the task before us, nor to the exertions still to be made and the privations and tribulations still to be endured and over-

coast of France. An immense armada of upwards of 4,000
ships, together with several thousand smaller craft, crossed
the Channel. Massed air-borne landings have been successfully effected behind the enemy lines, and landings on the
beaches are proceeding at various points at the present
time. The fire of the shore batteries has been largely
quelled. The obstacles that were constructed in the sea
have not proved so difficult as was apprehended. The
Anglo-American Allies are sustained by about 11,000 first-
line aircraft, which can be drawn upon as may be needed
for the purposes of the battle. I cannot, of course, commit
myself to any particular details. Reports are coming in in
rapid succession. So far the Commanders who are engaged
report that everything is proceeding according to plan.
And what a plan! This vast operation is undoubtedly the
most complicated and difficult that has ever taken place.
It involves tides, wind, waves, visibility, both from the air
and the sea standpoint, and the combined employment of
land, air and sea forces in the highest degree of intimacy
and in contact with conditions which could not and cannot
be fully foreseen.

There are already hopes that actual tactical surprise has
been attained, and we hope to furnish the enemy with a
succession of surprises during the course of the fighting.
The battle that has now begun will grow constantly in
scale and intensity for many weeks to come, and I shall not
attempt to speculate upon its course. This I must say,
however. Complete unity prevails throughout the Allied
Armies. There is a brotherhood in arms between us and
our friends of the United States. There is complete confidence in the supreme commander, General Eisenhower,
and his lieutenants, and also in the commander of the
Expeditionary Force, General Montgomery. The ardour

and spirit of the troops, as I saw myself, embarking in these last few days was splendid to witness. Nothing that equipment, science or forethought could do has been neglected, and the whole process of opening this great new front will be pursued with the utmost resolution both by the commanders and by the United States and British Governments whom they serve.

I have been at the centres where the latest information is received, and I can state to the House that this operation is proceeding in a thoroughly satisfactory manner. Many dangers and difficulties which at this time last night appeared extremely formidable are behind us. The passage of the sea has been made with far less loss than we apprehended. The resistance of the batteries has been greatly weakened by the bombing of the Air Force, and the superior bombardment of our ships quickly reduced their fire to dimensions which did not affect the problem. The landings of the troops on a broad front, both British and American—Allied troops, I will not give lists of all the different nationalities they represent—but the landings along the whole front have been effective, and our troops have penetrated, in some cases, several miles inland. Lodgments exist on a broad front.

The outstanding feature has been the landings of the airborne troops, which were on a scale far larger than anything that has been seen so far in the world. These landings took place with extremely little loss and with great accuracy. Particular anxiety attached to them, because the conditions of light prevailing in the very limited period of the dawn—just before the dawn—the conditions of visibility made all the difference. Indeed, there might have been something happening at the last minute which would have prevented air-borne troops from playing their part.

A very great degree of risk had to be taken in respect of the weather.

But General Eisenhower's courage is equal to all the necessary decisions that have to be taken in these extremely difficult and uncontrollable matters. The air-borne troops are well established, and the landings and the follow-ups are all proceeding with much less loss—very much less—than we expected. Fighting is in progress at various points. We have captured various bridges which were of importance, and which were not blown up. There is even fighting proceeding in the town of Caen, inland. But all this, although a very valuable first step—a vital and essential first step—gives no indication of what may be the course of the battle in the next days and weeks, because the enemy will now probably endeavour to concentrate on this area, and in that event heavy fighting will soon begin and will continue without end, as we can push troops in and he can bring other troops up. It is therefore, a most serious time that we enter upon. Thank God, we enter upon it with our great Allies all in good heart and all in good friendship.

THE FLYING BOMB

July 6th 1944

This form of attack is, no doubt, of a trying character, a worrisome character, because of its being spread out throughout the whole of the 24 hours, but people have just got to get used to that. Everyone must go about his duty and his business, whatever it may be—every man or woman —and then, when the long day is done, they should seek the safest shelter that they can find and forget their cares in well-earned sleep. We must neither underrate nor exaggerate. In all up to six a.m. to-day, about 2,750 flying bombs have been discharged from the launching stations along the French coast. A very large proportion of these have either failed to cross the Channel or have been shot down and destroyed by various methods, including the great deployment of batteries, aircraft and balloons which have been very rapidly placed in position. Batteries move to any position in which they are required and take up their positions rapidly, but once on the site great improvements can be made in the electrical connections and so forth ; and the Air Force, confronted with the somewhat novel problem of chasing a projectile, has found new methods every day.

As to evacuation, as I have said, everyone must remain at his post and discharge his daily duty. The House would be affronted if any suggestion were made to it that it should change its location from London. Here we began the war, and here we will see it ended. We are not, however, discouraging people who have no essential work to do from leaving London at their own expense if they feel inclined to do so by the arrangements they make. In fact, they assist our affairs by taking such action at their own expense. We do not need more people in London than are required for business purposes of peace and war. For people of small means, who are not engaged in war work and wish to leave, registers have been opened and arrangements will be made for their transfer as speedily as possible to safer areas. Children are already being sent at their parents' wish out of the danger areas, which are by no means exclusively confined to the Metropolis. There is, of course, the bomb highway over which the robots all pass before reaching that point of southern England which I

have ventured to particularize this morning. Children are
being sent, if their parents wish, out of the danger areas,
and in all cases mothers with small children, or pregnant
women, will be given full facilities by the State. And we
do not propose to separate the mother from the child
except by her wish, but a terrible thing happened last time.
Mothers were separated from children of two or three
years of age, and, after a period, when they had saved up
money and got time to go down and see them, the children
hardly knew them. I hope now with our growing strength,
reserves and facilities for removal, we shall be able to say
to a mother of three or four children, " If you wish to
leave, it is perfectly possible. Arrangements will be made
to take you into the country with your children. If you
wish them to go by themselves and you wish to stay here
with your husband, or because of your son, then arrangements can be made that way too ".

The House will ask, What of the future? Is this attack
going to get worse, or is it going to be beat like the magnetic mine, or beat like the attempted destruction of
Britain by the aeroplane, or beat as the U-boat campaign
was beat? Will new developments, on the other hand, of
a far more formidable character, come upon us? Will the
rocket bomb come? Will improved explosives come? Will
greater ranges, faster speeds, and larger war-heads come
upon us? I can give no guarantee that any of these evils
will be entirely prevented before the time comes, as come
it will, when the soil from which these attacks are launched
has been finally liberated from the enemy's grip. In the
meantime I can only say that when I visited various scenes
of bomb explosions on Saturday, only one man of many
hundreds whom I saw asked a question. The question
was, " What are you going to do about it? " I replied,

" Everything in human power, and we have never failed yet." He seemed contented with the reply. That is the only promise I can make.

I must, however, make it perfectly plain—I do not want there to be any misunderstanding on this point—that we shall not allow the battle operations in Normandy or the attacks we are making against special targets in Germany to suffer. They come first, and we must fit our own domestic arrangements into the general scheme of war operations. There can be no question of allowing the slightest weakening of the battle in order to diminish in scale injuries which, though they may inflict grievous suffering on many people and change to some extent the normal, regular life and industry of London, will never stand between the British nation and their duty in the van of a victorious and avenging world. It may be a comfort to some to feel that they are sharing in no small degree the perils of our soldiers overseas, and that the blows which fall on them diminish those which in other forms would have smitten our fighting men and their Allies. But I am sure of one thing, that London will never be conquered and will never fail, and that her renown, triumphing over every ordeal, will long shine among men.

THE INVASION OF FRANCE

August 2nd 1944

A volume would be required to recount the story of the crossing of the Channel and the landing of the Armies of Liberation upon the soil of France. I have only a few minutes, and therefore I must practise the selective art as far as possible. In April, 1943, General Morgan, of the British Army, became the head of the British and American Planning Staff, which surveyed the whole project by the decision of the Combined Chiefs of Staff Committee. They made a plan, which I took with me last year to Quebec, where it was submitted to the President and the Combined British and American Chiefs of Staff. This plan selected the beaches for the attack and presented the outlines of the scheme, together with a mass of detail to support it. It received, in principle, complete agreement. It is rather remarkable that a secret of this character which had to be entrusted from the beginning to scores, very soon to hundreds and ultimately to thousands of people, never leaked out either in these Islands or the wide expanses of the United States.

At Teheran, we promised Marshal Stalin we would put this plan, or something like it, into operation at the end of May or the beginning of June, and he for his part promised that the whole of the Russian Armies would be thrown, as indeed they have been, into the general battle in the East. In January of this year, the commanders were appointed. The Mediterranean had a British commander, General Wilson, and General Eisenhower assumed the command of the Expeditionary Forces gathered in Britain. No man has ever laboured more skilfully or intensely for the unification and goodwill of the great forces under his command than General Eisenhower. He has a genius for bringing all the Allies together, and is proud to consider himself an Allied as well as a United States Commander. The names of all the distinguished commanders are already familiar to the House and the country.

General Eisenhower forthwith appointed the Commander-in-Chief of the British Expeditionary Army,

General Montgomery, to the command of all the invading troops, British and American. For more than a year past, American stores, equipment and men have been moving steadily into these Islands, and we ourselves have selected from the British Armies here an expeditionary force which was practically as large as that of the United States in the opening stage. Great reinforcements which flow in from America have already altered, and will continually alter that balance, but in the great adventure we were practically equal. The training of all these troops was undertaken in a most strenuous fashion. The plan also provided for the successive landings which were to be made in relation to the major thrust. The great episode seemed to everyone to be the crossing of the Channel, with its stormy waters, swift currents and 18-foot rise and fall of the tide, and above all the changes of weather, which when an operation as big as this has to be undertaken might easily cut a portion of the Army off upon the shore for several days without anyone being able to get to them to reinforce them or even to withdraw them, and thus leave them at the mercy of a superior enemy. That was the element, this possible change in the weather, which certainly hung like a vulture poised in the sky over the thoughts of the most sanguine.

In all these matters, the work of the Combined Operations Headquarters, founded in 1940 under Admiral Keyes for the purpose of amphibious warfare, and developed since 1942 by Admiral Mountbatten, proved its value. As is well-known, I was opposed to making this great invasion across the Channel in 1942, and thereafter it was plainly impossible in 1943, owing to our having chosen the Mediterranean and our amphibious resources all being concentrated there. Now we were all agreed, and the Commanders took the vast mass of knowledge which had been accumulated and put their own stamp upon it, improving the plan in many ways and animating and training their troops to fit in to its different phases and features.

I do not believe myself that this vast enterprise could have been executed earlier. We had not the experience. We had not the tackle. But before we launched the attack in 1944 we had made five successful opposed landings in the Mediterranean, and a mass of wonderful craft of all kinds had been devised by our services and by our United States colleagues on the other side of the ocean. The bulk of these had to be constructed in the United States, although our own yards were strained and gorged to the utmost. There are more than 60 variants of these landing craft and escort vessels, and they provide for the landing, not only of an army, but of everything that an army can need.

For instance, I myself saw a few days after the landing was complete six of these large landing craft—I should say, medium landing craft, vessels of considerable size—charge up in line together till they were stopped by the sloping sandy beach; down fell their drawbridges, out poured their vehicles, and in a few minutes an entire heavy battery was drawn up in column of route ready for immediate action. I had this timed, because I certainly thought it would be a matter of hours, but in less than 15 minutes these heavy craft had pushed themselves off the shore and were returning to England for another consignment. This is a new atmosphere, a new light upon the possibility of an invasion across the Channel, which I hope will not be altogether lost upon our own people in the days when many of us have handed over our burdens to others. The marvellous American invention spelt D.U.K.W. is a heavy lorry which goes at between 40 and 50 miles an hour along the road, and can plunge into the water and swim out for miles to sea in quite choppy weather, returning with a load of several tons, coming ashore and going off to wherever it is specially needed.

An immense system of harbours, breakwaters and landing stages was also prepared which, as soon as the foothold was gained, could be disposed in their appropriate places to give large sheltered water space. In less than a month, harbours had been created compared with which Dover seems small. At these harbours, and on the beaches they protect, a very large army, with the entire elaborate equipment of modern armies, which have about one vehicle for every four or five men, was landed, and by the end of June, in spite of the worst June gale for 40 years, a solid base had been created which gave us the certainty of being able to conduct an offensive campaign on the largest scale against any forces which, according to our calculations, the enemy was likely to bring.

These operations were protected and supported by a considerable British Fleet, assisted by a strong detachment of the American Fleet, the whole under Admiral Ramsay. In spite of gales, in spite of mines, in spite of more than 100 German submarines waiting baffled in the Biscay Ports, and a swarm of E-boats and other marauders, ceaseless traffic has been maintained over the 100-miles stretch of channel, and General Eisenhower, with his lieutenant, General Montgomery, now stands at the head of a very large and powerful Army, equipped as no army has ever been equipped before.

Overwhelming air power was, of course, as indispensable as sea power to the carrying out of such an operation.

The strategic bombing by the combined British and American Bomber Forces, and the use of the medium bomber and fighter forces, was the essential prelude to our landing in Normandy. Preparations definitely began for the battle in April, and, not only at the point of attack, for that would have revealed too much, but necessarily impartially all along the coast and far in the rear. Thus when our ships crossed the Channel, unseen and un-molested, half the guns that were to have blown them out of the water were already dismantled or silent, and when the counter-attack began on the land and under the sea, the Tactical and Coastal air forces held it back while our foothold on shore and our sea-lanes were being firmly established.

These deeds of the Air Force were not done without losses, which, in killed, and in proportion to the number of flying personnel, far exceeded those of any branch of the Services. If we take April 1 as the opening of the air campaign and from then till June 30, over 7,000 men of the Home Command from the R.A.F. alone have been killed or are missing. United States losses are also most severe. The devotion of the pilots and the air crews of both countries was sublime.

Since those days we have been in constant battle, General Omar Bradley clearing the Cherbourg Peninsula, and General Dempsey occupying the area around Caen. We have inflicted losses on the enemy which are about double those we have suffered ourselves. It is remarkable considering we were the challengers, and unusual com-pared with the experiences of the last war. We have been hampered continually by the most unseasonable weather, which by its early mists and low clouds has day after day put off operations by rendering impossible the avalanche of fire and steel with which our air power prepares for an attack. Now at last we are gaining that space in which to deploy which is necessary for armies of the size that we are using.

VICTORY
"GOD BLESS YOU ALL"
May 9th 1945

God bless you all! This is your victory! It is the victory of the cause of freedom in every land. In all our long history we have never seen a greater day than this. Everyone, man or woman, has done their best. Every one has tried. Neither the long years, nor the dangers, nor the fierce attacks of the enemy, have in any way weakened the independent resolve of the British nation. God bless you all!

"BACK THRO' THE JAWS OF DEATH"
May 9th 1945

We were the first in this innocent land to draw the sword against Germany. After a while we were left alone against the most tremendous military power that has been seen. We were alone for a whole year. There we stood. Did anyone want to give in? Were we down-hearted? The lights went out, and the bombs came down, but every man, woman and child in this country had no thought of quitting the struggle. London could take it. So we came back after long months, " Back thro' the jaws of Death, Back from the mouth of Hell," while " All the world wonder'd ".

When shall the reputation and faith of this generation of English men and women fail? I say that in the long years to come not only the people of this island, but from all over the world, wherever the bird of freedom chirps in human hearts, they will look back to what we have done, and they will say " Don't despair. Don't yield to violence and tyranny. March straight forward and die, if need be, unconquered".

IS IT THE END?

The story of the human race is War. Except for brief and precarious interludes there has never been peace in the world ; and before history began murderous strife was universal and unending. But the modern developments surely require severe and active attention.

Up to the present time the means of destruction at the disposal of man have not kept pace with his ferocity. Reciprocal extermination was impossible in the Stone Age. One cannot do much with a clumsy club. Besides, men were so scarce and hid so well that they were hard to find. They fled so fast that they were hard to catch. Human legs could only cover a certain distance each day. With the best will in the world to destroy his species, each man was restricted to a very limited field of activity. It was impossible to make any effective progress on these lines,

Meanwhile one had to live and hunt and sleep. So on the balance the life-forces kept a steady lead over the forces of death, and gradually tribes, villages, and Governments were evolved.

The effort at destruction then entered upon a new phase. War became a collective enterprise. Roads were made which facilitated the movement of large numbers of men. Armies were organized. Many improvements in the apparatus of slaughter were devised. In particular the use of metal, and above all, steel, for piercing and cutting human flesh, opened out a promising field. Bows and arrows, slings, chariots, horses, and elephants lent a valuable assistance. But here again another set of checks began to operate. The Governments were not sufficiently secure. The Armies were liable to violent internal disagreements. It was extremely difficult to feed large numbers of men once they were concentrated, and consequently the efficiency of the efforts at destruction became fitful and was tremendously hampered by defective organization. Thus again there was a balance on the credit side of life. The world rolled forward, and human society entered upon a vaster and more complex age.

It was not until the dawn of the twentieth century of the Christian era that War really began to enter into its kingdom as the potential destroyer of the human race. The organization of mankind into great States and Empires and the rise of nations to full collective consciousness enabled enterprises of slaughter to be planned and executed upon a scale, with a perseverance, never before imagined. All the noblest virtues of individuals were gathered together to strengthen the destructive capacity of the mass. Good finances, the resources of world-wide credit and trade, the accumulation of large capital reserves, made it possible to divert for considerable periods the energies of whole peoples to the task of Devastation. Democratic institutions gave expression to the will-power of millions. Education not only brought the course of the conflict within the comprehension of every one, but rendered each person serviceable in a high degree for the purpose in hand. The Press afforded a means of unification and of mutual encouragement; Religion, having discreetly avoided conflict on the fundamental issues, offered its encouragements and consolations, through all its forms, impartially to all the combatants. Lastly, Science unfolded her treasures and her secrets to the desperate demands of men and placed in their hands agencies and apparatus almost decisive in their character. . . .

Certain sombre facts emerge solid, inexorable, like the shapes of mountains from drifting mist. It is established that henceforward whole populations will take part in war, all doing their utmost, all subjected to the fury of the enemy. It is established that nations who believe their life is at stake will not be restrained from using any means to secure their existence. It is probable—nay, certain— that among the means which will next time be at their disposal will be agencies and processes of destruction wholesale, unlimited, and perhaps, once launched, uncontrollable.

Mankind has never been in this position before. Without having improved appreciably in virtue or enjoying wiser guidance, it has got into its hands for the first time the tools by which it can unfailingly accomplish its own extermination. That is the point in human destinies to which all the glories and toils of men have at last led them. They would do well to pause and ponder upon their new responsibilities. Death stands at attention, obedient, expectant, ready to serve, ready to shear away the peoples *en masse* ; ready, if called on, to pulverize, without hope of repair, what is left of civilization. He awaits only the word of command. He awaits it from a frail, bewildered being, long his victim, now—for one occasion only—his Master.

PAINTING AS A HOBBY

Change is the master key. A man can wear out a particular part of his mind by continually using it and tiring it, just in the same way as he can wear out the elbows of his coat. There is, however, this difference between the living cells of the brain and inanimate articles : one cannot mend the frayed elbows of a coat by rubbing the sleeves or shoulders ; but the tired parts of the mind can be rested and strengthened not merely by rest, but by using other parts. It is not enough merely to switch off the lights which play upon the main and ordinary field of interest ; a new field of interest must be illuminated. It is no use saying to the tired " mental muscles "—if one may coin such an expression—" I will give you a good rest ", " I will go for a long walk ", or " I will lie down and think of nothing ". The mind keeps busy just the same. If it has been weighing and measuring, it goes on weighing and measuring. If it has been worrying, it goes on worrying. It is only when new cells are called into activity, when new stars become the lords of the ascendant, that relief, repose, refreshment are afforded.

A gifted American psychologist has said, " Worry is a spasm of the emotion ; the mind catches hold of something and will not let it go ". It is useless to argue with the mind in this condition. The stronger the will, the more futile the task. One can only gently insinuate something else into its convulsive grasp. And if this something else is rightly chosen, if it is really attended by the illumination of another field of interest, gradually, and often quite swiftly, the old undue grip relaxes and the process of recuperation and repair begins.

The cultivation of a hobby and new forms of interest is therefore a policy of first importance to a public man. But this is not a business that can be undertaken in a day or swiftly improvised by a mere command of the will. The growth of alternative mental interests is a long process. The seeds must be carefully chosen ; they must fall on good ground ; they must be sedulously tended, if the vivifying fruits are to be at hand when needed.

To be really happy and really safe, one ought to have at least two or three hobbies, and they must all be real. It is no use starting late in life to say : " I will take an interest in this or that ". Such an attempt only aggravates the strain of mental effort. A man may acquire great knowledge of topics unconnected with his daily work, and yet hardly get any benefit or relief. It is no use doing what you like ; you have got to like what you do. Broadly speaking, human beings may be divided into three classes : those who are toiled to death, those who are worried to death, and those who are bored to death. It is no use offering the manual labourer, tired out with a hard week's sweat and effort, the chance of playing a game of football or baseball on Saturday afternoon. It is no use inviting the politician or the professional or business man, who has been working or worrying about serious things for six days, to work or worry about trifling things at the week-end.

As for the unfortunate people who can command everything they want, who can gratify every caprice and lay their hands on almost every object of desire—for them a new pleasure, a new excitement is only an additional satiation. In vain they rush frantically round from place to place, trying to escape from avenging boredom by mere clatter and motion. For them discipline in one form or another is the most hopeful path.

Choose well, choose wisely, and choose one. Concentrate upon that one. Do not be content until you find yourself reading in it with real enjoyment. The process of reading for pleasure in another language rests the mental muscles ; it enlivens the mind by a different sequence and emphasis of ideas. The mere form of speech excites the activity of separate brain-cells, relieving in the most effective manner the fatigue of those in hackneyed use. One may imagine that a man who blew the trumpet for his living would be glad to play the violin for his amusement. So it is with reading in another language than your own.

But reading and book-love in all their forms suffer from one serious defect : they are too nearly akin to the ordinary daily round of the brain-worker to give that element of change and contrast essential to real relief. To restore psychic equilibrium we should call into use those parts of the mind which direct both eye and hand. Many men have found great advantage in practising a handicraft for pleasure. Joinery, chemistry, book-binding, even bricklaying—if one were interested in them and skilful at them —would give a real relief to the over-tired brain. But, best of all and easiest to procure are sketching and painting in all their forms. I consider myself very lucky that late in life I have been able to develop this new taste and pastime.

When I left the Admiralty at the end of May, 1915, I still remained a member of the Cabinet and of the War Council. In this position I knew everything and could do nothing. The change from the intense executive activities of each day's work at the Admiralty to the narrowly-measured duties of a counsellor left me gasping. Like a sea-beast fished up from the depths, or a diver too suddenly hoisted, my veins threatened to burst from the fall in pressure. I had great anxiety and no means of relieving it ; I had vehement convictions and small power to give effect to them. I had to watch the unhappy casting-away of great opportunities, and the feeble execution of plans which I had launched and in which I heartily believed. I had long hours of utterly unwonted leisure in which to contemplate the frightful unfolding of the War. At a moment when every fibre of my being was inflamed to action, I was forced to remain a spectator of the tragedy, placed cruelly in a front seat. And then it was that the Muse of Painting came to my rescue—out of charity and out of chivalry, because after all she had nothing to do with me—and said, " Are these toys any good to you? They amuse some people ".

Some experiments one Sunday in the country with the children's paint-box led me to procure the next morning a complete outfit for painting in oils.

Having bought the colours, an easel, and a canvas, the next step was *to begin*. But what a step to take! The palette gleamed with beads of colour ; fair and white rose the canvas ; the empty brush hung poised, heavy with destiny, irresolute in the air. My hand seemed arrested by a silent veto. But after all the sky on this occasion was unquestion-ably blue, and a pale blue at that. There could be no doubt that blue paint mixed with white should be put on the top part of the canvas. One really does not need to have had an artist's training to see that. It is a starting-point open to all. So very gingerly I mixed a little blue paint on the palette with a very small brush, and then with infinite precaution made a mark about as big as a bean upon the affronted snow-white shield. It was a challenge, a deliberate challenge ; but so subdued, so halting, indeed so cataleptic, that it deserved no response. At that moment the loud approaching sound of a motor-car was heard in the drive. From this chariot there stepped swiftly and lightly none other than the gifted wife of Sir John Lavery. "Painting! But what are you hesitating about? Let me have a brush—the big one." Splash into the turpentine, wallop into the blue and white, frantic flourish on the palette— clean no longer—and then several large, fierce strokes and slashes of blue on the absolutely cowering canvas. Anyone could see that it could not hit back. No evil fate avenged the jaunty violence. The canvas grinned in helplessness before me. The spell was broken. The sickly inhibitions rolled away. I seized the largest brush and fell upon my victim with Berserk fury. I have never felt any awe of a canvas since.

Painting is a companion with whom one may hope to walk a great part of life's journey,

> *Age cannot wither her nor custom stale*
> *Her infinite variety.*

One by one the more vigorous sports and exacting games fall away. Exceptional exertions are purchased only by a more pronounced and more prolonged fatigue. Muscles may relax, and feet and hands slow down ; the nerve of youth and manhood may become less trusty. But painting is a friend who makes no undue demands, excites to no exhausting pursuits, keeps faithful pace even with feeble steps, and holds her canvas as a screen between us and the envious eyes of Time or the surly advance of Decrepitude.

Happy are the painters, for they shall not be lonely, Light and colour, peace and hope, will keep them company to the end, or almost to the end, of the day.

NOTES

FAMILY

The Rt. Hon. Winston Spencer Churchill, P.C. (1907), O.M. (1946), C.H. (1922), F.R.S. (1941), Lord Warden of the Cinque Ports since 1941, was born on November 30th, 1874. He was the eldest son of the late Rt. Hon. Lord Randolph Churchill, 3rd son of the 7th Duke of Marlborough, Secretary of State for India (1885–6), Chancellor of the Exchequer and Leader of the House of Commons (1886), and Jennie, daughter of Mr. Leonard Jerome of New York, U.S.A., whom Lord Randolph met and married at the British Embassy in Paris.

In 1909 Winston Churchill married Clementine Ogilvy, daughter of the late Sir Henry Hozier and the late Lady Blanche Hozier, daughter of the 9th Earl of Airlie.

There have been five children of the marriage: Captain Randolph Churchill, M.P. for Preston 1940–5 ; Diana, wife of Duncan Sandys, M.P ; Sarah, stage and screen actress, wife of Anthony Beauchamp ; Mary, wife of Captain Christopher Soames, M.P. for Bedford since February 1950 ; and Marigold, born 1918, died 1921.

CONSTITUENCIES

Winston Churchill has represented the following constituencies in Parliament :

As a Conservative :	Oldham, Lancashire, 1900–6.
As a Liberal :	Manchester, North-West, 1906–8.
	Dundee, 1908–22.
	Leicester, West, 1923.
As an Independent :	Westminster, Abbey Division, 1924.
As a Constitutionalist :	Essex, Epping Division, 1924–8.
As a Conservative :	Essex, Epping Division, 1929–45.
	Essex, Woodford Division, 1945–

OFFICES AND HONOURS

1906–8	Under-Secretary for the Colonies.
1908–10	President of the Board of Trade.
1910–11	Home Secretary.
1911–15	First Lord of the Admiralty
1915	Chancellor of the Duchy of Lancaster.
1917–18	Minister of Munitions.
1918–21	Secretary of State for War and for Air.
1921–22	Secretary for the Colonies.
1924–29	Chancellor of the Exchequer.
1939–40	First Lord of the Admiralty.
1940–45	Prime Minister and Minister of Defence.
1945–51	Leader of the Opposition.
1951	Prime Minister and Minister of Defence.

1907	Privy Councillor
1922	Companion of Honour
1929–32	Lord Rector of Aberdeen University.
1930	Chancellor of Bristol University.
1946	Order of Merit.
1948	Hon. Academician Extraordinary of the Royal Academy.

PUBLICATIONS

The Story of the Malakand Field Force, 1898.
The River War, 1899.
Savrola, a novel, 1909
London to Ladysmith via Pretoria, 1900.
Lord Randolph Churchill, 1906.
My African Journey, 1908.
Liberalism and the Social Problem, 1910.
The World Crisis, (1911–1918) 4 volumes, 1923–9.
The World Crisis : The Aftermath, 1929.
My Early Life, 1930.
The World Crisis: The Eastern Front, 1931.
Thoughts and Adventures, 1932.

NOTES

P. 1. *Fenians:* A secret society organised in 1866–7 among Irishmen in America ; after an attempt to invade Canada they tried unsuccessfully to start a rebellion in Ireland, to bring about the repeal of the Act of Union with England, 1800.

P. 12. *Battle of Omdurman:* 1898, the last decisive battle in the British campaign under Kitchener's command against the Dervishes in the Sudan.

P. 16. *Boer War:* 1899–1902. The " Boers " were descendants of the Dutch who settled at the Cape of Good Hope in 1650. They resented later British settlers, moved inland in 1836 in " The Great Trek ", and founded the Transvaal Republic. During the 1890's, Paul Kruger, their President, refused full citizens' rights to the English " foreigners " (" Uitlanders ") who were developing the diamond and gold mines in the Transvaal. Kruger, hoping to evict the British altogether, prepared for war. The situation was aggravated by an ineffective armed raid on the Transvaal by Uitlanders, led by Dr. Jameson, in 1896, which the Boers easily suppressed. War finally broke out in 1899. Churchill went to South Africa as principal War Correspondent of the *Morning Post.*

P. 23. *The Relief of Ladysmith:* In October, 1899, soon after the outbreak of war, three British forces were surrounded and besieged : the main force at Ladysmith in Natal, and two smaller forces at Kimberley and Mafeking. Ladysmith and Kimberley were eventually relieved by British reinforcements in February, Mafeking not until May 1900.

P. 27. *The House of Commons:* After an unsuccessful attempt the previous year, Mr. Churchill was returned to the House of Commons as Member for Oldham, Lancashire, in 1900.

P. 41. *Moltke:* Count Helmuth von Moltke (1800–91), Prussian soldier. Reorganiser of Prussian army 1858–63, and director of strategy in the Franco-Prussian War 1870–1 ; created field-marshal 1871.

P. 43. *Agadir Crisis:* After the Treaty of Algeciras (1906) France had control of the zone of Morocco, and had to send an expedition to maintain order in April 1911. Germany interpreted this move as a preliminary to France's annexing the territory, and promptly sent a gunboat to Agadir harbour, on the Atlantic coast of Morocco, to protect German interests, and demanded a share in a partitioned Morocco.

" *Bec de Canard*": The name given to the north-eastern corner of the German Cameroons because it was shaped like a duck's bill.

P. 44. *Wieringen:* an island on the Zuider Zee, to which the Crown Prince fled in 1918.

von Tirpitz: Alfred von Tirpitz (1849–1930) German admiral, creator of the modern German navy, and director of it during the First World War.

P. 45. *Mr. Haldane:* Richard Burdon Haldane (1856–1928) Viscount Haldane of Cloan (1911). Secretary of State for War 1905–1912 during which time he completely re-organised the British Army and created the Territorial Reserve.

P. 48. *Dual Monarchy:* System which came into effect in 1867 by which Austria and Hungary had separate governments but were united under the Emperor of Austria.

Sarajevo: capital city of Bosnia, situated in the south-east of the country.

P. 50. *Assassination of King Alexander and Queen Draga at Belgrade,* 1903: Alexander I of Serbia (1876-1903) succeeded to the throne in 1889. He became very unpopular after his marriage with Mme. Draga Mashin, and both were murdered by disaffected Serbian officers.

Nihilists: Members of an extreme anti-social Russian revolutionary party formed about 1870, Nihilism being a complete negation of everything in the order of things as then constituted.

P. 51. *Berchtold:* Count Leopold von Berchtold (1863-1942), Austro-Hungarian statesman, Foreign Minister 1912-1915.

P. 54. *Morganatic marriage:* A marriage where the man is of higher rank than the woman, and by which the wife and children have no share of the husband's rank and privilege.

P. 55. *Count Hoyos:* Permanent official at the head of the Austrian Foreign Office, and trusted confidant of Count Berchtold.

Herr von Bethmann-Hollweg: Theobald von Bethmann-Hollweg (1856-1921), German statesman, successor to von Bülow as Chancellor of the German Empire, 1909-1917.

P. 56. *Triple Entente:* Great Britain had settled differences with France (1904) and Russia (1907), and the three Powers became known as the Triple Entente, as against the Triple Alliance, a military agreement between Germany, Austria and Italy.

P. 57. *" Mailed fist " and " shining armour ":* Notorious phrases from boastful speeches about Germany's military power made by the Kaiser earlier in his reign.

Falkenhayn: Erich von Falkenhayn (1861-1922), German general, commander of one of the German armies invading Roumania in 1916.

P. 58. *Conrad:* Count Franz Conrad von Hötzendorf (1852–1925), Austrian field-marshal and chief of staff of the Austro-Hungarian Army.

Ballplatz: Seat of the Austrian Foreign Office.

P. 62. *Shenandoah Valley:* In 1862–4 this part of Virginia was the scene of several important engagements in the American Civil War.

P. 64. *Jagow:* Gottlieb von Jagow (1863–1935), German statesman, Foreign Secretary 1913–1916.

Tschirschky: H. von Tschirschky, German Ambassador in Vienna at the outbreak of the War.

P. 69. *Agonistes:* ἀγωνιστής, one who contends or struggles, as originally in Greece for a prize at public games. c.f. Milton's *Samson Agonistes.*

Battle of the Marne: " Germany lost the war at the Battle of the Marne, and it is only a question of how long it will take her to find it out."—Venizelos, Prime Minister of Greece, 1910–1920.

P. 71. *Castelnau:* Noël de Cusières de Castelnau (1851–1944), French general, chief of staff to General Joffre.

P. 72. *Admiral Sturdee:* Sir Frederick Charles Doveton Sturdee (1859–1925), British rear-admiral at the time, later Admiral of the Fleet.

P. 76. " *The silence following great words of Peace* ": Mr. Churchill's own footnote on these words reads : " Rupert Brooke—his last and most pregnant line."

P. 78. *Admiral Scheer:* Reinhard von Scheer (1863–1928), chief of staff of German High Seas Fleet, 1918.

P. 80. *Scapa Flow:* British naval base in the Orkney Islands.

Pompaedius Silo: In the Roman Social War Silo was leader of the Marsi, a people of the Sabellian race living in the Apennine hills. He was killed in battle against Metellus Pius, 88 B.C.

Marius: (157–86 B.C.) Seven times Consul, and in command when the Marsi were defeated in the Social War.

P. 81. *Pedrail and Caterpillar systems:* A pedrail has broad surfaces like feet attached to the rims of the wheels ; the caterpillar is an endless jointed steel band passing round both wheels.

Mr. Tennyson d'Eyncourt: Sir Eustace Henry William Tennyson d'Eyncourt naval architect, director of naval construction at the Admiralty, 1912–24, and leader of the committee which evolved the first tanks.

P. 86. *General Liman von Sanders:* Otto Liman von Sanders (1855–1929) German general in command of the 1st Turkish Army at the beginning of the War, and of the 5th Army in 1915.

P. 90 *Mustapha Kemal:* Later Kemal Atatürk (1881–1938), Turkish general and statesman, in command of Turkish divisions at Gallipoli. Became president of Turkish Republic (1923–38), during which time he inaugurated great reforms and was chiefly responsible for the modernisation of Turkey.

General Monro: Sir Charles Carmichael Monro (1860–1929) had been in command of an army in France, and succeeded Sir Ian Hamilton in October 1915 as commander of the Mediterranean expeditionary force at Gallipoli. He was subsequently Commander-in-Chief in India, and Governor of Gibraltar.

P. 92. *Captain Keyes:* (Sir) Roger John Brownlow Keyes (1872–1945), later Admiral of the Fleet Lord Keyes ; chief of staff, Eastern Mediterranean squadron, 1915.

P. 95. *General Joffre:* Joseph Jacques Césaire Joffre (1852–1931), Commander-in-Chief of the French armies at the outbreak of the War.

Sir Douglas Haig: (1861–1928) Later 1st Earl Haig. Commander-in-Chief of British expeditionary forces in France and Flanders, 1915–18.

Pétain: Henri Philippe Pétain (1856–1951), French general and statesman: defender in the First World War of Verdun, and created Marshal of France 1918, Minister of War 1934, Ambassador to Spain 1939. During the Second World War he became Premier of the French Government of Vichy,

K

and later Head of the State, after the defeat of France by the Germans in 1940. After the war he was condemned for treachery to imprisonment for life.

P. 98. *The Battle Cruiser Action:* The preliminary com- bat of the battle cruisers, before the battle of the main fleets off Jutland, was a self-contained episode.

P. 104. *Q-Ships:* Warships disguised as harmless mer- chantmen.

P. 109. *Mackensen:* August von Mackensen (1849–1945), field-marshal, in command of the German armies in Roumania in 1916.

Ludendorff: Erich Friedrich Wilhelm Ludendorff (1865– 1937), German general and politician; quartermaster-general of the German army in 1914, later in command of German armies in France, where his strategy in 1918 almost defeated the Allies.

P. 113. *Rasputin:* Grigori Efimovich Rasputin (1871?– 1916), Russian monk, son of a Siberian peasant. In St. Peters- burg from 1907 onwards he exerted a malign and magnetic influence over the Czarina and the Russian Court. He was assassinated by Russian noblemen in Dec., 1916.

Duma: Russian parliament.

P. 114. *Kerenski:* Alexander Feodorovich Kerenski, born 1881, Russian Socialist revolutionary, held ministerial positions after the first Revolution, becoming Prime Minister for a few months, till he was overthrown by the Bolshevik Revolu- tion at the end of 1917, when he fled to Paris.

Grand Duke Nicholas: (1856–1929) Commander of the Russian armies in the Caucasus from 1914. Later chosen as the leader of the Russian monarchists in exile in France.

P. 115. *Alexeiev:* Mikhail Vasilievich Alexeiev (1857– 1918), Russian general, chief of the Russian Imperial general staff, 1915–16.

Stavka: The Russian military headquarters.

Ruzski: Russian general, in command on the North-Western Front.

P. 117. *Zemstvos:* Centres of Russian local government.

Trotski: Leon Trotski (1877–1940), Russian Communist leader. Twice exiled to Siberia as a revolutionary, escaping first to England, secondly to Vienna. Returned to Russia after 1917 Revolution and was placed in charge of foreign affairs, later transferring to the War Ministry. He was a loyal associate of Lenin, and was defeated after Lenin's death by Stalin for leadership of the Communist party (1924). Having been expelled from the party and exiled from Russia in 1929, he lived in Mexico until he was murdered in 1940.

Zinoviev: Grigori Evseevich Zinoviev (1883–1936), Russian Communist leader ; worked with Lenin in forming the Bolshevik group in 1903. Returned from exile in 1917, and became leader of the Third International in 1919. A letter from him to British Communists in 1924, encouraging the subversion of the Armed Forces as a means of overthrowing existing British institutions, caused the defeat of the Socialist Government under Ramsay MacDonald.

P. 121. *Tudor:* General Tudor, Commander of the British 9th Division in France, 1918, and a friend of Churchill's since his days in the Army in India.

P. 123. *Jena:* Battle fought in central Germany on October 14th, 1806, when the Prussian armies were heavily defeated by the French under Napoleon.

Confederates under Lee: The Confederate States of America was the name adopted by the eleven Southern States which seceded from the American Union in 1861, forming a confederacy with their own President, and causing the Civil War, 1861–65. General Robert E. Lee (1807–70) of Virginia became the Commander of the Confederate Army in 1861.

P. 127. *Prince Max of Baden:* (1867–1929) Heir presumptive to the grand-ducal throne of Baden ; became Imperial Chancellor when the German Army collapsed, October 1918, and initiated negotiations for an Armistice.

The Fourteen Points: Principles enunciated in January 1918 by Woodrow Wilson, President of the United States, on which a Peace Treaty should be based.

K 2

Hindenburg: Paul von Hindenburg (1847–1934), German field-marshal, chief of staff 1916, co-director with Ludendorff of German strategy for the remainder of the War. In 1925 he was elected President of Germany and again in 1932, when he was forced to yield to the Nazis and appointed Hitler as Chancellor.

P. 133. *Vereeniging:* The Peace of Vereeniging, ending the South African War, was signed on May 31st, 1902.

P. 135. *Unarm, Eros; the long day's task is done. . . . :* Shakespeare, *Antony and Cleopatra*, IV, xiv, 35.

P. 138. *Flammenwerfer:* flame-throwers.

Karl Marx: (1818–83), German Socialist and Ph.D. (Berlin). He published in 1847 *The Communist Manifesto*. After being expelled from Prussia he lived the rest of his life in London, being for some years the moving spirit of the International Working Men's Association. In 1867 he published *Das Kapital*, the Bible of the German Socialists and Russian Bolsheviks.

Omar: (581?–644), Arabian caliph, originally opposed to Mahomet and the new religion, then converted to Islam and did a great deal to extend the Moslem Empire. He inaugurated the system of dating Mahometan events from the *hegira*, the date, Sept. 20th, 622, when Mahomet arrived in Medina, having fled from Mecca during the early persecutions of the Mahometan religion.

P. 139. *Populists:* Members of the American " People's Party ", formed in 1891, which advocated increase of currency, public ownership and operation of railways, telegraphs, income tax, limitation of land ownership, etc.

Tamerlane: or Timur (1336–1405), famous Eastern conqueror. After making himself King of Samarkand, he conquered Persia and Caucasia, and invaded India, Syria and China.

Jenghiz Khan: (1162–1227) Mongol Emperor. After twice over-running China, he started on a great career of conquest in 1219. He drove the Turks before him into South-East Europe and ravaged South Russia and North India.

P. 140. *Capercailzie:* The largest European game bird.

Professor Sarolea: a distinguished Belgian writer on literature and politics. Most of his life has been spent in this country.

P. 141. *Kremlin:* The Citadel of Moscow, a large enclosure which contains palaces, churches and an arsenal, and is now the seat of the Communist government.

P. 142. *Dis:* Pluto, the God of the Infernal Regions.

Koltchak: Admiral Koltchak, who took refuge in Japan at the outbreak of the Russian Revolution, returned to Siberia and accepted supreme power as dictator, forming a government in Siberia in an attempt to overthrow the Bolsheviks and restore law and order.

Denikin: Anton Ivanovich Denikin, born 1872, Russian general who fled to the Caucasus at the outbreak of the Revolution and set up a South Russian Government in opposition to the Bolsheviks, but failed to gain popular confidence.

Bolsheviks: Members of the extreme wing of the Russian Socialist Party, later known as the Communists.

P. 143. *Savinkov:* Boris Victorovich Savinkov (1879–1925), Russian politician, a leader in terrorist activities at the beginning of the century. Became a minister in Kerenski's government (1917); opposed the Bolsheviks, first in Russia, later in Poland and France; eventually was arrested and condemned to life imprisonment.

Soviet: A Russian word meaning " council ", originally a council of Russian workmen. Later " The Soviet " came to mean the system of government by a congress of representatives from local soviets.

P. 147. *General Wrangel:* Baron Peter Nikolaevich Wrangel (1878–1928), Russian general, allied with Denikin, superseding him as commander of the anti-Bolshevik army in South Russia in April 1920: reorganised the army at first with some success, but was eventually defeated and fled to Yugoslavia.

Beresina: A Russian river which was crossed by Napoleon's main French Army, after terrible losses, in November 1812, during the retreat from Moscow,

P. 150. *Black and Tans:* A body of 5,800 armed men sent from England in 1920 to take the place of the Irish police during the Anglo-Irish conflict : so called from the colour of their clothing.

Sinn Fein: The revolutionary Irish nationalist party, whose members refused to attend Parliament at Westminster after the 1918 election, and set up their own " Republican Government " in Dublin.

The Irish Settlement: The Treaty signed on December 6th, 1921, giving Ireland full Dominion Status under the style of the Irish Free State, preceded by long negotiations between the British Government and Mr. de Valera, the leader of the Southern Irish revolutionaries.

P. 151. *Mr. Griffith:* Arthur Griffith (1872–1922), Sinn Fein leader, became head of the Free State executive.

Michael Collins: (1890–1922) A daring leader of guerrilla warfare in Ireland, later became commander-in-chief of the Free State army, and was killed in an ambush by opponents of the Treaty.

P. 152. *Mr. Duggan:* Edmund John Duggan, afterwards Home Secretary in the Free State Government, and later a Senator.

Mr. Erskine Childers: (1870–1922) Anglo-Irish writer and political figure ; devoted himself to the cause of complete republican independence for Ireland, opposing the Anglo-Irish Treaty and becoming an active rebel within the Republican Army : he was eventually court-martialled and shot by Free State soldiers.

P. 154. *With Essex and with Strafford, with Pitt and with Gladstone*: Successive English statesmen, from Elizabethan to Victorian times, who failed in their various attempts to solve the Irish problem.

Lawrence of Arabia: Thomas Edward Lawrence (1888–1935), scholar and soldier, educated at Oxford High School and Jesus College, Oxford, became the romantic leader of the Arab revolt against the Turks, 1917–18. He attended the Paris Peace Conference in 1919 as adviser and interpreter to the

Emir Faisal of Syria, who was opposing the French demand for the mandate of Syria, which was eventually assigned to them. He described his adventures in the Palestine campaign in his great book *Seven Pillars of Wisdom* (1926) published in an abridged form as *Revolt in the Desert* (1927). He was disillusioned after the War by what he considered the Government's unsatisfactory treatment of the Arab demands. In 1922 he enlisted in the Royal Air Force as " J. H. Ross " but changed this name to " T. E. Shaw " in 1923. He was killed in May 1935, swerving on his high-speed motor-cycle to avoid two boys bicycling abreast.

P. 155. *Achilles' heel:* In Greek legend, Thetis held her son Achilles by his heel and dipped him in the River Styx, which made him invulnerable. He was slain by Paris whose arrow wounded him in the heel, which had not been touched by the water.

F. 159. *All is over! Fleet career....;* the opening lines of *The Last Leap,* by Adam Lindsay Gordon.

The Munich Agreement: The agreement signed in September 1938 between Germany, Great Britain, France and Italy, which averted the Second World War for a year, Germany being allowed to annex various zones of Czechoslovakia which Hitler had demanded on the grounds of the discontent of a number of Sudeten Germans living in Bohemia.

P. 160. *Herr Henlein:* Konrad Henlein (1898–1945), Sudeten-German politician, head of the Sudeten-German Party which headed the polls at the 1935 election in Czechoslovakia, and later Gauleiter of Sudetenland after the German occupation.

P. 164. *Tannenberg:* Decisive defeat in August 1914 of two Russian armies invading East Prussia by Hindenburg with Ludendorff as Chief of Staff.

John Bright: (1811–89) English orator and politician, actively connected in Parliament with movements for financial and electoral reform ; denounced the Crimean War ; advocated Irish disestablishment ; supported the North in the American Civil War ; was President of Board of Trade under Gladstone.

P. 165. *Sir Kingsley Wood:* (1881–1943) Postmaster-General 1931–35, Secretary of State for Air 1938–40, Chancellor of the Exchequer 1940 ff.

Lord Halifax: Viceroy of India 1926–31, Secretary of State for Foreign Affairs 1938–40, Ambassador to the United States 1941–46.

P. 167. *Schlieffen plan:* Named after its originator, the German field-marshal Count von Schlieffen; a strategy for defeating France in war, by which northern and southern armies, swinging from a central "hinge", would crush the French defences.

P. 176. *Arm yourselves. . . :* A version of *I. Maccabees,* 4, verses 58–60, in the Apocrypha.

P. 181. *Every morn brought forth . . . : The Passing of Arthur,* from *Idylls of the King,* 1,398, Tennyson.

P. 183. *He nothing common did . . . :* from *A Horatian de upon Cromwell's Return from Ireland,* Andrew Marvell.

P. 185. *General Weygand:* Maxime Weygand, born 1867, French soldier, took over the command in France during the 1940 retreat.

P. 188. *Mers-el-Kebir and Oran:* Military ports on the northern African coast of Morocco.

P. 204. *à neuf:* anew.

vantards: boasters.

Montmirail: Site, near the Marne in France, of an allied defeat by Napoleon on 11th February, 1814,

de leur vivant: in their lifetime.

piste: track.

âpre: bitter.

où qu'ils soient: wherever they may be.

la fierté: pride.

tressaillera: will leap.

P. 205. *Thiers:* Louis Adolphe Thiers (1797–1877) French statesman, negotiated peace treaty with Germany at the end of the Franco-Prussian War, and as first president of the Third Republic (1871–73) did much to rehabilitate France after that war.

1870: at the time of the Franco-Prussian war.

l'aube: the dawn.

P. 206. *Sail on, O Ship of State ! . . . :* last stanza of *The Building of the Ship* by Longfellow.

P. 207. *For while the tired waves . . . :* from *Say not the Struggle Nought Availeth* by Arthur Hugh Clough.

The Battle of the Atlantic: In this speech, perhaps his grimmest of the war, delivered to the House of Commons on June 25th, 1941, Mr. Churchill disclosed that during the previous twelve months 4,600,000 tons of Allied shipping had been sunk by enemy U-boats.

P. 208. *The Minister of Labour:* Ernest Bevin (1881–1951), formerly General Secretary of the Transport and General Workers' Union, became Minister of Labour and National Service in 1940, and Foreign Secretary in Mr. Attlee's Cabinet in 1945.

Degaussing: "A magnetic sweep is used to destroy magnetic mines. The sweeping vessel steams ahead towing astern an electrically charged sweep wire which fires the mines as it passes over them . . . Though the magnetic sweep is reliable, during the Second World War all ships were de-magnetised by winding electrically charged wires around the hull because the minesweepers could not always keep all fairways mine-free. Before demagnetizing or degaussing was introduced, only wooden vessels could be used for towing magnetic sweeps." (Chambers' Encyclopaedia, 1950).

P. 209. *Mr. Harriman:* President Roosevelt's Special Representative to Great Britain with rank of Minister, 1941 ; Special Representative of the President and Chairman of the President's Special Mission to U.S.S.R. with rank of Ambassador, 1941. U.S. Representative in London of the Combined Shipping Adjustment Board, 1942. Member of the London Combined Production and Resources Board, 1942. U.S. Ambassador to U.S.S.R. from 1943–46, and to Britain, 1946.

P. 212. *Vichy:* The Armistice requested by Marshal Pétain was ratified by the National Assembly at Vichy on July 9th, 1940. Laval, Flandin and Admiral Darlan were successively Pétain's Prime Ministers in the " Vichy Governments " which existed from 1940–44 by grace of the German invaders.

P. 214. *Some chicken, some neck:* from a speech to the Canadian Senate and House of Commons at Ottawa, broadcast to the world on December 30th, 1941.

P. 215. *Rommel:* Erwin Rommel (1891–1944), German field-marshal, commander of the German forces in North Africa, 1941–43 : he was eventually driven out of Egypt, Cyrenaica and Tripolitania by the British, and recalled to Germany. Later held command against allies in Normandy. Died in 1944 after being forced to take poison, on Hitler's orders, for having been privy to the plot against Hitler.

P. 221. *The Fall of Singapore:* Singapore Island is sepa-rated from the southern tip of the mainland of Malaya by the narrow Johore Strait. By the Treaty of London, 1824, the Dutch handed over Singapore to the British, gaining con-trol of Sumatra in return. In 1922 Singapore was selected as a naval base and key to Empire defence in the Far East.

Earlier in this speech, Mr. Churchill had revealed that when Singapore fell in February, 1942, 100,000 British troops had surrendered to only 30,000 Japanese.

P. 222. *General Wavell:* Sir Archibald Percival Wavell, later Field-Marshal Earl Wavell, (1883–1950). Commander-in-chief of British forces in Middle East, 1939–41 ; supreme commander of allied forces in India and Burma, 1942 ; Vice-roy of India, 1943–7.

P. 223. *The End of Mussolini:* Two days before this speech was delivered Mussolini had resigned and after twenty-one years' existence the Fascist regime in Italy came to an end. The King of Italy took command of the Forces, and Marshal Badoglio became Prime Minister.

Fascists: A group of Italian nationalists, led by Mussolini, who banded together in 1919 to oppose Bolshevism, forming the first Fascio di Combattimento. (Latin *fasces*, a bundle of rods, a symbol used by Roman magistrates signifying power over life and death ; Italian *fascista*, a group.)

P. 228. *D-Day:* On June 6th, 1944, Allied Navies and Air Forces in great strength landed the first troops of the

Invasion Army on the Normandy coast: a penetration of several miles was made on the first day, while airborne troops also landed behind the enemy lines.

P. 231. *This form of attack:* The flying bombs were jet-propelled, pilotless planes, launched from firing-points along the French coast, and weighing about one ton. The explosions caused extensive blast damage.

P. 235. *Teheran:* The capital city of Persia, where from Nov. 28th—Dec. 1st, 1943, a conference was held between President Roosevelt, Mr. Churchill and Marshal Stalin, at which outlines of strategy for the defeat of Germany were agreed.

P. 248. *Age cannot wither her . . . :* Shakespeare. *Antony and Cleopatra,* II, 11, 235.

PRINTED IN GREAT BRITAIN
BY ROBERT MACLEHOSE AND CO. LTD.
THE UNIVERSITY PRESS, GLASGOW